THE AMERICAN DREAM IN NINETEENTH-CENTURY QUEBEC:
IDEOLOGIES AND UTOPIA IN ANTOINE GÉRIN-LAJOIE'S
JEAN RIVARD

THEORY / CULTURE

Editors
Linda Hutcheon, Gary Leonard, Jill Matus,
Janet Paterson, and Paul Perron

ROBERT MAJOR

The American Dream in Nineteenth-Century Quebec: Ideologies and Utopia in Antoine Gérin-Lajoie's *Jean Rivard*

UNIVERSITY OF TORONTO PRESS
Toronto Buffalo London

© University of Toronto Press Incorporated 1996
Toronto Buffalo London
Printed in Canada
Reprinted in 2018
ISBN 0-8020-0766-x
ISBN 978-1-4875-7712-4 (paper)
Originally published in French in 1991 as *'Jean Rivard' ou l'Art de réussir. Idéologies et utopie dans l'œuvre d'Antoine Gérin-Lajoie* by Les Presses de l'université Laval, Sainte-Foy, Québec, and revised by the author for publication in English.

The work was translated by David Smith, Department of French, University of Toronto, with the help of Linda Ballstadt, Jean-Jérôme Beaudry, Shirley Bockner, Anna-Lyn Di Paolo, Laura Frew, Pamela Pollack, Mercedes Sawosch, and Wanda Woods.

Printed on acid-free paper

Canadian Cataloguing in Publication Data

Major, Robert, 1946–
    The American dream in nineteenth-century Quebec : ideologies and utopia in Antoine Gérin-Lajoie's *Jean Rivard*

(Theory/culture)
Translation of: Jean Rivard, ou, L'art de réussir : idéologies et utopie dans l'oeuvre d'Antoine Gérin-Lajoie.
Includes bibliographical references and index.
ISBN 0-8020-0766-x

1. Gérin-Lajoie, Antoine, 1824–1882. Jean Rivard. 2. Gérin-Lajoie, Antoine, 1824–1882 – Political and social views. 3. Frontier and pioneer life in literature. 4. Quebec (Province) in literature. 5. Ideology in literature. 6. Utopias in literature. I. Title. II. Series.

PS8413.E7J44513 1996   c843'.3   c96-930245-2
PQ3919.G4J43513 1996

University of Toronto Press acknowledges the financial assistance to its publishing program of the Canada Council and the Ontario Arts Council.

This book has been published with the help of a grant from the Faculty of Arts, University of Ottawa.

TO MY PARENTS

Contents

PREFACE ix

Introduction 3
  Quebec-America 3
  Jean Rivard and Its Author 7
  Why *Jean Rivard*? 12
  Ideologies and Literature 14
  Jean Rivard and Ideologies 16

1 The Genesis of a Discourse. Gérin-Lajoie and the United States: Biographical and Historical Indicators 23
  Two Trips to the United States 24
  The College Years: Father Ferland, Anglophile 26
  Étienne Parent and the American Example 32
  A Topos: The French Canadian as a Foil for the American 41
  L'air du temps 52

2 Paratext and Plot: What Happens in *Jean Rivard*? 56
  The Paratext 57
    The Titles 57
    The Prefatory Discourse 64
  Jean Rivard: An American Dream 72
    The Quest for Wealth 72
    An Exemplary Capitalist 77
  The American Intertext 88

viii   Contents

3 Intertextuality I: Jean Rivard's Library   97
   An Exemplary Reader, a Remarkable Library   97
   Robinson Crusoe, Homo Oeconomicus   106
      Travel Narrative and Novel   106
      Robinson Crusoe and Jean Rivard: A Similar Fate, Similar
      Values   108
   Napoleon: The Conqueror, the 'Self-Made Man,' The Liberal   120
      Napoleon, a Constant Analogue   121
      Napoleon's Century   126
      Clearing the Land or Waging War   130
      Success!   133
      Liberalism on Quebec Soil   136

4 Intertextuality II: *Jean Rivard* as a Utopia   144
   Utopia in the Nineteenth Century   144
   The Ambiguities of the Notion of Utopia   148
   A Definition of Utopia   152
   Jean Rivard as a Utopia   155
   Utopia and Pedagogy: *Jean Rivard* and Education   164
   A 'Pure Laine' American Utopia   172

5 Republicanism or Feudalism in Laurentia?   181
   A Reactionary, Elitist Dream?   185
   The Ramparts of the Parish   188
   The Meaning of the Gulf between Classes   192
   A Mauve Novel   195

6 Conclusion   197

NOTES   207
BIBLIOGRAPHY   231
INDEX   249

Preface

This study is a reworked version of a book first published in French under the title *'Jean Rivard' ou l'Art de réussir. Idéologies et utopie dans l'oeuvre d'Antoine Gérin-Lajoie* (Sainte-Foy: Les Presses de l'Université Laval, 1991). The greatest changes made for the English edition are found in the Introduction, which has been considerably modified, in the Conclusion, and in the original appendix, now integrated into Chapter 2. Also, Chapter 3 of the original study has been eliminated, and parts of its content used elsewhere. Furthermore, the text has been revised in a number of places: all kinds of additions and omissions, as well as changes both in style and substance, have been made.

These changes became necessary for two reasons. First, the study had to be adapted for English-speaking readers by adding information or clarifying details. Second, the polemical stance of the original version had to be toned down, since its aim had been to present a necessary rereading of a landmark work in Quebec literature, in terms of and in opposition to a long-standing critical tradition.

However, the polemical dimension of the study, albeit softened, has not completely disappeared. Indeed, there is an accepted or standard way of reading nineteenth-century Quebec novels. They are readily seen as agrarian, historical, or adventure novels, but, regardless of the genre, they have always been considered to be inspired by conservative and reactionary nationalism and patriotism, thus showing how French Canadians supposedly turned inwards after the crushing of the Patriotes' revolt in 1837 and 1838.[1] This collective withdrawal is then said to have led Quebec society to construct several compensating myths, including that of the agricultural and spiritual vocation of French Canadians on the American continent.

The supposed conservatism of these works was first acclaimed by critics in Quebec, then vehemently decried from the Quiet Revolution onwards, when modern Quebec, in the 1960s, turned its back on its traditionalist past. For its part, English Canada was quite willing to accept the Quebeckers' perception of their literature, since it corresponded closely to its own view of Quebec at the time as a 'priest-ridden society' and of its inhabitants as worthy fellows and 'brave habitants' like those so well described by William Henry Drummond in his *Habitant Poems* or Hugh MacLennan in *Two Solitudes*.

However, nineteenth-century Quebec seemed to me to be far richer and more complex than this now caricatural picture. I therefore proposed a new reading of *Jean Rivard* that I considered innovative and hoped was salutary. It thus became necessary to examine previous critical readings of the novel in order to challenge them. Part of this intention remains in this version. What is more, as I explain in the Introduction, it is impossible in sociocriticism not to treat a work's reception when analysing it. Any important work becomes part of the 'literary institution' (in the sense in which Dubois and Bourdieu use that term), and is transmitted to us, laden with the significance attributed by previous readings. It would be impossible to disregard them.

When the editors of the Theory/Culture collection sought to include my book in their series, they no doubt judged that a study of this kind would not be out of place. Indeed, it illustrates a theoretical experience: a multifaceted sociocritical reading of a crucial work in Quebec literature, a reading that has a certain heuristic value. In keeping with the second part of the collection's title, it also seeks to redraw, through this literary reading, the very profile of nineteenth-century Quebec culture.

The translation of this study is the result of an unusual pedagogical experiment. Professor David Smith, a specialist in eighteenth-century French thought, carried out the task with a team of students at the University of Toronto: Linda Ballstadt, Jean-Jérôme Beaudry, Shirley Bockner, Anna-Lyn Di Paolo, Laura Frew, Pamela Pollack, Mercedes Sawosch, and Wanda Woods. I would like to extend my thanks to him and his students for having undertaken and completed this work. Professor Smith and Pamela Pollack, in particular, saw this project through to the end. The many questions raised and suggestions made by Professor Smith and his students have undoubtedly made this study a less imperfect one. I would also like to thank Laval University Press for graciously permitting this translation, and the Faculty of Arts at the University of Ottawa for granting funds for the revision of this study. Finally, I would like to thank Latté-Bégnon Lawson-Hellu for his help as my research assistant.

ROBERT MAJOR

TRANSLATORS' NOTE: All translations of quotations are our own. Translations that we have found useful, notably Vida Bruce's translation of *Jean Rivard*, are listed in the bibliography. Book titles are kept in the original language, save for those of classical works (e.g., *Don Quixote*) written in a language other than French or English, and the two titles of Gérin-Lajoie's work: *Jean Rivard, the Pioneer* and *Jean Rivard, Economist*.

THE AMERICAN DREAM IN NINETEENTH-CENTURY QUEBEC

Introduction

Quebec-America

When Ishmael, at the beginning of *Moby Dick*, goes to the whaleman's chapel before boarding the *Pequod* and embarking on his epic hunt, he witnesses an astonishing scene. He is surprised neither by the appearance of the chapel which is completely adapted to its maritime environment, nor by the look of the preacher, an old seafarer, nor even by the design of the pulpit, which the minister can reach only by climbing up a rope ladder. What amazes him, however, is the preacher's action once he reaches his podium and look-out post:

For I was not prepared to see Father Mapple after gaining the height, slowly turn round, and stooping over the pulpit, deliberately drag up the ladder step by step, till the whole was deposited within, leaving him impregnable in his little Quebec.[1]

Ishmael's astonishment at this methodical way of isolating oneself is equalled only by our own at the chosen metaphor: 'impregnable in his little Quebec.'

The reader may well ask what Quebec is doing in Melville's novel. For Americans, Quebec must have represented isolation and solitude, since this image sprang to the novelist's mind! The metaphor is daring and brilliant, both startling and logical. Quebec (the town, of course, but, by extension, the whole of Quebec society also) is described as a fortress, isolated from the world around it, impregnable (and no doubt, too, a home for the Word of God), withstanding every attack by English-speaking America or modern materialism.

Was this really the case in the nineteenth century? Was this ever the case? The great American novelist may have judged that Quebec, with its own language, its special institutions, its culture and traditions, was an enclave, the last unassailable bastion in North America of the French, who had once spanned the continent. Historians know that the reality was more complex. In fact, the walls of the citadel were porous, and its isolation was more apparent than real. So long as appearances could be kept up, Quebec offered little or no resistance to the American invasion. Aside from the protests of the elite, which in any case were neither unanimous nor consistent, the population, throughout history, was inclined to warmly accept what came from 'les États,' and was only too ready to leave its 'little Quebec' and venture forth into a faraway land. In fact, it would be difficult to find a Quebec family with no branches long established in the United States.

How could it be otherwise? Quebeckers are North American francophones. They know in the bottom of their hearts that they are heirs to a dual tradition, both French and American, or rather to a *single* tradition that gradually took root in this environment and became distinctive. It set itself apart, then, at the same time from both the original culture and the other traditions that were being established in these vast and increasingly settled lands. Quebeckers – 'improved Frenchmen,' as former Quebec premier Maurice Duplessis called them – have always been aware of this environment, which was initially an adoptive one but eventually came to be considered their own. From the Jesuit priest Father Le Jeune, whose hand shook with fear and fascination as he signed his 1632 *Relation* 'in the middle of a forest more than 800 leagues across,'[2] to Gilles Vigneault bellowing out the unreachable limits of Quebec's winters, from Jacques Cartier, amazed by the 'eternal silence of these endless spaces' that lay before him, to contemporary novelists, flinging their characters along all the roads across the continent, America has been part and parcel of Quebec's identity.

However, Quebec's and Quebeckers' deep relationship with America is not without ambiguities. In most cases, until very recently at least, America was seen by many vocal critics as a threat, the incarnation of undesirable values. The critic might be a seventeenth-century administrator concerned that contact with American forests transformed His Most Christian Majesty's loyal subjects into rebels resisting all authority.[3] He might be a nineteenth-century parish priest, preaching against the abandonment of the countryside and emigration to New England's factories or California's gold-mines. Or he might be a contemporary leftist nationalist, railing against the degradation of Quebec culture, language, and traditional values.[4] In all three cases, America plays the role of the villain with remarkable consistency. America is a foil for Quebec.

Not long ago the remarkable essayist Ernest Gagnon contrasted France and America as the spirit and body of Quebec:

We are American French. American French: a spirit and a body. The spirit was transmitted at a moment blessed with balance and vigour. But here this thought came to assume a body that was no such thing: a Nordic country with inaccessible faraway territories, where vast forests, vast plains, and vast inland seas ignore man and fix him at the mysterious crossroads of contrary distances.[5]

It is perhaps not surprising that Father Gagnon, a Jesuit writing in the 1950s, heir to a long Augustinian tradition, should evoke this duality of spirit (balanced, healthy, and vigorous, like classical France) and of body (inhuman and savage, like mysterious and boundless America) to define Quebec. However, even more recently, Jacques Godbout, secular though he may be, admits to having indulged in the same dualism:

My mother's name was Hollywood. My father's was Saint-Germain-des-Prés ... For me, all writers were French by definition. Ideas were all French. But actors, industrialists, millionaires, heroes, politicians, and depraved women were all American. Everything technical was American.[6]

Jean Larose, pondering the same phenomenon, came to the conclusion that 'France and America represent, for Quebeckers, the two classic poles of the metaphysical cleavage.'[7]

This contrast is sometimes sharp and stark. For Pierre Vadeboncoeur, another leading Quebec essayist, the United States is responsible for the death of humanism and has brought to an end the history, art, and rich philosophical and religious tradition of the West. It is a monster that swallows everything in its path and reduces consciousness to the immediate and the factual, condemning thought to uncertainty and threatening humanity with spiritual death.[8] The condemnation is absolute. Its very excessiveness invites us to recognize therein the sign of an attraction or a fascination that the essayist will not or cannot accept.

In fact, whatever the values attributed to the American pole in the official discourse of established Quebec ideologues (colonial administrators, Catholic clergymen, or leftist intellectuals, depending on the century), it must be recognized that America has been the object of an intense fascination. 'America is fashionable in Quebec today,' Benoît Melançon notes in a recent article that takes stock of the numerous studies (books, colloquia, special issues of periodicals) devoted to the relationship between America and Quebec.[9] This profusion should not be surprising. The subdued consciousness of a profoundly American identity has left its mark on literature. And writers, very sensitive to this fact, had preceded critics in the search for a problematic American-ness. Yves Thériault, Claude Jasmin, André Major, Marie-Claire Blais, Jacques Godbout, Jacques Poulin, Victor-Lévy Beaulieu, Gilles Archambault are all American writers, sometimes against their will and even though they resolutely claim to be rejecting American civilization.[10] They are Americans despite their resistance to Americanization.

It would be wrong to believe that this fascination is a recent phenomenon or a simple fad. 'From New France to today, Quebec has always possessed an American way of thinking,' as Guildo Rousseau notes in *L'image des États-Unis dans la littérature québécoise (1775–1930)*.[11] This American way of thinking has left its mark on many recent works (poems, novels, songs, films). But it has also found its way into the earliest works, where one is surprised to find it – in good nationalist novels, for example, which seem to preach the virtues of life in the fields, in the steeple's shadow, feet in the furrow and eyes lifted heavenward.

The purpose of this study is indeed to examine the profoundly American nature of one of Quebec's masterpieces of the land: *Jean Rivard* by Antoine Gérin-Lajoie. The American theme in the works of Victor-Lévy Beaulieu, who has devoted forceful essays to Herman Melville, but also to Jack Kerouac, is quite obvious, as is the attraction of America in the novels of Jacques Poulin, who sends his characters along the roads to California; likewise, it is quite possible to pick out American rhythms in the novels of Gilles Archambault, a professed jazz lover. These literary works readily claim to be deeply American. For example, a distinctive feature in novelist and essayist Victor-Lévy Beaulieu's work is his fascination with Melville, which drove him to relentlessly pursue the American author in his life and in his work, and to finally appropriate and symbolically integrate him into Quebec. One can readily recognize this feature, and afterwards analyse it if it is so desired. It is also possible, as Paul-André Bourque[12] or Ronald Sutherland[13] propose, to establish some instructive parallels between Quebec and American novelists who share strikingly similar themes. Such is the case with Yves Thériault and Ernest Hemingway, Marie-Claire Blais and William Faulkner, Jacques Poulin and J.D. Salinger, Victor-Lévy Beaulieu and Henry Miller, André

Major and Faulkner again. 'So many parallels remain to be established, so many comparisons remain to be drawn [in order to define] the American nature of the Quebec novel,' notes Paul-André Bourque.[14] More names could be added to the list: Jacques Godbout and Salinger, Victor-Lévy Beaulieu and William Burroughs, Michel Tremblay and Tennessee Williams. Furthermore, if one were to list all the Quebec works that speak explicitly about the United States, usually critically, the list would be long, from Henri-Raymond Casgrain (*Lettres américaines*) through Ringuet and Marcel Dubé to Réjean Ducharme (*Le nez qui voque*).

The interest of such analyses is undeniable. This study, however, proposes something else: to define an American-ness that did not make itself conspicuous. Is America present in nineteenth-century Quebec works even when it is not explicitly mentioned? Does ideological analysis allow this fascination to be detected, even when it lurks between the lines of books apparently above suspicion, books that seem to be leagues away from such an influence?

Jean Rivard is indeed a work that could be described as above suspicion in this respect. The two sections of the work are called *Jean Rivard, the Pioneer (A Real-Life Narrative)* and *Jean Rivard, Economist*. But perhaps it would be more appropriate to give the two-part work a single title: *Jean Rivard, the American*, so clearly does the hero of this diptych embody the American dream.

Jean Rivard and Its Author

When Antoine Gérin-Lajoie published the two sections of his book in 1862 and 1864, he had just entered his forties (he was born in 1824) and was one of the most prominent Quebec intellectuals of his generation. A brilliant student at the Collège de Nicolet (1837–44), he had composed the popular patriotic song, 'Un Canadien errant,' at the age of eighteen, and an equally patriotic Cornelian drama, *Le jeune Latour*, when he was twenty. The precociousness of his talent had been greeted with enthusiasm by his contemporaries. Before the publication of *Jean Rivard*, his best-known work, he had written a *Catéchisme politique* (1851) and compiled a large part of the *Catalogue de la Bibliothèque du Parlement* (1857–8). A founding member of the Institut canadien in Montreal in 1844 and one of its most dynamic supporters, he was also the most ardent and efficient organizer of Quebec's first literary movement during the 1860s. In fact, it was in one of the two periodicals created by this generation's writers that he published his novel: *Jean Rivard, le défricheur canadien* in

Les Soirées canadiennes (recueil de littérature nationale) in 1862, and *Jean Rivard, économiste* in *Le Foyer canadien (recueil littéraire et historique)* in 1864. He was the Parliament librarian, a serious man of culture, the great Étienne Parent's son-in-law, a friend of the best Quebec men of letters of the time; he was well known, despite his discretion and modesty. His novel established his fame.

The work is simple and effective. In the first section, Jean Rivard, the eldest child of a farming family, loses his father at eighteen. Courageously, he interrupts his studies, leaves the village of Grandpré, crosses the St Lawrence River and plunges into the forests of the Eastern Townships with a hired hand, Pierre Gagnon. He clears 100 acres of land purchased in the township of Bristol, sows the first cleared parcels, sells the potash produced when the trees are burned, extracts and then sells sugar from the maples, and after two years of continuous work, can marry his childhood friend Louise Routhier and bring her back to his new home, which he has built with his own hands. In the second section of the book, Jean Rivard continues his work. His land gradually becomes the centre of a flourishing village that he helps establish. Because of his eminent qualities, the protagonist assumes numerous civic responsibilities: counsellor to everyone, school administrator, mayor, and magistrate. This second part, dealing with consolidation and expansion, ends with Jean Rivard's election as a member of the Quebec legislature. A few years later, the narrator arrives in Rivardville, meets the hero, and can assess this remarkable career in which a fatherless youth became the founder of a town and a prosperous man. The work ends with the announcement that the narrator will one day write this story, a promise that was kept, since we are reading it.

The narrator, however, is not the only narrative voice. The work is also partly an epistolary novel. Jean Rivard exchanges several letters with his college friend Gustave Charmenil and thus narrates his own adventure. What is more, Gustave Charmenil, who struggles along in the city as a penniless lawyer, presents a contrasting destiny that could have been Jean Rivard's if he had lacked the courage to venture into the forest. This exchange of letters allows a constant comparison on many levels between a man who chooses a saturated profession in the city and one who decides to brave prejudice and become a pioneer and a simple land-clearer, despite his education.

Along with this core of characters (the hero, his wife, his subordinate companion, his correspondent) are a number of secondary characters. Some of these are opponents, like Jean Rivard's family: his mother, sisters, and brothers who question or criticize his decision. Most, however, are supportive: the venerable priest from his native parish who counsels the protagonist; the merchants who extend credit and encouragement; another college friend, Octave Doucet, who becomes the priest in the new parish and supports him in his efforts as mayor and magistrate; the neighbours who settle near him and, in his shadow, share a similar destiny. Therefore, the novel is the story both of an energetic, resolute individual who creates a domain in the forest, and of the establishment of a town that carries his name, Rivardville, since it is a little republic created in his own image.

This unassuming and direct work is one of the most important Quebec novels of the century, not necessarily because of its intrinsic merits, but, rather, because of its wide circulation and its seminal quality. According to Monsignor Camille Roy (whose *Manuel d'histoire de la littérature canadienne de langue française* appeared in twenty editions from 1920 to 1962, thus conferring on his judgment considerable authority), 'this novel made the rounds of Canadian homes'; it was a 'widely-read book.'[15] Gérard Tougas (*Histoire de la littérature canadienne-française*) recognized it as one of Quebec's most important nineteenth-century novels, a fundamental text, the first to articulate the didactic and patriotic themes that would later be used in so many novels. René Dionne identifies the novel as one that gave rise to the most comment in the nineteenth century:

Of all the novels of the nineteenth century, *Jean Rivard* is, after *Les anciens Canadiens* by Philippe Aubert de Gaspé père, and along with Laure Conan's *Angéline de Montbrun*, the one that has received the most critical attention.[16]

The novel was quickly institutionalized, distributed en masse in schools and colleges, publicized by Quebec's non-literary ideologues and taken up by the powers-that-be, who recognized its potential as a useful instrument in furthering precise policies and values. It has appeared in twenty-seven editions or reprints since it was first published in serial form. It was the first Quebec novel to be published in France. Few Quebec novels have enjoyed such a wide circulation.

It is true, however, that *Jean Rivard* is not well known to English-speaking readers. The novel has been translated by Vida Bruce (McClelland and Stewart, New Canadian Library, 1977), but this edition is out of print, and apparently did not increase familiarity with *Jean Rivard*, a novel rarely found on undergraduate or graduate reading lists of Quebec literature. It does not compete with the works of Gabrielle Roy, Yves Thériault, Anne Hébert, Marie-Claire Blais, Michel Tremblay, or Roch Carrier.

At a certain level, this exclusion is perhaps of little or no significance. Programs of study emphasize modern works at the expense of texts from the past and of any sense of history. An illustration of this phenomenon can be found in Mary Kandiuk's bibliography,[17] which includes no work before 1884, thus consigning to oblivion not only Antoine Gérin-Lajoie, but also Louis Fréchette, Octave Crémazie, Philippe Aubert de Gaspé, François-Xavier Garneau, P.-J.-O. Chauveau: in short, all of the writers associated with the first Quebec literary movement.

This deliberate amnesia and historical shallowness in programs of study is regrettable. But the fact remains that *Jean Rivard* has never been and probably never will be the best-selling Quebec work in translation. It cannot compete with its contemporary, Philippe Aubert de Gaspé's *Les anciens Canadiens*, which was translated immediately after its publication. It could compete even less successfully with more recent works, which better conform to modern sensibilities.

English-speaking critics, however, are not unaware of the work or the author. As early as 1862, Antoine Gérin-Lajoie appeared in Henry J. Morgan's *Sketches of Celebrated Canadians*; a longer entry was devoted to him in his *Bibliotheca Canadensis*.[18] Morgan specifies: 'His chief work is the novel of *Jean Rivard*.'

> In this work he has successfully endeavoured to give a true picture of French-Canadian life and character. The hero ... conceives the idea of entering the backwoods as a pioneer of civilization and by hard work, energy and pluck carve out a name and a fortune for himself in the primeval forest ... The story is a simple one simply told and therein is its chief charm and attraction, but the romance is not wanting.

To support his judgment, Morgan quotes an article by a Reverend W. Elder published in the *Journal* in Saint John, New Brunswick:

> We heartily wish that every young man in our Province who feels tempted to try his fortune in a foreign land, or in the more common of the learned Professions, rather than win his way to independence by the cultivation of the soil, had an opportunity of perusing the pages of this admirable story.

The tone had been set. In Henry Morgan's subsequent biographical handbooks, Antoine Gérin-Lajoie was called 'a noted *littérateur*,' 'a distinguished man of letters.'[19] It was on this account that, from then on, his work was included in various anthologies[20] and studied by a number of critics. This was the case for Lorne Pierce in his *Outline of Canadian Literature*, Ian Forbes Fraser in *The Spirit of French Canada: A Study of the Literature*, and Jack Warwick in *The Long Journey: Literary Themes of French Canada*. A volume (in French) of the *Makers of Canadian Literature* (Ryerson Press, 1925) was devoted to Gérin-Lajoie, and he was the subject of entries in the most serious handbooks: *The Oxford Companion to Canadian History and Literature* (Toronto, 1967) and *The Oxford Companion to Canadian Literature* (Toronto, 1983).

Opinion of the work is nuanced and variable: all in all a rather favourable reception, with a harsh reprimand every now and then. Most often, the work's regionalism is stressed: '*Jean Rivard*, the first French-Canadian book to be published in Paris, idealizes rural life, domestic felicity, the language, religion and traditions of the race in a simple and sincere manner.'[21] The didactic qualities of the work are also emphasized: 'Gérin-Lajoie's novel is really a demonstration of the practicality of this kind of pioneering, and an illustration of its rewards.'[22] Sometimes, the work is condemned in terms of aesthetic canons, especially by recent, uncompromising critics who lay great stress on *littérarité*:

Both [books of *Jean Rivard*] deal with rural Quebec, but they are propaganda for the movement to stop emigration to the United States by settling organized groups of French Canadians in the back districts of Quebec. In both books Gérin-Lajoie's use of propaganda is too obtrusive for the reader to retain an interest in the development of the theme.[23]

He is the author of *Jean Rivard*, a dull novel of pioneer life.[24]

The severity of these last comments need not cause offence. Quebec critics are equally, if not more uncompromisingly, harsh.

In any case, the novel's reception in English Canada follows much the same lines as in Quebec. This is not to say that one imitates the other, but that, since critical discourse answers to social imperatives (if not to fashions) and since the two Canadian collectivities have evolved more or less in unison, it is not surprising to find in both critical traditions essentially the same values and preoccupations. Quebec critical discourse is, however, as could be expected, much more abundant, and reflects the importance of the work within the literary tradition.

The novel's reception in Quebec falls into three stages. Gérin-Lajoie's contemporaries were quick to recognize the novel's merits: not just its potentially beneficial effect on society, but also its intrinsic qualities as a well-written book. In the course of the twentieth century, however, this reception evolved into two successive attitudes that are both opposed and complementary. In the first half of this century the chorus of praise was virtually unanimous, peaking sharply in 1924 with the centenary of Gérin-Lajoie's birth. There was plenty in this work that the dominant agriculturalist and conservative ideology of the day could turn to its advantage. The novel was widely assessed as a tribute to Quebec's traditional values and as encouraging French Canadians to live the agrarian life, which was supposedly their preferred vocation. In reaction to this institutionalization, literary critics in the last thirty years or so are virtually unanimous in condemning the work, dismissing it as a thesis novel that poorly disguises its didactic nature with its constant awkwardness.

In fact, aside from its plot, which is simple, *Jean Rivard* has the dubious honour of providing, in its purest form so to speak, a condensed version of all the shortcomings of the nineteenth-century Canadian novel: one-dimensional characters devoid of any subtlety, apostrophes to the reader, moralizing discourses, stilted, oratorical dialogues and a dull, laborious style. Only its pioneering quality and its testimonial value guarantee it a place in our literary history.[25]

Thus, the fortunes of this novel are no doubt exemplary and worthy of further study. A book unanimously acclaimed by serious readers at the time of its publication ends up, less than a century later, after having enjoyed a remarkably wide circulation and having received an official seal of approval, by being almost unanimously condemned by literary critics of our time.

Certainly, contemporary critics do not totally deprecate it. Less extreme rereadings of *Jean Rivard* have been done recently by Antoine Sirois, René Dionne, Martin Dubé, and Rosanne Furgiuele.[26] All the same, however, severe literary judgments on the work by numerous critics make it necessary to justify my choice of this novel for this study.

Why *Jean Rivard*?

For a sociocritic, the choice of a more or less successful novel (or one so judged) as the object of analysis may well be fraught with ambiguities.

Indeed, on the one hand, minor works, whether secondary or simply badly written, have long been considered the only appropriate material for a sociological type of analysis: they become documents for the sociologist after having been dismissed by the literary scholar. On the other hand, the best-known representatives of the various sociocritical trends (in the widest sense of the term) have gone to great pains to stress that sociocritical studies should preferably be based on masterpieces.

It was under these circumstances that, in *Le dieu caché*, Lucien Goldman maintained the importance of studying great texts, because there and only there could one find the coherent world view of the writer's social group. Similarly, Claude Duchet strongly disagrees with the common presumption that 'a work considered to be minor represents society more accurately and more faithfully, because it is less elaborate' and that 'the documentary content of a novel varies in inverse proportion to its literary value.' On the contrary, he believes that the minor work does not necessarily achieve reality: it conveys only a 'discourse on reality.' Such a work reproduces a discourse that exists independently: a group's dominant ideology or sociolects, its generally accepted ideas or stereotypes. The minor work does not 'work' on this discourse; reality is not kneaded, worked on, or 'thought out' the way it is in a major novel, where a strong, authentic, enunciative voice fashions new meanings. Therefore, minor works can be informative, can teach us about what is ready-made and ready-thought, what already exists, but they are lacking a fundamental aspect: the 'dialectic relationship between the text and society' that is established when, in a good novel, reality is totalized in a particular space-time, that of the novel, where a new socialization is effected.[27]

These reflections show clearly that critics, especially sociocritics, must watch out for many pitfalls if they decide to study a novel like *Jean Rivard*. On one hand, belletrists (if such a clan exists outside of salons) can maliciously congratulate the scholar who makes such a choice: here is a 'worthless' work, clearly suited to a sociological type of study. On the other hand, sociocritics might reproach the scholar for fostering ambiguities and harming the discipline by making such a choice. Either way, it is agreed that *Jean Rivard* is a terrible novel.

But that is the point: what exactly is a masterpiece? Few critics would accept the view of Hoggart, who eliminates any distinction between masterpieces and other works.[28] The Bordeaux School's studies have nevertheless clearly shown that the choice of a masterpiece owes a lot to chance, that the criteria for selection are extremely vague; that certain people and certain institutions make these decisions according to arbitrary rules, conforming to canons that are never clarified or are a disgrace (it always comes down to a matter of taste, if not of fashion!); and that at any rate the lifetime of the masterpiece is extremely problematic. Neither success nor timelessness makes a masterpiece: success often is a hindrance. If *Jean Rivard* is compared with the works of the great nineteenth-century French writers – an inappropriate comparison, admittedly: I will make more relevant comparisons further on in this study – it is obvious that Gérin-Lajoie is no Balzac or Chateaubriand. But the same can be said about many sound writers.

However, the question is not so much to determine whether *Jean Rivard* is a masterpiece (no critic has dared to claim that), as to see if the work can be called a novel and whether a re-examination of it is justified. An affirmative answer can unhesitatingly be given to both questions. This novel definitely deserves to be reread.

Jean Rivard is admittedly a thesis novel. But one might be tempted to ask: What of it? The label should in no way be considered dishonourable, as Susan Suleiman clearly demonstrates in an excellent book devoted to this unappreciated and scorned genre.[29] There are good and bad thesis novels, but the genre has existed for a long time, like it or not, and to demand for the novel an illusory 'gratuitousness' or 'purity' is no doubt a confession of ignorance of the workings of literature as an institution and of the ambiguous ties that link every work with the ideologies of its time.

Jean Rivard is a very good thesis novel. Furthermore, if 'a work is deemed great when it becomes part of the literary canon and participates as such in the reproduction of a culture'[30] – certainly a more valid criterion than a timeless beauty that is impossible to define – then *Jean Rivard* is a great Quebec novel. It is an important work, both in the history of Quebec literature and as an ideological phenomenon. The latter aspect is particularly deserving of further study.

Ideologies and Literature

The connection between ideology and literature, as Jacques Dubois points out in his excellent study on Zola,[31] is a contentious and exciting issue that divides literary critics of various sociological schools. Conceived as a 'relatively coherent set of ideas and beliefs, of values and representations, in reference to a group, which situates it within society as a whole and justifies its existence,'[32] ideology maintains numerous complex and profound relationships with literature. In fact, ideology and the ideological field are at the origin of a work, and it is from these sources that the novel is put together, not from a raw, pure, 'true reality' that only the novelist, by some special gift, would allegedly be able to see and grasp. It has long been known, at least since Mannheim,[33] that knowledge is sociological; that perception, while subject to the laws of logic and psychology, does not escape sociological screening. 'Subject to social control, situated in an intellectual field, themselves social beings and cultural agents, novelists first hear and grasp, not reality itself, but a discourse about reality resulting from different human activities.'[34] 'For literature, ideology is a fundamental fact, a substratum that it cannot help but integrate, like its own place of origin. Ideology, which permeates language, representations and mythical configurations, is the basis upon which literature is able to function.'[35]

Such statements, when applied to *Jean Rivard*, will encounter no opposition. The explicit purpose of the novel is to convey a message, to advance a 'thesis,' an ideology. It is in tune with the ideology emerging at the time in response to the massive emigration of French Canadians to the United States: settlement. It is relatively easy to establish links between the novel and contemporary documents (sermons, speeches, studies, commissions of inquiry) that are 'more purely' ideological equivalents of some of the representations constituted by novelistic fiction. We are obviously dealing, then, with a text that is constantly metatextualizing, that seeks, artlessly but honestly, to deliver a message. The number of repetitions, the narrator's interventions, the deployment of characters, the one-dimensional quality of the protagonist and other techniques, including the paratext itself (especially the prefaces), are evidence of the author's desire to make a point, of his didactic intentions. Above all, the novel seeks to be useful. This pragmatism necessarily implies univocity, absolute denotation, a constant effort to eliminate ambiguity or any literary complexity, while at the same time implying a certain populist aim: clarity and intelligibility are essential if the greatest number are to be served. It is therefore evident that it was not Gérin-Lajoie's intention to provide several levels of meaning in his novel, and this aspect will later be examined more closely.

However, we know that even a text that metatextualizes itself to excess and that is constantly over-defining itself still leaves 'chinks in its armour.'[36] Even while aiming at a univocal surface reading, even while seeking to eliminate purely novelistic aspects in an effort to refine the message as well as the reader (only serious patriotic readers will persist, and there is no guarantee that even they will keep at it!), there is still a tendency for a novel like *Jean Rivard* to offer a multiplicity of meanings.

First, in an absolute sense. With the passage of time, a novel inevitably becomes polysemic, fitting into different cultural sequences, playing different roles for different readers. For example, my reading, quite simply, could never be the same as that of Camille Roy, a priest and monsignor, a university president and as ardent a nationalist as they came in Quebec in the first half of the twentieth century. But in a special sense, as well, this is a polysemic novel. Indeed, its highly developed intertextuality causes the novel to be intertwined, as Michel Foucault puts it, 'in a system of references to other books, other texts, other sentences.'[37] Most of these reference texts are indicated explicitly, but others only implicitly, which is sometimes very revealing. A contemporary rereading must necessarily bring them to light.

So let it be clearly established from the start: I am not interested in *Jean Rivard*'s alleged triviality, or relative failure, nor in its status as a minor work. This novel is not for me just a 'document' with no novelistic dimension. The novel exists, it has exerted considerable influence, it has given rise to more critical commentary, it is better known than most works of nineteenth-century Quebec, and it is of a complexity that has never really been acknowledged.

Jean Rivard and Ideologies

This novel offers not so much a pretext as an opportunity to study, in the most French Canadian of novels, in the most virtuous of patriotic works, in what may seem a borderline monological novel, the workings of an apparently exogenous ideology (or at least one that was refused recognition). It also provides an opportunity to put to the test a number of different approaches (literary history, textual analysis, ideological analysis, intertextuality) that constitute a sociocritical reading and enable us to clarify a work's significance.

An ideological reading of *Jean Rivard* must necessarily analyse the ideology explicitly advocated in the text and isolate its components. At the same time, it must bear in mind previous interpretations and judge them, not simply for the satisfaction of crossing swords – in any case, it is impossible to pick a quarrel with critics who, for the most part, are no longer alive – but rather because these readings, which were proposed, spread, and 'imposed' for various reasons, are 'networks of ideological permeation'[38] that must be dismantled. But above and beyond this overt ideology, which more often than not has merely been reaffirmed by critics following the author's lead, other ideological currents run through the book. A quarter of a century ago, Sartre was already passionately proclaiming in *Questions de méthode*, in response to dogmatic, simplistic Marxist criticism: 'Most works of the mind are complex objects difficult to categorize; they can rarely be 'situated' in relation to a single class ideology, but they rather reproduce, in their deep structure, the contradictions and the struggles of contemporary ideologies.'[39] Sociocriticism has made this one of its basic principles: 'A work is never permeated or driven by a single ideological tendency.'[40] Indeed, even a work that professes an ideology always manages, at the same time, to challenge that ideology, because it sets its limits and by so doing, denounces it. Thus, Pierre Machery is right to consider as absurd the attempt on the part of critics to 'demystify' a work: 'Literary works are themselves, of essence, demystifing.'[41] However, let us acknowledge that if one cannot 'demystify' a work, one can demystify interpretations of it.

Settlement, or the need to develop the virgin territories of Canada, is *Jean Rivard*'s massive and public referent. It is the referent *against* which the novel is constructed. The ambivalence of the preposition must be noted: *Jean Rivard* is admittedly based *on* settlement, but at the same time it speaks *against* it. The novelist does not seek to disguise his preferences, nor the militant character of his book, nor its topicality. On the contrary. All the same, it must be realized that this referent, settlement, is simultaneously the object of an inquiry conducted in the novel and through fiction. The referent is analysed and reinterpreted. Critics, always busily classifying this supposed 'novel of the land' as a vehicle for an ideology of the *status quo*, of backwardness, have often been unable (or unwilling) to perceive that this referent takes on new meanings. In their minds, being a settler, a backwoodsman, necessarily leads to backwardness! However, it seems to me that this work says exactly the opposite.

In fact, the initial hypothesis of this study is the profoundly American character of the novel. Reading *Jean Rivard* for the first time a few years ago, with a limited knowledge of nineteenth-century Quebec ideologies but a wider knowledge of American literature and the 'American spirit,' I was struck by the 'American classic' quality of its discourse. This novel seemed an excellent example of what Americans call a *success story* or, since the great vogue of Horatio Alger novels in the second half of the nineteenth century, a 'rags-to-riches story.' A virtuous, enterprising, brave young man, whose only capital is in his merits, achieves a brilliant success, forerunning the Rockefellers, Fords, Vanderbilts, Morgans, and Kennedys who were later to be brought to the attention of the masses by the Dale Carnegies, the Lee Iacoccas, and the other theoreticians of American success. In other words, the novel advocates the ideology of economic liberalism, as practised by the individual, based on the Protestant work ethic, which has been well analysed by Max Weber. Thus I find it significant, but also quite predictable, that the English-Canadian translator of *Jean Rivard* should come straight to the point in her brief introduction: '*Jean Rivard* is essentially a success story.'[42] And we know that for an English speaker, a success story is a story of *economic* success: gaining influence in the business world, building up a personal fortune.

Thus the second focus of this study emerges, a focus that will require closer examination than the first. The novel is more than a tale of settlement or pioneer life. It must be analysed as an American tale, imbued with the American spirit, and even as a utopia, obeying the laws of the utopian genre, but a utopia that proves to be typically American. An ideology that is staged, performed, and displayed is superimposed on the ideology that is expressed: the representation of one ideology (success) goes hand in hand with the expression of another (settlement).

Since the words 'American utopia' have been uttered, it is perhaps appropriate at this point to justify briefly this second component of the subtitle. Long ago, in one of the great critical texts of the Renaissance, Sir Philip Sidney reflected on utopia as a rhetorical form and a road to knowledge. He associated utopia with poetry and placed both at the forefront of humanist studies, well ahead of history and philosophy. They shared for him the same definition – 'a speaking picture, with this end to teach and delight' – although utopia was intended for the community rather than the individual: 'But even in the most excellent determination of goodness, what ... can so readily direct ... a whole commonwealt, as the way of sir Thomas Moore's Utopia.'[43]

In short, utopia is a pleasant way to shape and direct communities. It is not hard to accept this definition and this purpose. The special ties that link utopia with ideology are instantly apparent. Utopia *is* ideology, and ideology in its most radical form: the totalizing reinvention of the city ('direct ... a whole commonwealt'). Just like ideology, utopia is a weapon in the social struggle; perhaps not as fraught a weapon, but its apparent lack of power is deceptive. Utopia is a long-range canon, far-reaching, aiming at a future totalizing reconstruction of society. Mannheim was right to see in it a revolutionary force in all periods of history: the expression of people who want to create the future. Or, as Georges

Introduction 19

Duveau said: 'Groups of people whose energy is stifled or has no outlet get their revenge by conjuring up somewhat complex fantasies, imagining victories to be won at fairly distant dates, in this world or the next. This is how utopias are born. They may be the expression of a guilty conscience, but they are above all a remedy for wounds or disappointments.'[44]

This is exactly the situation experienced by Gérin-Lajoie's contemporaries. Antoine Gérin-Lajoie was a member of a community that felt injured, disappointed, and victimized. French Canada had been militarily conquered in 1760 when Wolfe defeated Montcalm on the Plains of Abraham and British forces overran the fortified city of Quebec, thus gaining the whole of French possessions in America; it was crushed in 1837 and 1838, after a brief revolt against British imperial rule led by Papineau and Nelson (the Patriotes' Revolt); thereafter Quebec (or Lower Canada, as it was then called) was linked by force in 1842 to the neighbouring province of Upper Canada (present-day Ontario) with the explicit intention, under the Union, of promoting the assimilation of the French population. Lord Durham's proposals in his famous 1839 report pursuant to the previous years' revolts were very clear on this point; in order to solve the Canadian problem, Britain had to achieve, in its colony, the assimilation of the French Canadians:

I entertain no doubts as to the national character which must be given to Lower Canada; it must be that of the British Empire; that of the majority of the population of British America; that of the great race which must, in the lapse of no long period of time, be predominant over the whole North American Continent.[45]

French Canadians were therefore quite conscious that they had to constantly fight to maintain and protect their language, their faith, their laws, and their traditional values: in short, their identity. Furthermore, the community was threatened by the prospect of an even more comprehensive association, the 1867 Confederation of all the British colonies north of the United States. In this new country, the Quebeckers would be permanently relegated to a minority status. Quebec was, in fact, hemmed into a narrow stretch of territory along the St Lawrence, every day losing its human resources, its youth, and its most dynamic and adventurous elements because of the constant erosion that emigration to the United States represented. In the 1850s, the decade preceding the writing of *Jean Rivard*, 70 000 Quebeckers, that is, '15 000 more people than the population of Montreal at the time, the most heavily populated city in Quebec,' emigrated to the United States. Two hundred thousand Quebeckers emigrated between 1840 and 1870.[46] The overpopulated Laurentian countryside could no longer feed its population.

Antoine Gérin-Lajoie was painfully aware of his fellow citizens' situation. How could he not be? His was one of the most thoughtful minds of his time; he had experienced first hand the temptation to emigrate and the misery of dead-end jobs; he was politically active under the Union of Upper and Lower Canada; he was directly involved with parliamentary life; his father-in-law was imprisoned during the Patriotes' revolt; his friends and acquaintances were some of the most enlightened men of the time. Individually or collectively, they sought to restore the health of a community in disarray. This was a favourable time for writing utopias.

How is it possible for mid-nineteenth-century French Canadians to survive under these conditions? Even more importantly (particularly for a utopian), how can power be seized? The answer given by *Jean Rivard* is a radical one, and effects a reversal of traditional roles. For the century following the Conquest, the struggle had been constitutional and had taken place in the political arena, where generations of French-Canadian republican leaders had sought to gain true democracy, or at least proper representation, and curtailing of British rule. But *Jean Rivard* tells us that power is not political, but economic. Power is money, power is wealth. The first step must be to build a personal fortune, and the rest will follow. The proposed model is an American one.

This study, then, has two foci: settlement and an American utopia, with the second being more important than the first. Linked thereto is a whole network of ideological developments. This study will seem quite 'mottled' at times, the approach being to advance by successive approximations or via concentric circles. Attempting to determine the ideological scope of a work – feeling one's way, as one must, partly at least because of the hesitancy inherent in a developing discipline, not to mention the analyst's own limitations – is like trying to kill several birds with one stone at the obvious risk of missing them all. But I think that this way of proceeding, aside from the methodological or heuristic interest that it may offer – after all, it does convey the dynamism of discovery – is justified by the very nature of ideological research and especially by the theory of intertextuality: the texts, the clusters of meanings of various origins that speak in this novel, that are echoed in it or that prolong that echo, cry out for an explanation.

Does Gérin-Lajoie's novel thus become just an excuse for discussing outside phenomena? I do not think so. It seems to me that it goes without saying – but it is perhaps worth repeating – that 'it is neither a betrayal nor an abandonment of literature to see in it something that is elucidated by today's theory and ideology, but that also predated them and was present in the text without our knowing it.'[47] My analysis of the book will be literary, and the ideological discourse must be sought in and beneath the literary text. The novel can only be properly investigated by respecting what makes it a work of a particular genre. In short, I subscribe to Marc Angenot's and Darko Suvin's thesis, which is somewhat militant but has the advantage of clarity:

> It is true that literature can be understood only by considering the morphological properties that give it literary status. It is equally true that the 'immanent' or 'formal' analysis of texts can be significant only if it is part and parcel of a 'sociological,' so-called 'extrinsic' analysis and not just mechanically complemented by it. In fact, we must consider the terms within quotation marks to be outdated: there is no valid literary theory, history, or criticism that is not simultaneously formal and social. This means that historical semantics and sociosemantics (modelled after 'sociolinguistics') are prerequisites for any other type of analysis, whether diegetic or textual, of fiction and of dramatic texts.[48]

A prerequisite and, let me add, a constant companion.

Jean Rivard is vigorously highlighted by the social and political background of its time: political battles, massive emigration, settlement crusades, a desperate search for a better future in depressing circumstances. It is therefore tempting to see it only as a document – the author even invites us to do so – a sort of study in social science (using the methods of Le Play, for example, which were being developed at the time and aroused much interest). But this work remains a novel, a work of fiction, and it must not be forgotten that if this novel claims to offer us knowledge (and refers to a whole collection of validating 'hors-texte' to support its pretension), if it claims to don the austere livery of serious, informative, educational, and stirring works, this claim lies *within* the text of the novel and constitutes the text of the novel: it is ideological and calls for analysis.

An ideological analysis of *Jean Rivard* is therefore necessary. While suggesting new meanings,[49] this analysis may contribute – at least such is my hope – to the rehabilitation of a novel that has been given quite a hard time in current criticism. It is even possible that the study of the novel's utopian dimension will lead to a better appreciation of some of its so-called weaknesses. Such a study will make the novel and the author better known; it will throw some new light on nineteenth-century ideologies and on one of the Quebec's most remarkable intellectual families: Étienne Parent's clan.[50] By stressing the American nature of the work (in both senses of the word: it is rooted in the North American continent and its spirit is that of the United States), this study will seek to transcend what strikes me all too often as a lamentable ethnocentrism in Quebec literary studies.

My aspirations are no doubt too ambitious. But, to tell the truth, ambitions are not so much at issue as are the partial and limited aspects of this study. I would nevertheless like to point out, in conclusion, that if this study takes up many challenges, perhaps it does not fulfil any of them completely. This is no doubt to be expected, because this study stands at the intersection of a whole network of approaches that are all in their infancy. Indeed, research into the complex relationship between literature and society, between novels and ideologies, has only just begun and is embroiled in methodological debate; the history of the settlement of the backwoods of Quebec, according to one of its best specialists, Gabriel Dussault, is just starting up;[51] the history of agriculture, according to Norman Séguin, still has to be written;[52] almost nothing has been said about relations between the United States and French Canada, particularly about the nineteenth-century popular perception of the United States.[53] As Pierre Savard indicates in his study on Tardivel, historians and literary scholars readily shift the responsibility to each other in the search for hard facts. Ideally, one would like to use historical sources to understand certain important phenomena presented in different nineteenth-century novels – settlement, agriculture, Americanization – but historians, in a nice paradox, refer us back to the novel as a fertile source of information![54] In short, whichever way we turn, we find ourselves on shifting ground. But obviously this should not stop us from moving ahead.

1

The Genesis of a Discourse.
Gérin-Lajoie and the United States:
Biographical and Historical Indicators

We would like to think that an author's ideological position is clearly discernible in his biography. Jacques Dubois, for example, seems to take for granted that an author's ideology is made manifest in his life.[1] In other words, a person's origins, experiences, and relationships provide information that does not need to be unscrambled, whereas the literary work is an encoded text that has to be deciphered and painstakingly interpreted.

I do not believe that is the case. The discourse of a biography is not that of a literary work, but it, too, is a discourse nonetheless, to be read and interpreted, and it reaches us as a text, either biographical or autobiographical. I do not use the terms 'text' and 'discourse' metaphorically, since an author's life, the events that have sketched his profile, reach us in the form of writings such as letters, memoirs, firsthand accounts, and biographies, each with its own author. In the case of Gérin-Lajoie, we have his *Mémoires*, that is, his autobiography, with all the fundamental ambiguity of the genre, and, what is more, filtered, edited, and commented upon as the text proceeds, by a Father Casgrain, who transmits only what he sees fit to disclose. Since the original manuscript has been lost, there is no way of knowing how much this pious and self-serving biographer and commentator left out. We also have Léon Gérin's *Souvenirs*, but they are the memories of a respectful, loving son, published moreover at a time (the centenary of Gérin-Lajoie's birth) that encourages flawlessly tender filial sentiments, if not hagiography. Thus, Gérin-Lajoie's biography has come down to us in fragments, passed on by respectful family members and close friends, patiently reconstructed by a literary critic,[2] but nevertheless full of gaps resulting as much from the author's own reticence as from the circumstances in which these accounts of his life have been transmitted to us.

In a word, this biography, like so many others, is not explicit. Still, a few signposts can be found that are relevant to this study, providing a concrete basis, both biographical and factual, for my reading of the novel. They signal the presence of a discreet yet very persistent thread running through Gérin-Lajoie's life: his enormous fascination with the United States of America and with the Anglo-Saxon as a type.

Two Trips to the United States

Gérin-Lajoie took two trips to the United States, the first at the age of twenty, upon leaving college, and the second seven years later. The first trip lasted only seventeen days (14–30 August 1844) and the second, six months (3 September 1851–15 March 1852). The student's escapade has provided us with a lively, colourful account, rich in biographical details and humorous insights.[3] On the other hand, the six-month study trip is summed up by Father Casgrain in two paragraphs and he is very skimpy on detail, no doubt because the manuscript, which was the outcome of this long stay, was a separate text from the *Mémoires* used by Casgrain, and was intended, at least originally, for publication.[4] According to Léon Gérin, his father went to live in Boston but travelled widely in Massachusetts, taking notes as he went.[5] Casgrain, who saw the manuscript, said it 'would make a sizeable volume,' and was 'an indepth study of American institutions, primarily of those in Massachusetts, the oldest and most noteworthy state in the Union. The political, social, religious, commercial, and industrial condition of the American people is assessed here both accurately and impartially.'[6]

The journal of this trip, written in English, and the sociopolitical manuscript on which Gérin-Lajoie worked for a time with the intention of publishing it in *La Minerve* are now lost. The loss seems to me a considerable one. These writings would no doubt have added an important chapter to our knowledge of Quebec intellectual life in the nineteenth century. What was the attraction of the United States for a young intellectual who belonged to the founding generation of the Institut canadien, and was both a convinced nationalist and an ardent patriot? How could one be a nationalist, be stirred by patriotic songs, even compose some oneself, as did Gérin-Lajoie when he wrote 'Un Canadien errant,' and flirt with the United States?

First, a distinction must be made between the two trips. At first glance, the student's trip comes as no great surprise. His youth, a taste for adventure, the need to escape after some years at college, but also ambition, the thirst for knowledge, and the conviction he would make a quick fortune impelled him to cross the border. 'His main goal was to study English there and to earn enough money to continue his legal studies,' Father Casgrain tells us. '[I was] convinced that once I got there, I would have only to offer my services in order to earn more than enough money to survive,' Gérin-Lajoie candidly admits.[7] In short, the student believed that the United States was Cockaigne country, where one had only to reach out one's hand. Furthermore, this seems to have been a widespread belief. The projected trip met with no objections from either Gérin-Lajoie's family or his teachers. The appeal of the United States seemed self-evident in the early 1840s, when the enormous wave of emigration of French Canadians began. America, land of opportunity!

What is surprising, however, is that Gérin-Lajoie went back to the United States, even though his first trip was a disaster. His aborted seventeen-day first trip, 'very short' but long enough to clear his head of 'all the illusions he had cherished for several years,'[8] gradually lost its dissuasive effect on the author. It seems that there was a gradual dulling of the disappointments suffered by this latter-day Candide, 'full of illusions and daydreams,'[9] but roughly awakened, without friends and soon without funds, in a country nothing like Eldorado, and whose first concern upon returning to Canada was to go to church, fall to his knees, and give thanks to God.[10]

Seven years later Gérin-Lajoie responded once again to the call of America and this time stayed in New England for six months. The fascination of the United States must have been truly powerful to overcome the disillusionments of the first trip. All the more so since this six-month stay must have required a considerable outlay in those days for a young man without a steady job, who had practised for a few years the underpaid profession of journalist, and who probably had no real savings. Moreover, his admissions of poverty, which are true cries of distress, abound at this time in his *Mémoires*.

In order to understand all the resonances of these two trips, it is necessary to backtrack somewhat to Gérin-Lajoie's formative years, which shed some light on the first, and to his meeting with Étienne Parent, which elucidates in part the second. This retrospective look will perhaps enable us to understand, by studying a single case history, the fascination the United States held for a whole generation of Quebec intellectuals.

The College Years: Father Ferland, Anglophile

Gérin-Lajoie was a student at the Collège de Nicolet from 1837 to 1844. He arrived there 'just as its educational resources, both human and material, were being replaced and improved, as they were in most of the other colleges in Lower Canada.'[11] René Dionne has written a fine study of these years as a whole; I will focus on the presence of English at the college and on the awakening to Americanism that Gérin-Lajoie must have experienced there.

English had been taught at the college since its opening. 'From 1808 to 1822, it was a subject like any other, except that it was aimed at everyone without distinction of age or class.'[12] From 1822, 'English became a school subject like Latin and Greek, that was taught in all years including the business class. The amount of time that was devoted to it varied from one class to another.'[13] Translation into English was the basic exercise of this teaching; grammar was studied and pronunciation practised. The textbooks were accurate and fairly well done. Along with this teaching of the language, the presence of English-speaking students, both Canadian and American, must be noted throughout the history of the college. 'On the list of students at the Nicolet Seminary, quite a few English, Scottish, and Irish names can be found. They amounted to ten percent of the total number of students between 1803 and 1969. The first English speakers had arrived at the college in 1813.'[14]

The real quality of this teaching and the educational effectiveness of these English speakers may, of course, be questioned in light of the difficulty Gérin-Lajoie, a gifted student, admits he experienced in speaking English at the time of his first trip to the United States. But this admission is to be treated with caution; his professed ignorance serves as a comic effect and is used to paint, throughout the pages of his *Mémoires*, a topos of tried and true narrative effectiveness, that of an innocent abroad. The penniless student is no doubt much more ignorant of the outside world and, in particular, of this foreign country and its customs, than he is of the English language. Gérin-Lajoie had learned English, no doubt imperfectly and in a bookish manner, but he had learned it nonetheless. It was even among the priorities of the college and one of the specialties of the vice-principal from 1841 on, Father J.B.A. Ferland. His influence on Gérin-Lajoie was so great that it merits further examination.

Indeed, Father Ferland, one of the outstanding men of nineteenth-century Quebec, made Gérin-Lajoie his protégé, then his friend and collaborator. Father Casgrain stresses this influence:

Among the teachers at Nicolet was a man of fine intellect, of even more unusual erudition and with a heart more exceptional still. He was Father Ferland, the kind author of stories entitled *Le Labrador, L'Histoire de Gamache, La Gaspésie*, etc., not to mention an *Histoire du Canada* which placed him among the ranks of our best historians. Father Ferland, the vice-principal, treated Gérin-Lajoie more as a friend than a student. He enlightened him with his advice, fired him with his patriotism, and passed on to him something of his priestly selflessness.[15]

Léon Gérin also sees him as his father's mentor:

The year 1865 was filled with grief for him. Early in January, Father Ferland, whom he had held in great veneration since his days in the Collège de Nicolet, died of a stroke. Deeply affected, Gérin-Lajoie devoted the next issue of *Le Foyer canadien* to a eulogy and a biography of his mentor and faithful collaborator.[16]

This influential teacher, then friend, was an anglophile whose English was flawless. The obituary published in *Le Courrier du Canada* on 13 January 1865, mentions his facility in speaking the country's two languages:

In 1813, M. Ferland went to live in Kingston with his mother [he was then eight years old] and stayed there for three years. It was there that he became proficient in the English language ... Many of our English-speaking fellow citizens told us that they would have thought that M. Ferland, to judge him only by his English, had been raised on the banks of the Thames.[17]

An obituary, admittedly, is not the place for subtlety and reservations. It is the case, however, that the arrival of Father Ferland at Nicolet was directly related to his knowledge of English. He was invited to take over the vice-principalship because he spoke English, because an English commercial school was wanted at the college, and because in general the teaching of English was desired by the public. Father Harper, the college bursar, states this unequivocally in a letter to his bishop, written in 1840:

Seeking to contribute, to the best of my limited abilities, towards restoring the college's financial health, I applied myself to finding the principal causes of the trouble. Apart from bad harvests, the poverty in the region, etc., etc., it seems to me that the deplorable condition in which the Seminary finds itself can be attributed to the fact that the education given in this institution responds to neither the needs nor the wishes of those very people who would be the most favourably disposed towards it. The children from both this parish and the neighbouring ones, who are sent elsewhere to get what they cannot find at the Seminary, are a convincing proof of this ... It would be desirable to have one [a vice-principal] who himself had a practical knowledge of the English language. The teachers, or at least most of them, besides possessing the qualities and knowledge necessary for teaching, should also be able to speak English. With a teaching body made up in this way and headed by a man of M. Ferland's calibre, for example, I have no doubt that Nicolet would not only overcome its difficulties, but would also become the most popular educational institution in Canada.[18]

The English school was established that same fall with 'two talented young Irish teachers.' Well publicized in *La Gazette de Québec*, it attracted a number of students: twenty out of a total school population of eighty. The following autumn, Father Ferland arrived, to the bursar's great relief:

I do not need to tell Your Lordship that it is with the deepest satisfaction that I have learned of M. Ferland's favourable decision ... But it seems to me that it is necessary to announce at once the appointment of M. Ferland as vice-principal at Nicolet. If this were known, I'm sure it would attract many new students who might otherwise go elsewhere.[19]

The new vice-principal's first report to his bishop (a letter dated 1 January 1842, after the first trimester exams) shows the importance Ferland attached to English, not only during the exams themselves, but also outside of courses, an importance that reflects the bishop's concerns and indicates clearly the specific nature of Ferland's mission:

Grade Twelve: it is, in every respect, one of the best classes I have ever encountered. They have a good knowledge of English. Recently I had them work, on the spot, on a speech by Pitt. They hadn't seen it before, but nevertheless, without any preparation, they translated into French, easily and exactly, this piece of oratory that is quite difficult to understand ... The most intelligent student in the class, and probably in the entire community, is Antoine Gérin-Lajoie from Yamachiche ... *Tenth*: It is a very good class. Édouard Martineau, Léandre Gill and J.O. Béland are doing very well. The first applies himself well to the study of English ... *The English school* has twelve boarders and a few day-students. At the moment, I am in charge of it, along with Mr Trevor during Mr O'Reilly's absence ... This school is going well. A few of the students are making remarkable progress ... A couple of times a week, during a half-hour taken from evening recess, I meet in a room with those senior boys who volunteer, and I read to them sometimes in English, sometimes in French, the summary of political and ecclesiastical news in the *Mélanges* and Nelson's *Gazette*. About fifteen of the community's best students attend. Upon my recommendation, several have begun to keep in English a private journal of noteworthy facts. These journals are to be offered to Your Lordship at the end of the year. This project will engrave contemporary history on their minds, will teach them to write in English and will make them accustomed to keeping a journal of memorable events.[20]

We know that Gérin-Lajoie never gave up his habit of keeping a journal in English. During his second trip to the United States, his journal was indeed written in English. According to Gérin-Lajoie, Father Ferland used these voluntary meetings to fill the gaps in the teaching, particularly in modern history and in English. This 'informal little class in modern history and politics' was enormously beneficial to the students. More than twenty years later, the fervour of his former student's prose clearly reveals the strong influence that Father Ferland had on those around him. 'He found countless ways to promote emulation among the students ... A large number of students followed these lessons eagerly and several derived genuine benefit from them.'[21]

An exceptional educator, Father Ferland was also a scholar whose reputation was firmly established even before the publication of his historical works. A quick survey of the American content of these writings gives us some insight into some of the subjects possibly touched upon during the informal lectures given at the Collège de Nicolet. A reading of his *Cours d'histoire du Canada* reveals that his knowledge of the English language led him to read American historians assiduously and to study in depth New England, its inhabitants and their temperament. Ferland readily cites the historians of every state in the Union, their chroniclers and memorialists. He knew American history down to the last detail, in so far as was possible at the time. This history is obviously linked with that of New France, so numerous and often conflicting were the relationships between them. His historical honesty led him, therefore, to study scrupulously the documents and histories of the American colonies and, on more than one occasion, to get the American version of the facts.

But his knowledge and his use of these sources went beyond a concern for objectivity. He enjoyed dwelling upon certain episodes that had only a tenuous connection with Canadian history but that must have aroused in the humanist, the believer, and the priest a certain intellectual curiosity. A good example is the witch-hunt of 1692 in Salem, orchestrated by Cotton Mather, which resulted in twenty people being executed and fifty or more being tortured. These events had deeply moved public opinion in New England and would leave a profound mark on American literature, as Nathaniel Hawthorne's work adequately demonstrates.[22] Father Ferland also describes in detail the Puritan foundation of Plymouth and the independent foundation of Boston and seems to marvel at their rapid progress in both population and wealth. In his notes he can dwell just as readily on the founding of Harvard[23] as on the etymology of the word Yankee.[24]

This familiarity with American writings did not result solely from Ferland's need to write as complete a history of Canada as possible. From his earliest works, Ferland demonstrates his knowledge of the United States. In 1853, when he made his debut as a historian by soundly criticizing the acrimonious work of Father Brasseur, he could already draw upon his information about Boston and count on his knowledge of the American mentality in order to describe the French abbé's pretensions as 'humbug.'[25] The following year, commenting on the beginnings of the Jesuit college in Quebec in 1636, Ferland quite naturally compares it with Harvard College, which was already prestigious in his day:

Canada thus had the advantage of having a school before the New England states. For it was only in 1637 that the Massachusetts legislature resolved to found one, and decided that it would be established at Newton. John Harvard, a minister who died in 1638, left an inheritance of £770.17.2 to the public school at Newton. To honour this generous benefactor, the school by order of the court was named Harvard College and Newton changed its name to Cambridge. What is remarkable is that the first professor to be put in charge of this rich and famous institution, in 1637, was Nathaniel Eaton who had been trained by the Jesuits. This is reported by a contemporary writer, Governor Winthrop.[26]

The 'Governor Winthrop' whom Ferland mentions is John Winthrop the First (his son and grandson would also have the first name John and also be governors in New England), whose journal was published in 1853, just a year before Ferland's note, by J.K. Hosmer with the title *The History of New England from 1630 to 1649*. Thus Ferland was well aware of American publications from the moment they were published.

The Genesis of a Discourse 31

Many factors sparked Ferland's interest in the United States: his research as a historian, conscious of the numerous links forged over two-and-a-half centuries between Canada and the United States; his position as a priest, curious about these pragmatic Protestants; and his status as an open-minded Canadian, fascinated by this enterprising, ambitious people. As a result, the comparative portrait that he draws of French Canadians and Yankees is very revealing. It deserves to be quoted at length, in particular its conclusion, which stresses their common yet contrasting American heritage, and, above and beyond their different temperaments, blood relationships seldom noted by others, which were the result of guerrilla warfare and rapine:

Most of the founders of the English colonies, the ones who most influenced the destiny of New France, came from one of these two main places – Plymouth and Boston. The French in Canada and the English in New England grew in number on American soil, living sometimes in peace, but more often than not openly warring or harassing one another with acts of undeclared aggression. Restless, bold, and eager for adventure and travel, the French set foot among the indigenous western nations at an early stage and discovered the whole interior of the continent from the Gulf of Mexico to Hudson Bay; full of cheerfulness and good-heartedness, they earned and managed to keep the friendship of native tribes; sincerely Catholic and consequently conservative, they maintained the customs, traditions and beliefs of their ancestors and at the same time their physical characteristics. Prudent, diligent, and skilful at predicting the success of a commercial enterprise and at seizing every opportunity, the English population became rich through trade. But they were never liked by their indigenous neighbours to whom they were too impassive and cold. Calvinism stamped them with its sanctimoniousness and coldness from which they have still not shaken free. As for their physique, they no longer conform to the type that their ancestors brought over from England. Today, the true Yankee, tall and thin, his face pale and his chest narrow, no longer resembles the heavy, robust and ruddy Englishman. It is interesting to note that New England provided Canada with a fair number of its children, who mixed with the French population and became indistinguishable from it. Indeed, for nearly a century after the establishment of English colonies in the north of the United States, few years went by without the French and native raiding parties bringing back to Canada women and children captured in enemy villages. Ordinarily, the women were returned after a time in captivity while the children were usually adopted by the colony. Many Canadian families today, then, include among their ancestors individuals born and partly raised in New England.[27]

It would have been surprising, to say the least, if this remarkable man and influential professor had not passed on his great interest in the neighbouring nation to his students and, in particular, to the one he considered the most intelligent of them all. There is perhaps no need to look further for Gérin-Lajoie's motives when, immediately after his graduation from Nicolet, he headed for the United States.

Étienne Parent and the American Example

In November 1842, with Father Ferland's encouragement, Gérin-Lajoie had founded an Academy at the Collège de Nicolet, that is, 'a literary and discussion society.'[28] Many students were to develop their oratorical and literary talents in this Academy,[29] beginning with its founder, who, taking advantage of these intellectual exercises (lectures, discussions, debates, creative works) became 'a new man.'[30] Barely out of college, in December 1844, Gérin-Lajoie helped found an equivalent body, but on a larger scale: the Institut canadien, no doubt the best-known literary society to have existed in French Canada. Moreover, he was to play an active role in the early years of the Institut. He was its secretary-archivist, then second vice-president, president for three terms, and secretary-correspondent; he even made the first speech to be given there (16 January 1845) and took part in all its discussions.[31]

It was during the presidency of Gérin-Lajoie (and, it could well be, at his initiative, so great were his eagerness and dedication) that Étienne Parent delivered the first of his five lectures at the Institut. Parent was then in his prime; he had been a very influential journalist for close to twenty years with *Le Canadien*, the journal that had been the voice of French Canada. His patriotic convictions, though moderate, had brought about his imprisonment during the insurrection of 1838; this jailing had given even more lustre to his renown. He had sat as Member of Parliament during the Union before becoming a high-level civil servant. At the time of his lectures at the Institut, he was clerk to the Executive Council, then under-secretary of the Province of Canada. He was 'one of the most respected and most listened-to among the older generation of the French-Canadian elite' of the time, 'one of the great figures in [French-Canadian] history' whose 'personality and thought ... dominate the entire first half of nineteenth-century Quebec,' as Jean-Charles Falardeau rightly says in his biography.[32] Parent would become Gérin-Lajoie's father-in-law in 1858, adding a special dimension to his influence. A precise study of his impact on the genesis of *Jean Rivard*, taking into account not only his activities as a journalist and his lectures, but also his correspondence, in particular with Rameau de Saint-Père from 1860, would be of the greatest interest. Some aspects of this influence will be dealt with in subsequent chapters. For the moment, however, let us consider only these early lectures, which were given just before Gérin-Lajoie's second trip to the United States, and particularly the first three, in which one theme is especially developed: America as an example to be imitated.[33]

These lectures, it must be emphasized, were widely circulated at the time. Delivered before an elite audience, the cream of the Montreal youth of the period, in a context of national reconstruction after the ordeal of the Act of the Union, reprinted in several newspapers (*Le Canadien, La Minerve, Mélanges religieux, Le Journal de Québec*) and in James Huston's *Le répertoire national* (1848) before being printed in book form in 1850,[34] they were intended for 'the French-Canadian people as a whole'[35] and proposed a precise and articulate program for the nation's present and its future. In the intense early years of the Institut canadien, they were greeted with fervour and enthusiasm.

Étienne Parent's first three lectures are presented as three chapters devoted to the same subject, as is clearly indicated by the title of the first one ('Industry Considered as a Means of Conserving Our Nationality'): 'means' not only to 'conserve' the French-Canadian identity, but also to insure for it a prosperous and happy future. Parent considers three means – industry, study, and work – for the purpose of his analysis. But in fact he proposes only one: the need to follow the example of the Anglo-Saxons and, in particular, of the American branch of this race, the only model for a people concerned about its future.

'Industry Considered as a Means of Conserving Our Nationality' (22 January 1846) distinguishes, in all, three categories of ways to uphold the nation: religious, political, and social. However, only the social means – that is, those within the reach of individuals, that everyone can use – interest the speaker. In this first lecture, he sets out to show the importance of a social means, namely industry, and to destroy French-Canadian prejudices with regard to it. These prejudices are seen as a poisonous legacy from the French nobility (Parent's resentment against the nobility is a constant in his lectures) and from the French nation as a whole. French Canadians, in his view, are too fond of titles (aspiring to the nobility or throwing oneself into an overcrowded profession are only two manifestations of the same 'fondness for titles' [118]) and look down on manual labour. For such is the definition of industry for

Étienne Parent: 'manual labour driven by intelligence' (119). The true power in America is the power of practical intelligence that is practised in profitable work. Industry conquers America: 'Industrialists, men whose manual labour is driven by intelligence – these are the noblemen of America' (119). Rather than extol careers that are prestigious but have no future, rather than leave the less talented to try their hands at industry, the nation should encourage the most intelligent to open workshops or factories, to start businesses or farms.

Parent stresses two points in particular: 'the little care that [French Canadians] generally take to preserve, from one generation to the next, businesses and other concerns, which [their] active and intelligent countrymen sometimes succeed in establishing' (120), and their reluctance to get agriculture out of 'the rut of outdated routines' (122) and to clear the 'uncultivated land that abounds in [their] country' (122). The stagnation of agriculture and colonization particularly arouses his indignation. While Quebec is inactive, others conquer America with their axes.

Throughout this lecture, indeed, the axe is the civilizing instrument par excellence, conquering wild nature to construct cities and empires. 'The axe, not the sword, is the weapon that truly conquered America. Industry is the founder of America's civilized societies.' 'The industrialist has created countless cities and empires out of the wilderness, not with the sword and the blood of other men, but with the axe and the sweat of his own brow' (119, 124, and passim). The eulogy of the axe scattered throughout this lecture repeats the idea and even the words of the tribute penned by James Fenimore Cooper in *The Chainbearer, or the Littlepage Manuscripts*: 'The American axe! It has made more real and lasting conquests than the sword of any warlike people that ever lived; but they have been conquests that have left civilization in their train instead of havoc and desolation.'[36]

The possibility of an influence is real, since Cooper was an author of international reputation, very much in favour, and *The Chainbearer* had been published in 1845, shortly before Parent's lecture. But even if there was no specific influence in this case, the idea was widely held at the time. The axe and those who wield it are awe-inspiring; they build a new world by overcoming wild nature. This eulogy is part of contemporary discourse on the New World – young, democratic, and vigorous – in opposition to the Old, which is aristocratic, warlike, and exhausted.

Thus, the pioneer and the worker in the fields, 'the breadwinners of the state' (123), are industrialists in the eyes of Parent. They are the true nobles, the builders who have nothing to be ashamed of when compared with the professions. The industrialist is 'the father of American civilization, without whom we would not exist' (123). In his conclusion, Étienne Parent conjures up an apocalyptic vision of what the future will hold for French Canadians if they do not follow the anglophones' example. The nation will be 'absorbed or smothered' by the English who 'have the advantage of a superior industrial education' and who are 'driven by the spirit of industry that characterizes their race' (125). Between nations, might is right. Industry is 'the only source of wealth' and wealth is 'the greatest if not the only way of acquiring social importance' (125).

The presence of the Anglo-Saxons, an industrious, trading race, eager to make money, and a model to be emulated, becomes an obsession in Parent's second lecture, entitled 'The Importance of Studying Political Economy' (19 November 1846). The basic idea of this lecture is simple but powerful. Quebec's struggle for political freedom is over. It has been won by the older generation. The war must now be fought on a new front, and the youth of Quebec (his listeners at the Institut) must battle on questions of material interest. In this new battle, however, their rivals are formidable. The Anglo-Saxons are the 'most industrious, the most commercially shrewd race of men in the world' (136). Indeed, the people surrounding the French Canadians

are descendants of a race of men who seem to have embarked upon the conquest or the modernization of the world by material interest. Their god is Mammon. Their children are born and live only to make money. They dream of nothing but making a fortune – a rapid and colossal fortune. There is no golden mean for them. And they satisfy this passion with all the fervour, activity, steadfastness, and persistence that men ordinarily devote to the pursuit of objects or to fulfilling the most intense and insatiable passions.

I am not being satirical here. On the contrary, I am only pointing out a fact that seems to me to be providential, and I am inclined to believe that this acquisitiveness in the Anglo-Saxon race, which, let it be said in passing, has only increased in the American branch of this people, is destined to write a chapter in the history of humanity, an age of industry, of material improvement, the age of positivism, the age of the glorification of work. But for the persistent and incessant work of the industrious nations, the world would have far fewer material and intellectual pleasures. Thus, far from envying them, we owe them gratitude. To avoid being overwhelmed, absorbed, or crushed by them, let us do as they do, let us work steadfastly, with enthusiasm, with intelligence, as they do. In the past, shiftless and feeble nations were the prey of warlike nations. Now idle and ignorant peoples will be exploited by industrious and intelligent peoples. (134)

Étienne Parent's idea is clear and powerful, and contradicts the traditional representation of Quebec at the time. He believes that wealth, comfort, and desire for gain are good and providential, intended by God to bring happiness to humanity. There is no sign here of a compensating discourse on the Messianic and spiritual role of the French-Canadian nation on the American continent. On the contrary, Étienne Parent wants his fellow citizens to become rich, to compete with the English speakers, and to this end, to imitate them, to become like them. 'Let us do as they do,' like these people Étienne Parent obviously admires unreservedly.

He had previously noted ruefully that French Canadians take delight in frivolous literature mass-produced in newspapers:

What benefit can be gained from the works of European serial writers by a people like ours, that has forests to clear, fields to improve, factories of all kinds to build, improvements of all sorts to make, whose mission, in a word, is to do with its inheritance on the American continent ... what our neighbours do so well with theirs? ... The time of lightweight literature has not yet come and will not arrive in Canada for quite some time. (130)

Faced with adversaries as tough as the Anglo-Saxons, it is imperative to read 'useful and instructive books,' and above all to study political economy. This is all the more important since England has just opted for free trade; henceforth, the nation's prosperity depends upon the decisions that will be made, and these decisions must be enlightened through the study of a science, political economy. It 'alone can put the statesman in a position to appreciate the significance and the effect of the different institutions and measures, and consequently to adopt those that are the most advantageous for the nation' (137–8). In support of his thesis, Parent cites several historical examples of poor decisions made out of ignorance. In his conclusion, he expresses the wish that colleges introduce courses in political economy into their programs of study, and he sings the praises of work that draws people nearer to the Creator and enables them to grow rich and make progress.

Indeed, it is to work that the third lecture, 'Of Man's Work' (23 September 1847), is devoted. As in the previous two, Parent frequently has recourse to the example of the Anglo-Saxons. This comparison is in a way the leitmotif of what Parent calls an 'improvisation,' borrowing the image of a 'rural stroll' as the organizing principle of his 'few considerations' (148). In reality, even if the lecture leaves an impression of disjointedness at times, it is quite clearly divided into two parts: criticism of those who scorn work, and refutation of the penal conception of work. In his introduction, Parent shows the tenor of his argument: French Canadians do not work *as much* as they should, whereas the English *like* work. Furthermore, French Canadians, with their 'stolid and routine spirit' (147) do not work *in the way* they should, whereas the Anglo-Saxons are always trying to improve their labour and to find ways to better themselves. This two-part comparison underlies the whole text. It leads to the menacing conclusion: 'No, do not delude yourself into thinking you can live as your fathers did when they were alone here. Hasten to pull yourselves up to the level of the newcomers, or else expect to become the servants of their servants, as many of you have already become in the areas surrounding the large cities' (148).

For Parent, and this he states unequivocally, an idle man is 'a degraded man, a very poor citizen, and an enemy of God' (149). Work, in fact, is in man's nature: human powers must be put to use. Work enables man to dominate creation and, by his discoveries, all of them the fruit of intelligent work, to conquer the universe. Along with the habits of order and application, and the cultivation of intelligence that it demands, work seems to ensure political freedom as well – the example of the United States is revealing for Parent. 'Thus the most industrious peoples were almost always the most free ... This is because industrious peoples need freedom more than all the others, and they find in their work the means to acquire it and to keep it' (157). Thus, disdain for work is for him a stupid prejudice typical of aristocrats or, as he adds at the end, of savages.

After his criticism of this 'harmful prejudice,' he launches into an attack on the 'absurd notion, as insulting to the divinity as it is harmful to humanity, that work is a punishment to which the Creator has condemned man' (155). For him, on the contrary, work has a divine but benevolent origin, because it is 'the continuation of God's work of creation' (155). Work brings happiness and progress to humanity, and Parent readily supports his theses with a short history of civilization. Moreover, the only way to prosper is to work – nobles and savages disappear before the industrious. The conclusion is self-evident: 'Gentlemen, I say again, let us work. It is only work that regenerates peoples' (169).

This lecture, with its fascinating mixture of religion and pragmatism, with its utilitarian moralism and its liberal optimism, would not be out of place in the collected works of a Franklin or a Defoe. God wills that we work, and he rewards the industrious. The true God is the God of work, of well-being, and of progress, since the fruits of labour are of benefit to humanity:

England, France, and the United States do not exist each for itself. Providence, in creating so much greatness, so much power, so much light, willed that a little of it should overflow outside these countries for the benefit of humanity. Moreover, it is less permissible for nations than for individuals to be selfish, predatory, and plunderous. (168)

This conviction gives rise to a rather curious passage in which Parent associates American republicanism and liberalism with a true theogony. In the best American tradition, inherited from the New England Puritans, God is associated with the birth of America and, in return, America offers the universe, now cleansed of the slag of the degenerate Old World, an authentic vision of God:

But one day America rose up with its young, robust peoples, presenting the world with another God – the God of free men, the God of workers. Europe, tottering in many ways in its ancient faith, has been quick to recognize that the God who appeared in the West was the true God of humanity ... And today you see Rome, the mistress of old-world politics, who has become the queen of modern-world religion; you see Rome, under the patronage of an enlightened pontiff, preparing the way for the enthronement of a new God. (163–4)

'Another God ... the true God of humanity ... the enthronement of a new God ...': the words quite obviously transcend the thought here. It would be more appropriate to speak of a new conception of God, a fresh look at the wishes of Providence and the social order willed by God. Parent's strict Catholic orthodoxy is unchallengeable, of course, yet his American optimism and his profound conviction that free, enterprising, and conquering America is doing God's will, lead him to express himself in terms that give us pause.

In another lecture, Parent returns to this fundamental conviction that God and America are partners, a conviction that is essentially Puritan (in the historical sense of the term) and is a component of the American mentality: 'People have laughed at the title that the old Pilgrims of New

England gave themselves in the lands of which they took possession, when they said that God had given the land to his saints. I find, for my part, that this title was just as apt as many others that seemed then and still seem unchallengeable' (232-3). With such thoughts, we are far removed from the French-Canadian Messianic thinking that associated God with the *spiritual* vocation of French Canada, positing New France as a mystical evangelizing enterprise that was to be prolonged by the anti-materialism of French Canada on a continent intoxicated by money. For Étienne Parent, the opposite is true: God is immediately associated with the pragmatic, commercial vocation of the American people. This is in the best tradition of the Puritans, who refused to dissociate spirit and profit, and who, as Bostonians were quick to point out, quite readily and rapidly confused God and cod.

Étienne Parent's admiration for the United States and for the English mentality persists undiminished in his other lectures. The sixth in particular, 'On the Importance and the Duties of Business,' delivered in Quebec on 15 January 1852, is very close to the first three. It aims to present 'what is beautiful, great and humanitarian in business' (229), by making it, 'after the Christian religion, the greatest instrument in the hands of God for man's moral and intellectual advancement' (232). This instrument, in Parent's mind, has been perfected by the English race: 'a nation of shopkeepers' (223), according to Napoleon, but who nonetheless succeeded in acquiring a vast empire and holding the Emperor in check. To the youth who were listening to him, Étienne Parent exclaims enthusiastically, using English for the last two words: 'Follow the motto of your century and of the New World: Go forward! Go ahead!' (229).

But even in his other lectures, however far removed they are from mercantilist or even strictly economic concerns, his admiration continually comes through. In his lecture on education in Lower Canada ('Reflections on Our Popular Education System, on Education in General and on the Legislative Means to Provide It,' Institut canadien, 19 February 1848) Parent launches into a very revealing digression ('By the way ...') that shows his clear preference for the English character:

In France they say: 'Do what has to be done, come what may.' It is chivalrous, it is nice. However, I prefer for the average man, the English adage, 'Honesty is the best policy.' It is more tangible, more practical, more true to human nature. Incidentally, it has been said that proverbs are the wisdom of nations. Don't you find that the two we have just cited paint fairly accurately the character of the two nations to which they belong? (191)

In his lecture on the priest ('On the Priest and on Spiritualism in Their Relationship with Society,' Institut canadien, 17 December 1848), he delivers a rousing apologia for individualism. Repeating the title of Ralph Waldo Emerson's famous lecture, he even indulges in scathing criticism of the contemplative orders:

But in this century at least, I would not understand the existence of communities of men practising a purely meditative life in hair shirts. In my eyes that would be a deplorable aberration of spiritualism. I would say the same about all religious practices that aim to weaken in man the feeling of independence or the *self-reliance* of the English, or that belittle both God and man by taking the place of the manly, active virtues that society requires. (207; italicized and in English in the original)

Finally, in his meatiest lecture ('On Intelligence in Its Relationship to Society,' Institut canadien in Quebec, 22 January and 7 February 1852), Parent draws a parallel between the United States of his day and ancient Greece. The 'quite natural' comparison comes to him during the course of a development on the efforts of intelligence to conquer the government of the world. 'It would be strange, although quite natural, if Greece's civilization, like America's, were attributable to the same cause, to the need for a freer and more liberal social state felt by people of well-tempered intelligence' (267). Suggesting in this lecture what is strictly speaking a utopia,[37] a radically new plan for the direction of society, Étienne Parent recognizes without hesitation that England embodies in part one of the main points of his program – that is, the aristocracy of intelligence:

I have just indicated that the English system offers in practice some similarity with the one I am proposing, and anyone who takes a close look at it will do little but generalize, and introduce everywhere something similar, in terms of useful results at least, to what time and the wisdom of several generations have achieved in England. This is worth thinking about, for the English system is synonymous with order, stability and freedom within; greatness, power, and glory without; finally industrial and commercial prosperity unheard of until our time. (284)

Thus, Étienne Parent constantly puts forward the English as an example for his listeners; at every opportunity he recommends the American model, which is always the first to come to his mind.

The Genesis of a Discourse   41

It therefore seems natural to assume that the author of *Jean Rivard* must have been influenced by the speeches of this great man, impassioned and convinced, balanced and reasonable, soon to be linked to him by marriage to his daughter, and thus close to him both temperamentally and emotionally. These early lectures by Étienne Parent added to the fascination that Gérin-Lajoie already felt for the United States. In all likelihood, the conjunction of these two elements is what persuaded Gérin-Lajoie to embark upon a study trip, his second journey to that country. And this determining influence no doubt prompted Gérin-Lajoie later to create a protagonist who, for the most part, is profoundly American, created in the image of the ideal proposed by his father-in-law: an industrious, brave, individualistic, practical, and resolute man, whose sole ambition is to be successful; a goal he will achieve thanks to manual labour guided by intelligence.

A Topos: The French Canadian as a Foil for the American

The constant parallel that Étienne Parent draws between his compatriots and the English speakers around them, in order to emphasize the former's failings and to whip up their fervour, was perhaps relatively new in a French-Canadian context. His systematic way of pursuing this parallel through various lectures, and the somewhat paradoxical lesson he drew from it (*to fight* effectively *against the other, one must become the other*, adopt the other's values and habits; in short, *one must be the other!*) are certainly something new in the history of French-Canadian ideologies. But the basic structure of the parallel itself was hardly original. In fact, it was inescapable. This was particularly true of writers who were still influenced by the figures of ancient rhetoric and who, to paint a satisfactory portrait of the type that interested them, were avidly searching for a foil. The comparison attracted them imperceptibly. The contrasting parallel is thus often found in French writers who visited America, saw the two races side by side, and were struck by the contrast in their fortunes.

Among the French travellers who were attracted to America and who have left contrasting portraits of this kind, two in particular are worthy of study: Volney and Tocqueville. Perceptive, intelligent observers, and men of science as well, they wrote works that were widely read.[38] Both authors are cited in *Jean Rivard*, which suggests that Gérin-Lajoie gave a great deal of thought to their observations, or at least enough to mention the fact in his novel – Volney in circumstances that it is important to make clear.

Constantin François de Chasseboeuf, Count of Volney, sailed from Le Havre in 1795, after being confined in the prisons of the French Revolution. 'Sad about the past, concerned about the future, I went with some hesitation to the home of a *free* people, to see if a friend of the freedom that France had desecrated could find, for his old age, a haven of peace that he could no longer hope to find in Europe.'[39] His goal was to settle in the United States. He stayed there only from October 1795 to June 1798, forced out finally by John Adams, at the time president of the United States, after having been Washington's vice-president. Volney explains Adams' nastiness as the resentment of an author hounding his critic.

Nevertheless, Volney brought back a manuscript, which he published in 1803. He had an ambitious plan. Starting with the climate and the soil of the United States, Volney wanted to study the customs and the political, economic, and social history of the diverse peoples of the United States. In the end, he published only the first part, *Tableau du climat et du sol des États-Unis d'Amérique*, but his preface shows the range of his thinking, the precision of his information, the rigour and reliability of his judgment, and makes the reader regret that he never wrote the work that he originally planned. The *Tableau* can be read with interest and profit today, but what is particularly relevant to this study is the genuinely ethnological 'Éclaircissements sur la Floride, sur la colonie française à Scioto, sur quelques colonies canadiennes et sur les sauvages.' The fourth article of these 'Éclaircissements,' which is devoted to a French colony in the American west, is cited at length by Gérin-Lajoie in the first edition of *Jean Rivard, Economist* (1864). As the passage is very revealing, was not kept in the definitive edition of the novel, and is fairly hard to find, it seems to me appropriate to quote it *in extenso* in spite of its length. It is found in the 'Last Part' of *Jean Rivard*. The narrator, having more or less 'run aground' by chance in Rivardville, meets Jean Rivard and looks around the town. In the fourth chapter of this part, Jean Rivard gladly reveals to him his secrets of success. The third secret, 'work,' leads him to deplore the huge amount of time wasted by French Canadians, 'one of the great evils of rural Canada' (334).[40]

On that subject, I must read you a passage from a book that I have just recently perused and that has left a deep impression on me. It is an excerpt from the voyage of the renowned thinker Volney, who, as you know, came to America in

1795 and visited several settlements, including one founded by French Canadians in the western United States. Here, briefly, is how he assesses the character and habits of the peoples of these colonies:

'The general decline of the French settlements on the frontier of Louisiana and even of Canada, compared to the equally general growth of those of the Anglo-Americans, has been for me a frequent subject of meditation ... The belief of some people that the French do not take well to this climate is an explanation that I can not share, for experience has convinced all the officers and doctors in the Rochambeau army that the French temperament is more resistant to cold, heat, temperature changes, and hardships than the Anglo-American temperament. It seems that our fibre has more elasticity and *vigour* than theirs ...

'In analysing this subject, one very worthy of interest, it seemed to me that the true reasons for the different results are to be found in the different ways of doing things and in the different use of time, that is to say, in what are called *habits* and *national character* ... A comparison between some aspects of the daily life of the settlers among the two peoples will demonstrate the truth of this opinion.

'The American settler, whether of English or German blood, is naturally cold and phlegmatic; he calmly works out a project for a farm. He concerns himself unceasingly yet unhurriedly with everything that relates to its creation or its improvement. If he becomes lazy, for which some travellers reproach him, it is only after having acquired what he has planned and what he considers necessary or sufficient. The Frenchman, on the other hand, with his exuberant, restless activity, gets enthusiastically caught up in a project, the costs and obstacles of which he has not considered. Perhaps more ingenious, he scoffs at his German or English rival's slowness, which he compares to that of an ox. But the Englishman and the German answer with cold good sense that, for ploughing, the patience of *oxen* is more suitable than the fieriness of frisky, mettlesome *steeds*. And in fact, it often happens that, after fretting about his desires and fears, the Frenchman winds up by getting sick and tired of it all and abandoning everything.

'The American settler, slow and silent, does not rise very early in the morning, but once he is up, he spends the whole day in an uninterrupted flow of useful work. At breakfast, he coldly gives his wife her orders and she receives them timidly and coldly, and carries them out without supervision. If the weather is good, he goes outside and ploughs, cuts trees, builds fences, etc. If the weather is bad, he takes inventory of house, barn, and stables, repairs doors, windows, and locks, hammers in nails, builds tables or chairs, and endlessly busies himself with making his home secure, comfortable, and clean. Given these traits, being self-reliant, if he finds an opportunity, he will sell his farm and go off into the woods, ten and twenty leagues beyond the frontier, to build himself a new settlement. There he will spend years felling trees, making himself first a hut, then a shed, then a barn, clearing the ground, sowing it, etc. For her part, his wife, as patient and hard-working as he, will help him and they will sometimes go six months without seeing a new face. But after four or five years they will have acquired enough land to make a living for their family.

'The French settler, on the other hand, gets up early in the morning, if only to brag about it. He confers with his wife about what he will do and he listens to her advice. It would be a miracle if they always agreed. The wife orders, checks, challenges; the husband is insistent or gives in, becomes angry or disheartened. Sometimes the home becomes a burden to him and he takes his gun and goes hunting or on a trip, or chats with his friends. Sometimes he stays home and spends his time chatting good-humouredly or quarrelling and scolding. The neighbours pay visits or return them – neighbourly chats are for the French such a pressing habitual need that, all along the frontier from Louisiana to Canada, it would be impossible to name a settler from this nation who is established out of the range and the sight of another. In several locations, having asked how far away was the most isolated colonist, "He is in the wilds," I was told, "with the bears, one league from all habitation, *with no one to talk to.*"'[41]

Gérin-Lajoie dropped this long quotation, along with the paragraphs that framed it, in the novel's second edition. Was it one of the 'slight blemishes' ('a certain wordiness, details of very little importance')[42] referred to by Father Casgrain that the author removed to shorten his work? No doubt. It should also be said that the French described by Volney were really not pioneers, but rather formed a long-established settlement in the American west, half assimilated into the Indian tribes' free and easy life, and a sort of remnant of a military post. Upon reflection, Gérin-Lajoie perhaps considered that the parallel with rural Canada was less relevant. It might well be, too – and this is the explanation I favour – that these very negative remarks were perceived for what they really are, that is to say, a line of thought diametrically opposed to the message conveyed by the novel. Volney's thesis is that the French race, because of its 'national character,' is afflicted with a congenital incapacity to become established and to prosper in America. At the end of the chapter preceding this description of Poste-Vincennes, after having described a French colony on the Ohio (Gallipolis), Volney concluded:

I thought I noticed in my trips to the United States that the French do not have the same aptitude for establishing agricultural settlements as the immigrants from England, Ireland, and Germany. Of fourteen or fifteen examples of French farmers that I have heard mentioned on this continent, only two or three looked as if they would succeed. And as for mass settlements of villages such as Gallipolis, all those that the French had earlier begun or established on the frontiers of Canada or Louisiana, and that have been left to their own devices, have languished and ended up being destroyed, while simple Irish, Scottish, or German individuals, plunging alone with their wives deep into the forests, and even on to the savages' land, generally succeeded in establishing sound farms and villages.[43]

Gallipolis, Poste-Vincennes – everywhere the French dwindle, while the Anglo-Saxons prosper. *Jean Rivard*, however, seeks to prove the very opposite. A young Canadian 'plunging alone into the forests,' living 'in the wilds with the bears' is a brilliant success. In short, if Gérin-Lajoie agrees with Volney in recording and lamenting the time wasted by French settlers, all the same he does not want to leave the impression that the French race is congenitally *incapable* of colonizing effectively and vigorously. Their inability stems from habits and thus can be reversed. Jean Rivard, Gérin-Lajoie's protagonist, indicates the route to follow.

It must also be noted that, with the elimination of the Volney text in the second edition, all mention of the Englishman disappears from the development on work as the 'secret' of Jean Rivard's success. In his lectures, Étienne Parent was wont to compare the French Canadians with the English speakers who were good, hard workers. Volney compares the improvident, sociable French with the industrious, persevering Anglo-Saxons. Gérin-Lajoie, after having pruned his text for the second edition of *Jean Rivard*, retains the fundamental structure found in his two precursors, that of a comparison, except that henceforth the bad Canadian settler is compared no longer to the Anglo-Saxons, but to Jean Rivard, who embodies the English pole of the topos: working without respite, not losing a second, persevering 'with great diligence' (333), attending to everything. Therefore, for two reasons Volney's text might have appeared useless or harmful when the author was revising the novel. On the one hand, by its pessimism and its fatalism it could be seen as contradicting the novel's lesson, whereas the young French Canadian can succeed as well as anybody else. On the other hand, since Jean Rivard embodies the values conveyed by the Anglo-Saxon, the parallel between the French Canadian and the latter seems unnecessary. It is Jean Rivard who embodies the ideal to be followed, a model steeped in English values: individualism, pragmatism, and tenacity.

Was Gérin-Lajoie really seeking to effect this transfer or transposition? It is no doubt premature, simply on the basis of his elimination of a quotation, albeit a very long one, to come to this conclusion. For the time being, let us simply note that the topos 'initiated' by Volney[44] is transmitted through a series of texts read by Gérin-Lajoie, up to *Jean Rivard*, where the English–French parallel is in a way sabotaged in favour of another bipolarity: Jean Rivard, replacing the American and embodying his values, becomes the model to be followed.

Volney's chapter on Poste-Vincennes will be cited by Tocqueville in his famous work *De la démocratie en Amérique*.[45] In the early chapters of *Jean Rivard*, Gérin-Lajoie will also mention Tocqueville. And when *Jean Rivard* is read in parallel with *De la démocratie en Amérique*, it is no exaggeration to maintain that the spirit of the great French sociologist, renowned since 1835, is a constant presence throughout Gérin-Lajoie's novel. Some passages in Tocqueville, in particular those concerning American self-reliance, the marriage of this individualism and public-spiritedness, the health of communal institutions, the passion for human welfare, will be indicated in subsequent chapters of this study, thus bringing out the richness of this intertextuality.[46] For the moment, let us stay with our topos: the marked contrast between French Canadians and Anglo-Americans, which brings out the inadequacies of the former ethnic group.

Two passages especially in *De la démocratie* contrast the two races. In the first, Tocqueville explains the United States' vigour and the strength of American expansionism in terms of Anglo-Saxon customs and the laws that reflect these customs, and he contrasts the Americans with French and Spanish peoples of the New World:

Physical causes thus do not influence the destiny of nations as much as one would like to think. I have met men from New England ready to abandon a homeland where they could have been confortably off, to go and seek their fortune in the wilds. Near there, I saw the French population of Canada crowding into a space too narrow for it, when the same wilderness was nearby. And while the emigrant in the United States acquired, for a few days' work, an extensive estate, the Canadian paid as much for the land as he would have done in France.

Thus nature, in delivering to the Europeans the solitudes of the New World, offers them riches that they do not always know how to exploit.

I see the same conditions for prosperity among other American peoples as among the Anglo-Americans, but without their laws and customs; and these people are poverty-stricken. Thus, the Anglo-Americans' laws and customs are the special reason for their greatness and the predominant cause I am seeking.[47]

The second passage is found in the masterly conclusion to the first two volumes (published in 1835). Tocqueville returns to this contrast, but he lays more stress on the French element, bringing out its fragility by comparison with a people more gifted for economic conquest:

There was once a time when we too could have created a great French nation in the American wilderness and counterbalanced the English in controlling the destinies of the New World. France once possessed territory in North America almost as vast as the whole of Europe. At that time the three largest rivers on the continent were entirely under French jurisdiction. The Indian nations living between the mouth of the St Lawrence and the Mississippi delta heard no language but ours. All the European settlements scattered over this immense area recalled the homeland: Louisbourg, Montmorency, Duquesne, Saint-Louis, Vincennes, Nouvelle Orléans, all names dear to France and familiar to our ears.

But a combination of circumstances that it would take too long to list has deprived us of this magnificent inheritance. Wherever the French were few in number and sparsely settled they have disappeared. The rest have come together in a small area and have become subject to the laws of others. The four hundred thousand Frenchmen of Lower Canada today constitute as it were the remnant of an ancient people lost in the middle of a new nation. The foreign population is growing around them unceasingly, it expands on all sides, it penetrates right into the ranks of the former masters of the soil, predominates in their cities and corrupts their language. This population is identical to that of the United States. I am therefore correct in saying that the English race is not confined within the borders of the Union but extends well beyond them toward the North-East.[48]

Tocqueville's travel journal, published in 1860, often stresses this contrast. In the wilds of Michigan, in the summer of 1831, Tocqueville and Beaumont encountered marvellous representatives of the type that was creating the United States: the industrious American settler.

His well-defined muscles and slender limbs make the inhabitant of New England recognizable at first glance. This man was not born in the solitude in which he lives, as you can tell by his physique alone. His early years were spent in an intellectual and reasoning society. It is his will that has impelled him to labour in the wilds for which he seems ill-suited. But if his physical strength seems inadequate for his venture, on his features furrowed by life's cares, an air of practical intelligence, of cold, persevering energy strikes you at first sight ... To prosper he has braved exile, solitude, and countless hardships in the wild ... He made this effort one day, he has renewed it for years, he will do so for possibly another twenty years without becoming discouraged and without complaining ... Concentrating on this one goal – making his fortune ...

A nation of conquerors who endure living in the wild without ever letting themselves be led astray by its charms, who appreciate about civilization and enlightenment only their usefulness for human well-being ... a people who, like all great peoples, has but one thing in mind, and who march toward the acquisition of wealth, the sole aim of its labours, with a perseverance and a disregard for life, that could be called heroic, if this term were suitable for things other than the efforts of virtue.[49]

Tocqueville also relates in detail the enlightening conversation he had with the inn-keeper in Pontiac, Michigan, then on the frontier of civilization:

'One final question: The general belief among us is that the American wilderness is populated as a result of European emigration. How is it then that, since we have been travelling through your woods, we have not come across a single European?' A smile of superiority and satisfied pride came across our host's face as he listened to this request. 'It is only Americans,' he responded bombastically, 'who can have the courage to endure such hardships and who are willing to pay this price for prosperity. The European emigrant stops in the big cities by the ocean or in the neighbouring areas. There he becomes a craftsman, a farm hand, a manservant. He leads an easier life than he did in Europe and appears satisfied to leave the same legacy to his children. The American, on the other hand, takes possession of the land and seeks to build a great future with it.'[50]

This portrait of the American, highlighted in this instance by contrasting him favourably with the Europeans, will be rapidly completed by an equally striking contrast with another race, long acclimatized to its environment. Pushing beyond the last settlements, Tocqueville and his companion, after a somewhat perilous journey, visit Saginaw, a sort of outpost of civilization. There they see English and French living side by side without mixing. Tocqueville's observation confirms in every detail (adding cheerfulness as well) what Volney had noted thirty-five years earlier at Poste-Vincennes. 'The men who live on this small cultivated plain belong to two races that for almost a century have coexisted on American soil and obey the same laws. They have, however, nothing else in common.' The French have a strong 'taste for social pleasures,' a very 'happy-go-lucky attitude toward life.' The Frenchman, for all intents and purposes, becomes an Indian, adopting his free and easy morals, intermingling with him; but 'this man has nonetheless remained a Frenchman, cheerful, enterprising, self-important, proud of his origins, a passionate lover of military glory, more vain than selfish, a man of instinct, following his first impressions rather than his reason, preferring noise to money.' Next to him is the 'cold, stubborn, ruthlessly argumentative Englishman; he takes over the land and extracts from the wild all that he can remove. He battles endlessly against it, every day he strips it of some of its attributes ... The immigrant in the United States maintains that ... man comes into the world only to acquire the comforts and conveniences of life.'[51]

Coming through Canada on his return trip, Tocqueville completes this parallel with a study of French Canadians. He remarks on two main things when he talks about French Canadians: first, their gaiety, liveliness, and taste for social pleasures,[52] and second, their stay-at-home spirit. In his conversations with M. Quiblier, superior of the Montreal seminary, and with M. Neilson, a Member of Parliament with close links to the people, as well as in his impromptu interviews with the people, for example as they come out of mass at Beauport, or in his observations on the price of land, the same remark recurs constantly: the French Canadian is a homebody and does not want to leave his native parish.

[The French-Canadian race] does not have this adventurous spirit and this contempt for family and birth ties that characterize the Americans. The [French] Canadian does not move away from his parish and his relatives unless he has no choice and he settles as close to them as possible.[53]

The French Canadian is fondly attached to the soil on which he was born, to his parish, to his family. This is why it is so difficult to persuade him to seek his fortune elsewhere.[54]

French Canadians are too afraid of shaking the dust of their native village off their feet. They are not shrewd enough. 'Oh! You are right, but what do you expect me to do?' Such are their answers.[55]

One day I asked a farmer why French Canadians were hemmed into narrow fields while just twenty leagues away they could find fertile, uncultivated land. 'Why,' he replied, 'do you prefer your wife, even though your neighbour's wife has prettier eyes?'[56]

We found there, especially in the villages far from the towns, ancient French habits and customs. Around a church crowned with a weather-cock and a cross decorated with fleurs-de-lis, the village houses are huddled together, for the Canadian land-owner does not like to isolate himself on his land like the English or the American in the United States.[57]

Like New England, Lower Canada is surrounded by unlimited fertile land. However, until our time, the French population in Canada, lacking enlightenment, crammed itself into a space far too narrow for it, and the price of land is almost as high on the outskirts of Quebec as it is in Paris, while right beside it, the land is worth ten francs an acre.[58]

These quotations from Tocqueville are somewhat long. They are, however, of great interest. My analysis of *Jean Rivard* will emphasize and echo the French sociologist's commentary; it is essentially for this reason that I felt it important to quote it. It is easy to see, even at a first reading of the novel, that Gérin-Lajoie's protagonist fits rather poorly Tocqueville's and Volney's description of French Canadians (the essential elements of which are also present but toned down in Étienne Parent's writings). In effect, Jean Rivard seems copied down to the last detail (except the physique) from the description that these French travellers have left us of the enterprising American. It is as if Gérin-Lajoie had decided to subvert the topos and to use it for his own purposes. Jean Rivard, who plunges alone into the forest and takes possession of the land, who clears and cultivates it, who becomes a rich landowner, the founder of a town, leader of his township and an MP, follows step by step the trail blazed by the enterprising Americans in the nineteenth century.[59]

Indeed, Tocqueville, in his famous work, had stressed the fact that it was the Americans who cleared the land, and not the recent immigrants from Europe. There were two distinct patterns of immigration that characterized American settlement. The European settled along the coast, established himself, hired himself out, gradually amassed enough capital to enable him (or his children) to own and clear land, while the American plunged straight into the forest. As a typical example of this ceaseless movement of the native population out of New England,

Tocqueville states that in 1830 thirty-six Congress representatives were natives of Connecticut. Connecticut, then, though having only one-forty-third of the population of the United States, had in a way an eighth of the representatives in Congress. But in reality, Connecticut had only five representatives – the others were natives of that state, but represented new western states.

If these thirty-one individuals had stayed in Connecticut, it is probable that instead of being wealthy landowners, they would have remained small-time farmers, they would have lived in obscurity without being able to embark on a political career, and far from becoming useful legislators, they would have been dangerous citizens.[60]

Similarly, if Jean Rivard had stayed at Grandpré, he would have had a poor, obscure life. Like the Americans, he leaves his native parish and plunges into the forest to make his fortune.

Moreover, the theme of the enterprising American contrasted with the small-time French Canadian is treated not only by French travellers and by Canadian intellectuals who, like Étienne Parent, could have read their works; Canadian observers who were Gérin-Lajoie's contemporaries also treat it, repeating the essential elements of the contrast. Hogan, in *Le Journal de Québec*, declares:

Nothing is more dissimilar than the habitant of Lower Canada and the farmer of Upper Canada. The character of the latter is enterprising, adventurous and cosmopolitan. He is always ready to change his property ... he will willingly abandon a hundred acres of cultivated land for 500 acres of forest, if he believes the woods will be more beneficial for his children. The habitant, on the other hand, has no other love than the one he feels for his farm, which is often small. Of all the places in the world, he prefers his birthplace, even though he sometimes lives very poorly there.[61]

Fernand Ouellet, who cites this account, adds immediately: 'The French Canadians did not form a people of pioneers. Up until the middle of the nineteenth century they had populated the St Lawrence lowlands, clearing them as their numbers grew ... Instead of setting out to conquer new areas, they had further subdivided their farms.'[62] Father Ferland, Gérin-Lajoie's teacher and friend, remarked in 1851 that French-Canadian farmers had every reason to imitate English-speaking farmers in order to break their routine and to progress:

Thus, the advantage French-Canadian farmers find in settling in townships already inhabited in part by foreigners is that they can learn from them a better system of agriculture ... We observed that the townships populated exclusively by French Canadians have not made the slightest progress, while in other townships ... French Canadians who have settled on similar land have succeeded very well, because they have adopted the methods of cultivation used by foreigners established in the vicinity. In a way, they had model farms before their eyes and they managed to profit from them.[63]

In light of these commentaries, Jean Rivard's choice of the Eastern Townships as a place to settle takes on certain new connotations. Of course, it is a choice that is justified both historically and geographically. From 1848, colonization societies were created with the express purpose of colonizing the townships; moreover, the latter are relatively close to the old seigneuries. But apart from the likelihood of this choice, it appears that it may have thematic significance. The townships were traditionally reserved for anglophones, and the descendants of the American loyalists prospered there. But here comes a young French Canadian, as intelligent, educated, hard-working, and shrewd as they are, possessing in short, to a fine degree, their own qualities of industry and of perseverance, who takes the struggle into their own kingdom. The stakes are as follows: the 'townships' must become 'les cantons.' The Gallicizing of the word, as seen in the novel's second note (Chapter 3, p. 15), is a sign of the Gallicizing of the Anglo-Saxon's conquering qualities, a vital necessity for the ultimate Gallicizing of the territory and for French Canada's survival.

L'air du temps

The quotations that pepper this chapter – words of those close to Gérin-Lajoie or of thinkers who could have strongly influenced him – all of which work toward a valorization of the conquering qualities of the American, outline a true *zeitgeist*. 'L'air du temps' – the notion is famous but little used because of its vagueness. However, it translates well a constant of French-Canadian thought in the nineteenth century that was encouraged by illustrious European travellers, themselves fascinated by America.[64] The amazing development of the United States, its inexorable progress westward, the growth of its peoples, its economic and industrial conquests, and its wealth constitute a fruitful subject of reflection for the French-Canadian elite, and also, no doubt, for the common people. The latter have left barely any written traces of their thoughts, but nevertheless thought and acted. Thus, it was in the hundreds of thousands that French Canadians emigrated, living out in concrete terms their fascination with the United States despite their attachment to their native land.

Today, it is well known that Canada lives in the orbit of the United States and that Canadians are economically, politically, socially, and culturally dependent on this powerful republic. But the phenomenon is not a recent one. It seems that throughout the nineteenth century deep and extensive links were forged between the two countries. The extent of French-Canadian emigration shows that the ties were numerous and very real.[65] The writings of Father Ferland reveal clearly that, from the very beginnings of the French presence in North America, there was a special relationship between Quebeckers and the United States. Benoît Brouillette's book on the penetration of the American continent by French Canadians leads one to believe that it is unfaithful to history to think that, after the Conquest, Quebeckers huddled together on their lands in order to reproduce madly and take shelter from everything that seemed foreign,[66] feeling, as Melville would have it, 'impregnable in their little Quebec.' Reality was quite different, and the historian Gustave Lanctôt has summed it up in a few striking sentences:

Following the military conflicts of the French regime and the political campaign of the revolution, came the third stage, the economic penetration that characterized the nineteenth century. In its beginnings, Americanism was practised through business by the settler in the Eastern Townships. Having cleared the hurdle of the War of 1812, Americanism, through its political example, influenced the Patriotes of 1837, and, by its material wealth, attracted the politically discontented and economically disadvantaged of 1849. Shortly thereafter, it displayed its free and flourishing democracy as a goal to the adversaries of Confederation.[67]

Gérin-Lajoie was one of those 'politically discontented and economically disadvantaged' of the 1848 generation who were attracted to the United States. He belonged to that active and loquacious minority for whom the United States was a vital point of reference. According to Jean Bruchési, admiration for the neighbouring republic, its wealth, its dynamism, its institutions, and its tradition of freedom and democracy, was perhaps not widespread. However, it was sufficiently extensive, in particular among the liberal youth, that it found frequent expression in newspapers, speeches, demonstrations, or bodies such as the Institut canadien. This admiration is a strong undercurrent reappearing often as a leitmotif and revealing this group's aspirations, in particular at certain critical times: during the 1830s, which were stirred by the insurrectional republican movement culminating in the Patriotes' Revolt; in the late 1840s, when the debate about annexation to the United States was raging; and after the late 1850s when the debate about Confederation began[68] and Quebec was faced with permanent minority status.

The nationalist elite, reluctant to emigrate and no doubt having more means than the common people to enable them to stay in the country, proposed either to import American habits, customs, and virtues onto Laurentian soil, or to resort to a more radical solution: dumping the entire country into the lap of Americans. Fernand Dumont, reflecting on 'the rapid switch, surprising at first glance' of the youth of the Institut canadien 'from nationalism to propaganda for annexation to the United States,' concludes that a 'Quebec society that would be progressive in its economy and democratic in its structures was no doubt possible only by its integration into the neighbouring republic.'[69] In short, in order to safeguard their race, Quebeckers should remain on their land, but tip the entire country into the neighbouring American republic. Thus they would remain among themselves, in a tight-knit group, yet incorporated into the fascinating and progressive giant as a new American state. Failing that, they should *become American*, but remain francophone, that is, adopt the values and behaviour of the Americans.

From annexationism to Americanophilia: this was Étienne Parent's intellectual itinerary. After being a reluctant and unhappy annexationist during the political debate preceding the uprising of 1837-8,[70] he became, after the Act of Union, an enthusiastic propagandist for the American mentality in his lectures. As for Gérin-Lajoie, he remained an annexationist throughout his life: an enthusiastic annexationist in his youth, a discreet annexationist in his adult life. Thus, he could write in his *Mémoires* on 31 December 1849: 'I do not believe that I am destined to get involved in politics before Canada is annexed to the American Union, a time that I desire with all my heart and that I will greet enthusiastically like the dawn of a new day.' According to his widow, Gérin-Lajoie privately expressed his annexationist sentiments until the end of his life, but his post as a federal civil servant obliged him to keep quiet about them in public.[71]

Annexationism and the idealization of values conveyed by the United States characterized the intellectual climate during Gérin-Lajoie's formative years and at the time he took his first steps into the world. The massive emigration of his fellow citizens to the United States marked Gérin-Lajoie's maturity at the time he wrote *Jean Rivard*. America as the horizon and future of French Canadians – this was the particular challenge that he took up in his novel.

2

Paratext and Plot: What Happens in *Jean Rivard*?

What happens in *Jean Rivard*? This question may seem either pointless or pretentious, and those who find the novel a long bore will be tempted to answer: 'Nothing, of course.' John Dover Wilson legitimately asked the question about a work as complex and ambiguous as *Hamlet*, since scholars cannot seem to agree on the existence of the ghost, the reality of the murder, Gertrude's adultery, Hamlet's madness or hallucinations, his love for Ophelia, the meaning of the pantomime, the likelihood of the play within a play, and dozens of other important issues. But what about *Jean Rivard*? The plot is simple and linear. The protagonist is rough-hewn and the other characters are equally one-dimensional, or else barely sketched. In any case, since the author himself tells us exactly what to think of his work, what remains to be said?

Yet it was not until sixty years after the novel's publication that an economist, Édouard Montpetit, a lone voice soon ignored, reminded literary critics of the obvious: Jean Rivard *founds a town*, a town that he wants to see compete one day with America's largest metropolitan centres. His dream, an American dream, is to push back the frontier, to make the forest recede. His goal is not cultivation of land, as the critics insist; that is only an immediate end. The true goal is to found a town. In Jean Rivard's first letter to his friend Gustave Charmenil, his ambition is naïvely and forcefully presented:

Who is to say that my plot of land will not be the centre of a great town twenty years from now? Fifty years ago, what were the cities and villages of Toronto, Bytown [Ottawa], Hamilton, London, Brockville in Upper Canada, and the majority of American cities? They were dense forests felled by the axes of valiant land-clearers. I feel I have the courage to do the same. (27)

It is to be noted that the model invoked is anglophone and American. Not one French-Canadian town or village comes to his mind that would adequately represent the dimensions of his ambition.

Nevertheless, literary criticism devoted to *Jean Rivard* persists in resolutely keeping this work within the narrow confines of the rural novel. Critics see nothing in the work except an agrarian mystique, a physiocratic ideology, and an agriculturalist way of thinking. For Monsignor Camille Roy and those critics who unhesitatingly accepted his reading, *Jean Rivard* is the novel of the settler, the best example of the novel of the land. The novel is seen only as an agrarian, reactionary work, a dogmatic reflection of the globalist image that critics still have of the nineteenth century.[1] Commentators quote the characters indiscriminately and blithely confuse the characters with the narrator, action with discourse about the action, text with paratext, none of which would be accepted when dealing with an 'authentic' novel. They feel entitled, however, to do so in this case, on the grounds that it is a thesis novel and that it is univocal. For this reason it seemed to me a useful exercise to examine what actually happens in this novel.

The Paratext

Let us establish first what the obvious intentions of the author are, as they are revealed by the paratext, that is, the guide to the reader that he provides to accompany his novel, either surrounding it (the titles, prefaces, forewords, notes, appendices) or invading it (the metatext or prescriptive interventions by the narrator) – in short, the elements that constitute the manifest intentions, the 'will to meaning' mentioned in the introduction to this study.

The Titles

The paratext of *Jean Rivard* is particularly rich and, as is normally the case, the titles first capture the reader's attention. It is well known that titles are complex artefacts fulfilling numerous requirements and as such are rich in meanings.[2] Their primary functions – 'referential (centred on the object), conative (centred on the receiver), and poetic (centred on the message)'[3] – determine that titles, as coded messages, are saturated with meanings. Indeed, titles radiate outward in numerous directions, operate on various levels, and try to satisfy all requirements: they 'capture the reader's attention, give an idea of the content, stimulate curiosity, and add an aesthetic touch to complete the seduction.'[4] In short, titles have two essential aspects: their relationship to the work, which they introduce and summarize, setting it in motion but also permeating it; and, second, what Duchet calls their 'hors-texte,' since titles reflect a socio-cultural context, respond to commercial practices, and fit into a corpus of titles (a metalanguage or a descriptive code) of which they are only one element.

Gérin-Lajoie is fully aware of this second aspect, when he declares in his foreword:

Beautiful, young townswomen, who spend all your time dreaming of clothes, balls and romantic conquests; you gallant young men who, joyful and carefree, whirl though worldly pleasures, this story is definitely not for you.

The title itself will surely bore you to tears.

Indeed, 'Jean Rivard' ... what a common name! Could anything more vulgar be imagined? 'Rivard' would still pass muster, if instead of 'Jean' it were 'Arthur,' or 'Alfred,' or 'Oscar,' or some other name from mythology or a foreign language.

And a pioneer ... could such a person provide a model of grace and gallantry? (1)

In short, in an ironic, playful way, Gérin-Lajoie confronts his readers head-on. From the outset he acknowledges in the title itself that his undertaking falls intentionally short of their expectations. This irony can be understood only by reference to statements of Étienne Parent or Father Casgrain regarding the frivolousness of readers of the time, or to Yves Dostaler's study on the trite, insignificant reading that was usually offered for their consumption.[5] By means of a deliberately banal, prosaic title, Gérin-Lajoie clearly signals his intention to 'go against the flow.' The title is a strategic initiative, an indication of the author's departure from tradition: it manifests clearly his ideological purpose.

In fact, my use of the singular is no doubt misleading, and if critics speak continually of *Jean Rivard*, it is for purposes of convenience. There are, in fact, two titles: *Jean Rivard, the Pioneer* and *Jean Rivard, Economist*. When it was first published in serial form in 1862, it bore the title *Jean Rivard, the Canadian Pioneer*. The first volume of the diptych also has a subtitle in brackets: 'a real-life narrative.' There are two titles, then, with the same grammatical structure: a proper name followed by a noun in apposition; an adjective, 'Canadian,' eliminated in subsequent editions; a subtitle that functions as a generic indicator, that is, classifying the work in a genre in the same way as such indicators as 'a novel of manners,' 'a historical novel,' or 'an episode in the reign of.' Each of these elements requires further explanation.

First of all, the dualism. Why are there two titles when the novel recounts the life of a single character, who embarks on a single adventure, and when it would have been possible, on various occasions, to recast the work using a single title? Chronologically, two titles can be justified, the first title acting as a trial balloon and the second fulfilling the expectations created. Indeed, at the end of *Jean Rivard, the Pioneer* (in *Les Soirées canadiennes* 2 [1862], 318), Gérin-Lajoie declares: 'This first part of the story of Jean Rivard, which, moreover, can easily be detached from the rest, is the only one that will be published in *Les Soirées canadiennes*; however, if the public shows interest in this narrative, the author proposes to make the rest of the hero's life known, as soon as he has some spare time.' The good-natured public seems to have really taken an interest in the story and asked for a sequel. The author thus announced, two years later: 'Since that time, various people, friends of obscure grandeur, who had taken some interest in the young man's fate, have asked me for news about him ... Everyone made their own conjectures, which were more or less slanderous, about our pioneer and the spirit of his worthy wife and helpmate. This is in part why I have chosen today to make known what became of Jean Rivard' (*Jean Rivard, Economist, Le Foyer canadien* 2 [1864], 16).

The length of time it took to write the sequel (the author's 'spare time'), naïve marketing, and the new novelist's hesitations all explain the first publication in two parts. Yet even when it was republished in volume form, despite revisions, corrections, and systematic pruning of his novel, Gérin-Lajoie kept the two titles. They must therefore correspond to an essential intention.

Indeed, there are two distinct stages in the protagonist's life. He is a pioneer and he is an economist – a pioneer for two years, and an economist for the next fifteen years (until the end of his fictional life). A pioneer cuts trees in a forest to create arable land; he transforms or modifies the natural order. Foresters and lumberjacks spend their entire lives in the bush felling trees: they are linked to the forest on which they depend. The pioneer, however, ventures into the forest to make it recede. Clearing trees is for him but a means to an end. Being a pioneer is by definition a transitory occupation.

Paradoxically and unexpectedly, however, Jean Rivard does not clear trees in order to farm, which would be the logical extension of his initial task; instead, he becomes an 'economist.' The message encoded in the titles is thus clear: since pioneering necessarily leads to another occupation, Jean Rivard is a pioneer in order to become an economist. He is a manual labourer whose work is guided by his intelligence; he then becomes a man of knowledge, or rather a man endowed with a special type of knowledge that is fundamental – what Étienne Parent had called for on behalf of the community some years before – an understanding of the laws that govern wealth. He is probably the first person to benefit from this knowledge, but the very meaning of the term implies the wealth of the collective whole: an 'economist' has knowledge that goes beyond the sound management of personal property.

Morever, the syntactic structure of the two titles, at once similar and slightly different, establishes two different links between the proper name and the nouns that are in apposition to it. In his classic 1821 treatise, Fontanier calls apposition a figure 'par exubérance,'[6] by which he means, apparently, an expansion of the phrase, an amplification or abundance that seeks, by its construction alone, to complete the meaning. This definition is somewhat lively but is useful, in the circumstances, especially if we consider that the proper name, in itself, has no real meaning. It is just a label that has a referent, but does not lend itself to semantic analysis, except for the most basic findings. The proper name 'Jean Rivard,' for example, indicates that the person is a man and, in a very vague manner, is someone of a certain social origin, a commoner. This second clue derives only from what is not present in the name: the aristocratic 'de' or a title (le chevalier de ..., Angeline de ...), indicating the absence of blue blood or high rank; the lack of originality in both his first name and his surname, pointing to a common origin. The appositional construction is in effect minimal (a simple juxtaposition). This simple addition of a noun gives substance and meaning to the proper name: *Jean Rivard, the Pioneer* and *Jean Rivard, Economist*.

To the apposition is added a particular use of the basic determinative, the article. Indeed, the presence followed by the absence of a definite article captures the reader's attention. In the three subsequent editions published during his lifetime the author had ample opportunity to eliminate this inconsistency; he chose to keep the article in the first title (*Jean Rivard, the Pioneer*) and to keep it out of the second one (*Jean Rivard, Economist*). Two different types of apposition are thus under consideration. The explanatory or 'identifying'[7] apposition, with the article included, is a way of highlighting a particular characteristic: the article stresses a certain exclusiveness in the identification.

Pioneering, it would seem, is something so unusual that Jean Rivard, a Canadian name, has practically an exclusive monopoly over it. As a result, the proper name, with an article modifying the noun that follows it, thus acquires a 'precise characterization that makes for certainty in identification.'[8] The absence of the article in the second title indicates, on the one hand, that the apposition has merely a 'descriptive' function: being an economist is thus not the sum total of Jean Rivard's existence. On the other hand, the absence of the article, as is always the case when the noun stands alone, without a determinative, implies that the concept must be taken in the broadest sense possible. Jean Rivard – the syntax of the title is precise – is *the* pioneer, the quintessential pioneer, one of a kind; next, he is *an* 'economist' in the broadest sense of the word.

The only other feature of the title, the adjective 'Canadian,' is another case in point. Indeed, at first glance, its elimination after the novel's first publication in serial form can be easily explained. The adjective seems redundant, since the target audience is Canadian (read 'French Canadian')[9] and likely to recognize the nationality of the name in the title. 'Canadian' would become essential, if, for example, the book were published in France, since readers would have to be informed, from the very outset, that the work had nothing to do with a woodsman such as one could find in the novels of George Sand. In fact, when *Jean Rivard* was published in *Le Monde*, the adjective was naturally revived for French readers.

However, this does not explain its inclusion in the first published version. Either clumsiness on the part of the author must be assumed, which is quite possible since it would not be an isolated case, or else – to give him some credit – the epithet's redundancy must be seen as intentional. That is the crux of the matter. To judge by the reports of French travellers such as Volney and Tocqueville, Étienne Parent's complaints in his lectures, the high rate of emigration from Canada to American industrial centres, the snail's pace of French-Canadian colonization, the failed attempts to persuade French Canadians to take to the forest, despite the concerted efforts of people of all ideological tendencies to promote this goal, and the evidence presented in the novel itself, the pioneer, in those years, was *not* French Canadian. He was American or English.

Indeed, to pursue the point, a few facts may be added to the evidence already gathered in the previous chapter. For example, Arthur Buies, the propagandist for the great colonizing priest, Father Labelle, declared enthusiastically in 1889: 'It is not in vain that we breathe the invigorating air of a free America: with our neighbours in the United States, we are swept away by the same torrential current that carries both people and things toward ever-changing, ever more remote shores.'[10] But actually the torrential current was American. An oil stain is a more appropriate image for French Canadians. Father Labelle himself recognized this fact: 'The United States grows apace because the Americans colonize by rail, whereas we go by cart.'[11] In his study of Father Labelle, Gabriel Dussault cites the following statistics:

In the absence of any precise data, the number of colonists settling new land between 1851 and 1901 has been provisionally estimated to be about 1000 per year, compared with a total population growth from 890 261 to 1 648 898 over the same period.[12]

Fifty thousand pioneers, then, in a fifty-year period: a number that must be compared with the 580 000 French Canadians who emigrated to the United States as well as with the remarkable birth rate over that very short period of time. When compared with the colonization of the United States, the 'oil stain' seems insignificant. The Northern Pacific Company alone had 1000 colonial recruiters in Europe; in 1874, the Santa Fe Railroad brought over 10 000 German Mennonites to Kansas; even during the Civil War, the population of nine western states increased by 843 000 people; in 1864, at the height of the Civil War, 75 000 people passed through Omaha alone en route to the West. Thus, not even war slowed the tide of immigrants. But it was between 1870 and 1890 that the tide was at its height with the arrival of eight million new inhabitants. By 1890, the frontier no longer existed, except in the collective imagination; the immense prairies stretching between Missouri and California had been settled. Oklahoma, opened at noon on 22 April 1889 with an epic race, had 60 000 inhabitants by November of the same year and ten years later, a population of 800 000 inhabitants.[13] The gigantic proportions of this relentless surge are staggering, demonstrating why contemporary observers were fascinated by it. Tocqueville was one of the first to be astounded:

It would be difficult to describe the avidity with which the American rushes forward to secure this immense booty that fortune offers ... Before him stretches an almost boundless continent, and he seems to hasten onward as if he were already afraid that land was running out and he might get there too late.[14]

In this context, it is not surprising that, in the first edition of his novel, Gérin-Lajoie chooses to stress the fact that his pioneer is Canadian, knowing he can revert to a more laconic use in subsequent editions. We are thus presented with a pioneer, a Canadian pioneer to be precise, one who can compete with the great pioneers of the continent. The epithet serves a purpose similar to that of the definite article. Just as the definite article indicates in the apposition 'something quite separate, exclusive, and clearly identified,'[15] so the somewhat redundant adjective further emphasizes the author's purpose. In a people of reluctant pioneers, Jean Rivard is *the* pioneer, the *Canadian* pioneer.

Moreover, the newspapers of the day are quite instructive on this issue. For example, an article in the *Mélanges religieux* of 10 September 1844 deplored the mass emigration of French Canadians while the Canadian forests still remained uncleared:

It is understandable that French Canadians rightly consider the support of religion to be vital if they are to move into these new woodland communities. If we see them joining our American neighbours and experiencing the sad fate of which we have spoken [the hard life of quasi-slavery in the factories] ... *instead of settling practically in the middle of the forest as do foreigners*, it is simply because they hope to acquire, during their exile, the resources to establish themselves among their fellow citizens and not to be deprived of the benefits of religion. *It is common knowledge that Canadians cannot live in isolation.* (my italics)

This passage recalls the statements made by both Volney and Tocqueville on the characteristic courage of Anglo-Saxons. The paradoxical reasoning is also noteworthy. Rather than live *like* the foreigners (pioneering on their own in the forest), French Canadians prefer to live *among* the foreigners, even if it means being penniless. Jean Rivard is thus an exceptional case – hence the article and the adjective, *the Canadian* pioneer – he does what the foreigners do.

Indeed, he belongs to the family of American pioneers described by Tocqueville. After spending his early years 'within an intellectual, reasoning society,' he braves 'exile, solitude, and the countless hardships in the wilderness' 'in order to gain prosperity.' 'It is his will that drove him to work in the wild' and not necessity.[16] Contrary to French-Canadian settlers who, at the time, were generally poor and uneducated,[17] Jean Rivard is modelled on the image of the pioneers found in Tocqueville's striking summary. He advances into 'the solitudes of America with an axe and some journals.'[18]

Gérin-Lajoie's contemporaries, more sensitive to this continental reality than subsequent literary critics, were not mistaken:

> Jean Rivard is a type, one of those bold pioneers who are not afraid to plunge into the virgin forests, tackle their giant trees, and bring down the pride of their haughty peaks, accustoming their outstretched branches to becoming useful, transforming into rustic dwellings, flourishing villages, and opulent cities, the verdant crests that swayed lazily for so long in the breeze.[19]

From the 'virgin forests' to the 'opulent city,' thanks to the exploits of this remarkable pioneer! – this is the lesson of *Jean Rivard* and the meaning of its titles.

The subtitle, 'a real-life narrative,' should be seen in relation to the prefatory discourse. Its presence follows 'the general practice, dating back to the eighteenth century, of using a double title, in which the first has the same weight as the second, each one reflecting, explaining, or deciphering the other.'[20] Title and second title (*Pamela, or Virtue Rewarded*) are often confused with title and subtitle (*Clarissa, or the History of a Young Lady*). The subtitle of *Jean Rivard* is composed of a generic introduction ('narrative') that defines the form, and a determinative ('real-life') that establishes the content of the work. Any other term that could have been used (anecdotes, adventures, chronicles, episodes, history, account, vignettes) is disclaimed, in particular, the term 'novel,' which is rejected in the preface for reasons that will now be seen.

The Prefatory Discourse

The titles are only one element of the paratext, but obviously they act as synecdoches of the text and as an initial contact between text and reader; they are powerful reading guides accompanying the text and shaping the way it is read. Conversely, the novel refers back to the titles, translating and decoding them. Immediately after the titles, however, and still at the level of paratext, a prefatory discourse unfolds that further clarifies the author's intentions and explains, among other things, the titles and subtitle. This prefatory discourse is divided into three stages – indeed, three distinct parts – of which only the first would ultimately be kept: the Foreword of *Jean Rivard, the Pioneer*; the untitled note that precedes *Jean Rivard, Economist*, in *Le Foyer canadien* (1864); and the Preface of the first edition in book form (1874) of *Jean Rivard, the Pioneer*. In all three, the same elements are found: (a) the author is not writing a novel;

(b) his narrative is the unvarnished truth; (c) his hero is remarkable, praiseworthy, or exemplary, and his adventure can be inspirational.

Gérin-Lajoie's assertion is peremptory: 'I am not writing a novel' (Foreword); 'if my intention had been to write a short story or novel' (Note, 1864); 'the intention of the author, however, has never been to write a novel' (Preface, 1874). His rejection of this generic label is absolute and is accompanied by a definition of the novel, at least so far as its content is concerned. A novel contains thrilling adventures, violence, tangled love affairs, and usually ends with marriage:

I am not writing a novel, and if readers are seeking wondrous adventures, duels, murders, suicides, or somewhat complicated romantic intrigues, I make the friendly suggestion that they look elsewhere. (Foreword)

If it had been my intention to write a short story or a novel, I would have been careful to venture no further; by ending my narrative with a marriage, I could have given it the most natural of endings, in accordance with the fashion and the conventions of the genre. (Note, 1864)

The short story and the novel are here lumped together because a prefatory discourse is essentially used for justificatory and polemical purposes and does not concern itself with nuances: both are fictional, a tissue of improbabilities, removed from reality. The novel is not rejected on religious or moral grounds, because it may set a bad example or undermine public morality. It is rejected for ideological reasons: as it was perceived at that time ('in accordance with the fashion and the conventions of the genre'), the novel was a frivolous literary exercise, fit only for entertainment. It lacked seriousness. The necessary corollary of Gérin-Lajoie's rejection of fiction is the equally peremptory assertion that *Jean Rivard* could not possibly interest the great majority of readers: 'This story is not for you ... I make the friendly suggestion they look elsewhere' (Foreword); 'my goal being not so much to entertain the frivolous reader' (Note, 1864); 'even at the risk of boring frivolous readers' (Preface, 1874). Gérin-Lajoie unequivocally rejects current trends and proven formulas and hence success, targeting a small group of potential readers, the happy few who alone matter to him.

Of course, Gérin-Lajoie's attacks on the novel and on the pretty young women and gallant young men who would be put off by his serious book may well be treated with scepticism. In part rhetorical (the necessary humility of a novelist who is making his debut and is anxious not to set his sights too high), partly justified (certainly the subject matter of the novel is often dry and not very novelistic), the author's protestations are also for the most part disingenuous. He assumes that only romantic intrigues will be of interest to his reader, whether male or female. And, in fact, he amply fulfils their expectations with Gustave Charmenil's long letters to Jean Rivard.[21] Gustave, for the most part, tells of his romantic disappointments: the young ladies he loves, who build up his hopes, whom he clumsily pursues, who make him suffer terribly. With this eminently novelistic material is mixed the very romantic topos of the young man venturing out into the world, seeking, despite his poverty and hardships, to make a place for himself in the social jungle. His long letters are obviously sugar coating for readers of the time. Paradoxically, it is this part of the novel that modern readers find most boring.

Be that as it may, this condemnation of the novel and its corollary, the corresponding elitist purpose of the present work, extend beyond the prefatory discourse. They affect the development of the novel, which is to be expected, since a preface is merely a reflection on the novel and a vindication of it; they also give rise to various authorial interventions in the course of the narrative, which are extensions of the preface within the text itself. It is above all during the accounts of Pierre Gagnon's courting that the novelistic genre is again criticized:

His imagination had not been warped or inflamed by reading novels ... He visualized a woman, not as an angel, or divinity, but as a helpmate, a work companion. (209)

We have no intrigue, no interesting events to record, in the history of the romance between Pierre Gagnon and Françoise. Everything happened in the simplest way; no lover's tiffs, no break-ups, hence no showdowns, no reconciliations. (213)

But throughout the work, the author's awareness of his readers' probable reactions and especially their frustrations is apparent. These frustrations are treated lightly, in an almost cavalier manner:

But here I must go into such prosaic details that I almost despair of even my most indulgent readers being willing to follow me.
  In any case, I candidly declare that the rest of this chapter can interest only pioneers and economists. (59)

The author even takes it for granted that readers who have disregarded his warnings and have valiantly tackled the work have no doubt become quite discouraged along the way:

... my young male and female readers, if there remain any among you who have followed our hero this far. (114)

Fortunately, our pretty lady readers and our young townsmen who put on poetic airs have disappeared long ago, abandoning our hero to his prosaic, laborious life, because I would not fail to hear them cry out at the sight of this title: 'How long, strange storyteller, will you abuse our patience.' (*Les Soirées canadiennes* 2, [1862], 172)[22]

If the paratext is to be believed, the novel's readers have been poorly served by the work. It is not a novel because it supposedly does not contain novelistic elements. It is a 'récit,' that is, a narrative. But it is not 'fiction,' since it is an 'account of real life.' This rejection of the 'fiction' label in the 1874 Preface is surprising:

In order to make the work less dry reading, the author saw fit to include in his account some personal details and various incidents, which resulted in this account being considered a work of fiction. The author's intention, however, had never been to write a novel.

Jean Rivard is obviously a fictitious character, as are Pierre Gagnon, Octave Doucet, Louise Routhier, and the others; Rivardville exists no more than Grandpré. This is therefore a fictional creation, an imaginary world. Gérin-Lajoie, however, rejects the term: fiction means novel, hence novelistic content, whereas his entire book is founded on reality. *Jean Rivard* is 'the simple, true story of a young man' (Foreword); the author 'has scrupulously applied himself, even at the risk of boring the frivolous reader, to saying only what was strictly consistent with reality' (Preface, 1874). This claim of strictly adhering to reality also recurs quite often throughout the novel: 'The figure just mentioned is absolutely accurate and could even be checked if necessary' (99); 'People who may be tempted to think that the figures we have just given are exaggerated are asked to reread the interesting brochure ...' (158, note); 'Many facts of the same kind could be cited if need be' (161, note).[23]

Literary scholars are very familiar with this claim. The realist aim of a literary work is one of the constants in Western literature and certainly the most common theme of prefatory discourse as a genre. All writers claim to be subscribing to realism, usually for polemical purposes, as Gérin-Lajoie does here: to justify their own literary practice and to differentiate it from the 'unrealism' of others.[24] Rarely, however, is this claim sustained with such rigour within the text itself. The Preface's rigorously positivist ideology ('scrupulous care ... to say nothing that does not strictly conform to reality') manifests itself in the novel in the form of a complete documentary apparatus (notes, tables, convincing examples), which make this novel an excellent example of the myth of realism taken to extremes. The novel becomes a study, a monograph, to such an extent that a contemporary of Gérin-Lajoie cites the novel – either the supreme accolade or the ultimate irony – in in-depth studies of colonization. He thus guarantees the authenticity of his work by using the novel as a statistical source for his own scientific presentation.[25] By the same token, a more recent reader believed for a time that Gérin-Lajoie was perhaps the inventor of the famous monographic method of sociological inquiry, which would then have been attributed wrongly to the French sociologist Le Play![26]

Jean Rivard is not just a study, as I hope to demonstrate, but a study it certainly is – the study of an exemplary case, as the paratext affirms. This is the third assertion of the prefatory discourse: Jean Rivard is a remarkable young man by any standard. As Gérin-Lajoie describes him in the Foreword, Jean Rivard is endowed with all the physical and moral qualities of the proper hero. However, he is not superhuman. What he has accomplished can also be achieved by others, especially those who clutter dead-end professions.

But what exactly does he accomplish? A 'career in agriculture'? Not really – this is just a means to an end for Gérin-Lajoie. The author's goal, according to the 1874 Preface, is to 'publicize the life and work of pioneers, and to encourage our Canadian youth to take up a career in agriculture, instead of cluttering the profession of lawyer, notary, and doctor, and the counters of shopkeepers, as they do with increasing frequency, to the great detriment of the public and national interest.' But why follow this career rather than the others? Simply because it offers the prospect of success and wealth – better than any other career at the time, it ensures independence and prosperity to individuals, as well as collective wealth. Every sector of the economy was congested except this one: people clustered in towns while the whole of the Canadian ecumen had yet to be cleared and populated. 'To take possession of the land' is not a reactionary slogan. The American innkeeper quoted by

Tocqueville was categorical – it is the cleverest way for an individual 'to carve out a great future for himself.'[27] In short, both the primary and secondary sectors must be secured before the tertiary. Young people are beginning careers in the service sector while the country has still to be built. The author takes it for granted that his readers are aware of the expectations of young Canadians – they seek to establish themselves and to succeed, but without realizing where their true interests lie. The author, therefore, presents them with a striking example.

In fact, the Foreword sums up the work in unequivocal terms. In a single sentence, Gérin-Lajoie presents a summary of his plot:

The reader will find in this narrative nothing but a simple and true account of a poor young man of humble origins who succeeded in making it to the top by his own merits, becoming financially independent and receiving his country's highest honours.

A single sentence is used, but every word is carefully weighed. From the outset, the main clause restricts the meaning of the work to a single sense: the negative expression ('the reader will find ... nothing but') clearly indicates that the author is admitting only one interpretation of his novel. This is a 'story' in which money – its absence ('a poor young man'), then its abundance ('financial independence') – is both the *terminus a quo* and the *terminus ad quem*. In the original French the word 'fortune' is even repeated ('sans fortune ... indépendance de fortune') – the only one to be repeated in the sentence – to highlight the starting and finishing points of this life. Critics who systematically disparage the nineteenth century would do well to note that this destiny is perceived in its entirety as an upward climb ('who succeeded in making it to the top') rather than a descent into material things. Furthermore, this advancement is accomplished entirely in accordance with the concept of self-reliance so dear to Emerson and Étienne Parent. The reflexive nature of the verb ('s'élever' – to pull oneself up, to make it to the top – the action being exercised on its agent, hence working in a closed circuit) and the prepositional phrases indicating the means ('by his own merits') and the goals ('independent') emphasize the supreme power of an energetic individual. We are here far removed from the French Canadians' gregarious instinct. Paradoxically, however, this extreme individualism is coupled with a commitment to society and to the nation ('independent ... his country's honours'). It is but a single sentence, but one that overdefines its meaning. The only interpretation admitted by the author is this: success is money, acquired by a self-reliant individual.

The balanced binary structure of this sentence is particularly remarkable. It has several binary groups, but these are in a way simply rhythmic; there is no change in meaning. Here we have a 'simple *and* true' story: a young man, doubly deprived ('poor ... of humble origins'), achieves a twofold success (wealth ... *and* ... honours). But we already know, having examined the prefatory discourse, that in the author's mind what is simple must be true. A simple story can never be false or, conversely, a complicated story can never be true. The simplicity of the story (diametrically opposed to the artificial complexities of a novel) is a guarantee of its truthfulness; or reversing the terms but maintaining the relationship between them, the truth of the story (its distance from novelistic fiction) necessarily ensures its simplicity. The other binary groups are equally univocal.

In an officially classless North American society, in which wealth or the lack of it determines an individual's social standing, being 'poor' necessarily implies 'humble origins,' and vice-versa. Moreover, in that society, the acquisition of wealth is the best proof of a person's ability to manage the state's affairs and thus to achieve honours. In a society where the aristocracy has been officially abolished, money becomes the means of social advancement and the unequivocal sign of success. By obtaining 'financial independence,' Jean Rivard secures 'his country's highest honours'; the two are inseparable and indistinguishable. Having accepted the political sense of the word 'honours,' which is certainly the first that comes to mind when this sentence is first read, the reader concludes that if this young man has succeeded in his private affairs, he deserves the country's trust in public affairs. This does not preclude the broader sense of the word, as defined by Tocqueville when he spoke of honour in America: since he is rich, Jean Rivard deserves to be esteemed and honoured in his country.[28]

A poor young man becomes rich. This, then, is the story of Jean Rivard, expressed in this sentence which, with all its convergent elements, is a summary of the prefatory discourse. The novel fully confirms this affirmation in the paratext.

However, if the novel confirms the affirmation of the preface, it is not because the writer of the preface *is* the author of the novel or because we must trust him blindly when he speaks of his own work. The prefatory discourse must not be confused with the narrative. Determining the ideology of the preface's author is not necessarily the same as describing the ideology of the novel. For example, from the outset, Marxist critics have been consistently interested in the problem of bad faith: Balzac's neglect of the two 'eternal truths' that were supposed to inform and guide his work, and Zola's failure to produce the mechanistic work promised in his preface. The author of the preface and of the novel are one and the same, but in two radically different illocutory situations: thus neither the medium nor the message is the same. To avoid all confusion, it could even be said, as Geneviève Idt reminds us, that the author of the preface is always different from the author of the novel, in a sense another person, and that the preface is always heterographic.[29]

That being said, it does not automatically follow that the author of the preface misunderstands his own novel. All prefaces are obviously reductive: they 'reduce' a novel of a few hundred pages to a few paragraphs, summarizing it by 'announcing' what is to come. But is this reduction a necessarily 'untruthful' or 'illusory' look at the novel, as Mitterand would have us believe,[30] or 'irrelevant' as Derrida would have it,[31] since it is outside of the novel and contradicts its polysemic nature? In absolute terms, they are no doubt right. It goes without saying that a few sentences cannot take the place of a few hundred pages. However, the preface can point out the essential character of the work; it could be that the novelist-prefacer is deceiving neither himself nor the reader, even if such transparency is totally incompatible with the sensibilities of the modern reader, who is more inclined to look for evidence of deceit and duplicity on the part of the author. The novelist-prefacer may be right, especially if the novelist aimed at univocity and had a didactic purpose (both injunctive and performative), constantly interrupting the narrative with metatextual interventions, never really allowing the narrative to assume its natural mode of expression.

In the case of *Jean Rivard*, we do indeed have an author who has read his novel thoroughly and summarizes it in one striking sentence, which has thus far been almost totally disregarded by critics. Gérin-Lajoie clearly states that his novel is about the acquisition of a fortune, the story of material success, but most critics, marching in serried ranks to Monsignor Roy's tune, have made it out to be an agrarian novel. The interpretation proposed in the Preface, the only one authorized by the prefacer ('the reader will find nothing but'), has not been respected.

Quite wrongly so, as can be shown by an examination of the plot, and in particular of the main character, through his actions and the various descriptions of him. As Susan Suleiman appropriately reminds us, the doctrinal element of a thesis novel is not found just in the commentaries, the interpretive text that accompanies the action; the thesis is equally present 'in the way the novel structures events and characters, independently of any commentary ... It is appropriate to deal with the question of semantic investment in terms of the characters, for in the *roman à thèse*, as in all traditional fiction, it is the characters who function as the chief carriers and organizers of meaning.'[32]

Jean Rivard: An American Dream

The Quest for Wealth

Jean Rivard is an American dream. Not in the pejorative or parodic sense of the expression as used by Norman Mailer, for example, when he bestowed that ironic title on one of his novels, but rather in the confident, optimistic, and conquering spirit that was common before the Civil War and is still very widespread today. It is a dream, but one that many people have actually lived, and is for that reason quite viable. It is the dream of succeeding through one's own ability and in hand-to-hand combat with nature, achieving both the prosperity and the happiness that must logically follow from it.

The first chapter clearly sets the stage. Jean Rivard is nineteen years old, the eldest of twelve children; the death of his father interrupts his classical studies and he receives fifty louis as his inheritance. His problem, simply put, is the following: 'With this sum he had to survive and establish himself' (4). These are the last words of Chapter 1, the conclusion of this expository chapter. All other problems fade in comparison with the fundamental one: how to make a living, a place for oneself, a success in life. *Primum vivere*.

It is important to note that in the early chapters, Jean Rivard is an anxious, tormented, and profoundly indecisive young man. For the narrator, he is 'poor Jean Rivard' (4, 5); for the parish priest, from whom he seeks advice and whose wise counsel takes up seven pages of the novel, he is 'my young friend' or 'my dear child' (6–13, passim). As early as the Foreword, the paratext describes him in terms that foreshadow the future hero ('He was a handsome young man'[2]). However, he is not yet a hero; at the very most he has the makings of one. He is rather to be pitied, like a child, spending months at loose ends. This important aspect in the narrative's chronology has been largely ignored by critics. Many months pass: 'So Jean Rivard spent several more months considering his situation, making plans of all kinds, looking for a way out of the predicament. Sometimes despair filled his soul and the future seemed rather bleak' (13).

His metamorphosis into a hero is as sudden as it is miraculous. As a result of a dream, Jean Rivard gets up early one morning with his plan in mind. In the same paragraph, he receives the title 'our hero' (15) for the first time. Once he has a plan, he becomes 'bold' and 'resolute': he expresses 'noble feelings,' his muscles tauten and the blood courses though his veins. A few pages later, after purchasing his hundred acres of land, he is described once again as 'our hero' (21), a title he keeps until the end of the novel.

The technique is a bit crude, but the meaning is clear. Jean Rivard remains young ('our young man' just before the dream), a child, a pitiful being, as long as he is uncertain about his career path; as soon as he takes action, and especially when he chooses a hard, adventurous life, he becomes a hero. However, the goal of this hard life is the creation of personal wealth. The change in meaning is noteworthy. The 'hero' no longer uses his remarkable abilities to serve a selfless cause. He does not embark on an adventure out of nobleheartedness or on an impulse of total self-sacrifice. His courage, his skill, and his strength are used for personal gain. The term 'hero' has a prosaic, bourgeois, and calculating sense here, a decidedly modern meaning, undoubtedly more justified than the old: heroism for personal gain (albeit long-term) is certainly not as chivalrous, but it is more accessible to the average person. In short, Jean Rivard is a new breed of hero, profoundly American.

Tocqueville had already emphasized the particular shape of American heroism, focused on making money and requiring an exceptional strength of will:

In the United States martial valour is but little prized; the courage that is best known and most esteemed is that which emboldens men to brave the fury of the ocean in order to arrive earlier in port, to bear the privations of the wilderness without complaint, and solitude more cruel than any privations, the courage that renders them almost insensitive to the sudden loss of a fortune laboriously acquired and instantly prompts them to fresh exertions to make another. Courage of this kind is particularly necessary for the maintenance and prosperity of the American union, and it is held by them in particular honour and esteem.[33]

This pursuit of gain, and nothing else, is what makes Jean Rivard a hero. He becomes a hero when he decides to make his fortune, and he confirms his status by succeeding.

There is no doubt that Jean Rivard's primary preoccupation (his passion, even) is to become rich. He says as much to anybody willing to listen; first to the priest, who had begun by outlining for him the advantages of a career in law when he was considering legal studies:

'I will confess to you, Father,' said Jean Rivard, 'that love of honours counts for nothing in the choice I wanted to make. I do not aspire to be a public speaker or politician. Alas! My goal is perhaps less high-minded and noble. I thought I saw in this profession a way of making money, a means of securing the futures of my younger brothers.' (8)

He then tells his family, but in a less roundabout way. He drops all pretence and feigned sighs, using striking, heroic language with such 'energy' and 'resolve' that he 'electrified his young listeners' (23):

I am nineteen years old and I am poor ... by the time I reach thirty, I will be rich, richer than my father ever was. What you mockingly call my magnificent establishment is worth barely twenty-five louis today ... it will be worth two thousand then. (22)

Finally, he informs Gustave Charmenil in his first letter to his college friend:

Yes, my dear friend, I have recently purchased, and own at this moment, in the township of Bristol, a superb plot of uncleared land that awaits only my arms to bring forth its wealth. Within three years perhaps I will be in a position to marry and in ten years I will be rich. (27)

'I will be rich' is a clarion call throughout the novel. It is as much a passionate conviction as a prophecy. In Jean's mind, wealth is closely linked to happiness: 'with a little money you could be so happy!' (143), he unhesitatingly writes to his friend. By the same token he fervidly advocates, to young pioneers who visit him, his 'sure-fire recipe' for 'acquiring prosperity and the happiness that goes with it' (131–2). This causal relationship (happiness as a 'result' of prosperity) is a constant theme in the book. For example, when proposing the name of Rivardville for the new parish, a neighbour, M. Landry, declares: 'It is to Jean Rivard that our children will owe their prosperity and happiness' (193). Happiness is the natural and logical consequence of prosperity, just as night follows day. Conversely, unhappiness – the case of Gustave Charmenil is a prime example – is being without money.

Likewise, the quest for money is intrinsically an honourable enterprise for Jean Rivard. Thus he eagerly declares to his new wife: 'You know, when I cleared a road for myself in this uncultivated region two years ago, I swore that within ten years this lot would be worth at least two thousand louis. I intend to keep my word' (185). He spontaneously uses, in American style, a vocabulary ('swear ... keep my word') previously associated with another code of conduct (chivalrous or feudal) to describe a strictly economic ambition: prosperity. His notion of wealth has even a profoundly Puritan or Protestant dimension. God rewards the elect, even here below. Wealth is a sign of being blessed by God:

Jean Rivard placed absolute confidence in the Divine Providence that had thus far protected him. 'May God grant me continued health,' he would say, 'and my fortune will grow year by year; every day's work will increase my wealth; and within ten years, I will see my dream come true, my prophecy fulfilled.' (162)

This passion, nevertheless, is a qualified one. Jean wants to be rich not just for his own sake, but also for his mother, a 'poor widow,' and for his brothers, and ultimately his wealth will be of benefit to the whole community. But his passion never lessens. He calculates everything 'accurately and precisely' (160), keeps a record of all his business activities, can produce 'on demand a reliable balance sheet' (160), and turns into money anything he touches or any situation that arises, no matter how insignificant. A prime example of this is his encounter with the bear, which could have devoured him, but is instead fortunately killed, then turned into ham, butter, and fur by the protagonist. In earlier times, the hero would have made a trophy out of the conquered beast, but he would never have had the idea of using it for ham! But in this financial success story, the American-style hero wastes nothing; danger, once vanquished, becomes an object to be consumed.

Jean also knows the monetary value of everything and has a knack for evaluating in hard-cash terms even objects and beings that seem least amenable to such conversion. When complimented on his library, his first reaction is to put a price on it: 'Well! as you see it now, it cost me little more than fifty louis' (329). This kind of assessment extends even to his wife, whom the narrator evaluates in detail to demonstrate the appropriateness of his choice. Louise Routhier not only brings a considerable dowry (both money and goods), but also 'habits of hard work, order, and thrift' (165) which make her 'a source of wealth' (166) and a worthy match for her husband.

Evidently, his real-estate holdings and the products they turn out are the favourite subjects of Jean Rivard's calculations. For his 100-acre lot he pays 500 shillings (21), that is, 25 louis (128) or 600 francs (161), in the other monetary units used in the novel. Since the louis was worth $4 at the time, he pays $100 or $1 per acre.[34] In a year, the value of the land doubles (128). After two years, his land is worth 300 louis (161) or $12 an acre, and his buildings and other assets another 200 louis ($800). In addition, his land produced, in the course of these two years, a net profit of 100 louis ($400) by the sale of all types of products. It is easy to understand that, with figures of this magnitude and a dizzying rate of growth, Jean takes pleasure in monitoring his business activities and maintaining tight accounting controls, a practice that to him is quite intoxicating.

Moreover, the narrator enjoys his voluptuous pleasure in the second-last chapter of *Jean Rivard, the Pioneer*. The first volume of the diptych ends with the wedding, a sentimental *novelistic* conclusion to the first part of the protagonist's life; but the penultimate chapter is devoted to the *financial* balance sheet of this first period. Everything culminates in these figures: they represent the indispensable climax, the logical outcome of a life focused on money and success, and are the best statement – since it can be audited – of the plot. The narrator gives it the following title: 'A scabrous chapter.' In the first edition (1862), the title was 'A chapter that should not be read.' By replacing the relative clause by an adjective, 'scabrous' – in other words, 'indecent' – with its clearly libertine and sexually licentious connotations, Gérin-Lajoie wanted to ensure that the chapter would be read. The metatext, however, quickly dashes any expectations created by the enticing, meretricious title. The chapter will be considered indecent only by enthusiasts of fine literature, who have, in any case, been frustrated from the very beginning: 'At the risk of incurring the wrath of the poets, I will allow myself to present in a concise table ...' (157). The narrator first presents 'the results of our hero's agricultural operations' (157) by concentrating on the land under cultivation and the different crops with their respective values; then he devotes 'a few lines to a detailed inventory of Jean Rivard's wealth' (160). To these lines is added a long note, another metatextual intrusion, in which Gérin-Lajoie anticipates any criticism charging him with exaggeration. He gives documented examples of remarkable successes and records the wealth of other pioneer families. This enjoyment of figures spills over into the wedding chapter, which, following the logical progression of the work, begins with a detailed description of the future Mrs Rivard's net worth. The marriage is likewise a good deal that may be accurately evaluated.

An Exemplary Capitalist

Thus, Jean Rivard ardently seeks his fortune. What is more, this 'quest' is what clearly distinguishes him from his college friends, who, in the words of his friend and correspondent Gustave Charmenil, '*await* a fortune that will probably never come' (225; my italics). Calculating everything and attributing extreme importance to his 'bookkeeping,' Jean Rivard therefore seems a masterful incarnation of the capitalist spirit. Furthermore, his conduct is governed by a whole series of values associated with the search for material gain. Two of these values in particular represent, as it were, the cornerstones of capitalism: individualism and hard work.

Jean Rivard relies only on himself. He sets out alone with just a servant: one man against the forest, an idea that conforms in every respect to the American example described by Tocqueville and Volney. He has nine brothers, of whom one is eighteen years old; the ages of the others are not specified, but since there are twelve children in the family, it is safe to assume that some of the other brothers closely follow him in age. Given the strength of family ties, and the tears that are freely shed at each of Jean's departures and returns, it may seem strange that he does not take with him any of his brothers who would have been old enough to help him, especially since he seeks to give them a comfortable life, too. This is quite remarkable and perhaps seems unlikely, at first reading.

Indeed, at the time, the clearing and settlement of land in French Canada was essentially a collective undertaking. The history of settlement is the history of the massive migration of people, usually directed by the clergy, to such an extent that in the minds of historians, the great settlers were priests (Monsignor Racine in the Bois-Francs, Monsignor Hébert in the Saguenay and Monsignor Labelle in the Laurentians), that is, leaders of groups, rather than the pioneers themselves. In an attempt to exploit the gregariousness of French Canadians, settlement associations and companies were founded to steer them *in groups* toward the forest. Left to himself, the lone settler, apparently, had no stamina. The *Mélanges religieux* from 1843 to 1844 and especially during 1847–8 are very clear on this point. Associations were therefore established in order to settle the Eastern Townships, the Saguenay, and the Lower St Lawrence. Here is one example among many:

A company ought to be formed to purchase some of the good plots of land that are still uncultivated and to sell them at the lowest possible price to the many young people who can no longer find positions or jobs in our parishes. When leaving the family home, *they would go with a large group* of brothers and friends; or they would *join those who had gone before them*. The chapel with its humble steeple and its cross that speaks so eloquently to the hearts of the miserable would soften *the harshness of exile*. A priest would accompany the small group of settlers and the children would not be separated from their fathers.[35]

Settlers must be organized, encouraged, helped by any means available: they are 'children,' 'miserable,' 'exiles' who are easily discouraged. All historians of settlement stress the vital role of the clergy; though not the most flattering portrayal of the settlers, their opinions are doubtless valid, given their unanimity:

In our province, settlement has always had a patriotic quality to it. The motivating force has always come from the top, since the majority of the army of settlers is poor and without influence; this courageous army needs leaders and guardians ...

Fifty years ago, when the first large settlement movement began, it was not the government that took care of clearing land: it was ordinary individuals, more often than not members of the clergy, who took the initiative and led the pioneers into the forest.[36]

In all fairness, it must be said that the *priest* was the *protagonist* par excellence of settlement, the best friend, the adviser and the supporter of the settler ... Who discovered the Bois-Francs and directed the excess population of the central region into the rich forests of the east? Yesterday it was a handful of heroic missionaries ... Who populated the Saguenay? It was once again a priest, M. Hébert. Was it not the clergy who opened up and settled the Eastern Townships with their eighty parishes? With the priest, there was no crude self-interest, no speculation for his own gain ... Settlement work draws only apostles, that is to say, men who are driven by religious and patriotic fervour to make all possible sacrifices for the success of the cause. *The habitants are not afraid to follow them, despite being timid and mistrustful by nature. Thus, whenever the priest takes the lead, settlement is successful,* parishes are established, churches are built, and the forest retreats.[37]

Even in the novel, the example of Jean Rivard notwithstanding, settlement is portrayed as a preferably collective effort. Jean's neighbour, Pascal Landry, who sells his fifty acres in Grandpré and purchases 500 acres in the township of Bristol for his four boys and himself, is cited as an example: 'All had agreed to work together at the outset. The father was to be established first' (86). The model that Gérin-Lajoie's contemporary propagandists put forward for clearing land in the Townships was the Boudreau brothers: seven brothers who built houses, roads, bridges, and watermills while clearing their 800 acres. The lesson that is taught is diametrically opposed to the example of Jean:

Working as a team and helping one another are just as effective in carrying out this type of work as the most sizeable capital. *Let us isolate ourselves as little as possible*, and move in families and groups to these new lands. Let us take with us as many of the things that are dear to us as we can. It is a way of staving off homesickness for the place we have left behind and becoming more quickly attached to the land we have adopted. It is there, especially in those solitudes not yet provided with the numerous goods of civilization, that we will need to feel we can count on the help of our brothers and friends.[38]

Jean Rivard has several brothers, of whom a few could have gone with him. He even has a friend who fancies becoming a pioneer. Nonetheless, he sets out alone, defying both probability and the national character. He is a relentless individualist, a supporter of self-reliance, an eloquent illustration of American individualism as described by Tocqueville: 'So Americans have often got an exaggerated opinion of themselves, but this is almost always to their benefit. They fearlessly trust in their own strength, which appears to them to be sufficient for anything.'[39] By the same token, Jean Rivard does not expect to be protected by the state, an organization, or other pioneers. He does not place himself under a priest's direction, does not become part of a 'large group,' does not try to convince parents or friends to accompany him, and is not going to join acquaintances already in the forest. He sets out alone, and he alone will be responsible for his success. He is confident that he will succeed and that others should do as he does. He confides to the narrator: 'One of our great faults, *one which we have probably inherited from our ancestors*, is that we are not sufficiently self-reliant' (357).[40] He reacts strongly against this character flaw. His credo is the superiority of the energetic individual. He enjoys advocating it to those around him, thus producing a 'magical effect' (132); having blazed a trail for others, he easily becomes the leader of the township, though only a young man. This optimistic individualism, as much as his desire to make a fortune, is what pushes him toward the forest: 'Hey, wait a minute!' he says to himself, 'am I to be condemned to work as a day labourer, slaving in the same parish where my father was a freehold farmer?' (13). A proud, independent, and energetic man sets his own course and makes his own fortune.

His success is due, however, to his great perseverance, his exemplary courage – the courage typical of the American who braves anything to get rich – and his tireless work, since success does not come easily. The work ethic is, in fact, one of the fundamental values of the novel. It follows the Anglo-Saxon lines envisaged by Étienne Parent: methodical, thought-out, intelligent work focused on the goal of personal and collective wealth, but also appreciated for itself, for the profound inner satisfaction it brings.

The first words of the novel are a eulogy to work. Two epigraphs placed immediately after the title and preceding the Foreword praise the hard-working man:

The thoughts of a strong, hard-working man always produce abundance; but all who are slothful are poor.   SOLOMON

Boldness and work overcome the greatest of obstacles.   FÉNELON

This privileged position, at the very beginning of the book, is emphasized by the typographical layout – a sort of incipit – and confers a particular importance on these words, all the more because Gérin-Lajoie does not overuse epigraphs: only three of the twenty-five chapters in *The Pioneer* have them, and the next epigraphs do not appear until Chapter 13. Moreover, these first quotations, placed directly after the novel's title, are not chapter epigraphs, but serve for the whole book.[41] They are thus the first words to be read, enhanced by the prestige of divine authority in the first case and of the priesthood and literary glory in the second. They also brilliantly illuminate the spirit of the novel: a glorification of work, the only true key to wealth.

'Work conquers all' is Jean Rivard's motto, his great code of conduct. To M. Lacasse, who subjects him to close questioning to see whether he has 'the courage and the heart' (29) to succeed, Jean replies: 'Sir, since the day I left school, I have always had in my mind the maxim that our great principal often repeated: through work it is possible to achieve any goal, or as he would say in Latin: *labor omnia vincit*. I made these three words my motto' (19). This motto, or its popular equivalent, 'God helps those who help themselves' (339), is 'the greatest and principal cause of (his) success' (335). This is his third secret when he divulges his recipes for success to the narrator at the end of the book. It is his third secret, but the first that depends on him, since the other two, a good plot of land and good health, are in a way external and beyond his control.

The great merit of work is that it leads to wealth. Jean constantly repeats this, to such a degree that on the one unusual and brief occasion when he is downhearted, he finds himself on the receiving end of his own advice. It is at this time that Pierre Gagnon reminds him that he is the best match for Louise Routhier, thanks to his zeal for work:

It is true that you are not as wealthy as many others, but you will be some day, because you are not afraid of working hard, and as you yourself always say, work leads to wealth. (53)

But work is also a source of profound personal satisfaction, quite apart from its material rewards. Gustave, who is condemned to idleness in the city and whose letters are a continuous series of lamentations, marvels at Jean's lightheartedness and joy, despite doing hard work. The answer to this paradox, however, soon strikes him:

It is true that work, any type of work, is one of the main requirements for happiness; and if we add the hope of improving and enhancing one's position with every passing day, one's inner satisfaction must be almost complete. (61)

How can something arduous and tedious be a source of happiness? The common explanations such as acquiring self-esteem and the esteem of others, a deep-felt satisfaction at overcoming difficulties, and so on, easily come to mind and are also proposed in the novel. However, the narrator goes further in a quite unusual passage that recalls the ancient theory of humours. He proposes a physiological explanation for this mystery:

O, you young people full of strength and intelligence, who spend the best years of your lives in idleness, dreading work as a slave dreads his chains, you do not realize what happiness you forsake! That vague uneasiness, that boredom, that disgust that obsess you, that unbearable sadness that sometimes overwhelms you, those insatiable desires for change and innovation, those tyrannical passions that make you unhappy, all this would disappear, as if by magic, under the salutary influence of work. There exists inside every man a secret fire destined to set in motion the whole mechanism that makes up his being. If this secret fire is pent up inside an idle man, it will devastate and ravage him from within, soon leading to his total destruction, but when it inspires an active, hardworking man it can be the source of the finest feelings and the motive behind the noblest actions. (100–1)

Therefore, work has, inside the very heart of man, the almost magical ability to produce riches, to turn negative into positive, destructive forces into creative ones, Thanatos into Eros. People who do not work self-destruct, so to speak! Idleness is more than a vice: it is suicidal.

It is, therefore, literally in the most elementary sense that work is a divine law. God has created people in such a way that work is indispensable to them, an integral part of their being. Not only does work produce wealth, independence, the collective good, and enormous satisfaction, but it also creates remarkable qualities of self-regeneration and self-preservation. Therefore, one critic's assertion that work has for Gérin-Lajoie an almost punitive character seems to me a serious misinterpretation; there is no 'complacency bordering on masochism'[42] in the narrator's description of a supposedly exhausted protagonist. Work for Jean Rivard is not a sentence; nor does he work to be redeemed or to become worthy, through a progressive purification, of the joys of the hereafter. He works in order to become wealthy 'in the here and now'; he works because he experiences joy in creating and making nature productive; he works because he is deeply convinced that man is on this earth to toil and leave his mark; he works because he knows – he has been reminded by Gustave Charmenil's letters to the point of satiation, and he has learned from his own experience of hesitation about his future life, without a job – that those who are idle are unhappy, 'degraded human beings,' and in the words of Étienne Parent, are punished in both body and soul for their 'flagrant crime of resisting the will of the Creator.'[43]

The apostrophe to the reader, which contains the curious physiology lesson noted above, immediately follows an exposition on the power of work, one of many such passages in the novel. In this one in particular, the language is high-flown, producing a true paean of praise. The awe inspired by the omnipotence of work bursts forth with a style and imagery that recall an ancient rite or the Christian Eucharist:[44]

Paratext and Plot 83

Let us stop for a moment before the awesome power of work. What have we seen? A young man ... alone ... We saw him when ... God ... touched by his courage, said to him: 'See this land which I have created; it contains within it unknown treasures.' ... The young man heeded this voice ... Imagine the pure sweet bliss of enjoying the first fruits of his labour! 'Without me,' he says to himself, 'all these riches would still be buried in the bosom of the earth ... thanks to my efforts ... through my work.' (100)

The exclamations, the recollection of concrete facts introduced by rhetorical questions, the enthusiastic admiration for these wonders, give this passage a clearly doxological character. However, it is a doxology to the combined glory of God and the hard-working people who know how to exploit the 'treasures' and 'riches' hidden by the Creator. Those who work extend creation, and it is in this sense (the very same sense that Étienne Parent advocated) that work is divine law. Work and religion, in the best Puritan tradition, are inseparable. Work *is* a religion! Devout people are hard-working; capitalists, who make the most of their gifts and nature's riches, who make their capital grow (in short, who do not bury their 'talents') are the only ones deserving of praise.

It is precisely this type of capitalist spirit that Jean Rivard embodies. His goal, we have seen, is wealth; his behaviour is governed by the central values of capitalist liberalism: individualism and work. What is more, in the precise meaning of the word 'capitalist,' he is a person who puts his capital to work. It seems this dimension of the work was readily grasped when the book was first published. L.M. Darveau stated impartially:

With a starting capital of only 200 dollars, he sets out to establish a homestead, a name, and a fortune in the virgin forests of the Eastern Townships. He devotes himself to being the pioneer of civilization and the instrument of his own fortune.

Despite obstacles and disappointments of all kinds, he manages, thanks to his tireless energy, to overcome all obstacles which lie between him and his goal.

In the end fortune smiles on the pioneer's courage, on the untiring lumberjack.

He has secured his future.[45]

Moreover, for Gérin-Lajoie's contemporaries, this goes without saying. As Tocqueville would have it: 'One could not clear the bush without capital or credit.'[46] Jean Rivard needs both, and, like all shrewd capitalists, knows the value of credit and how to get it. But very quickly, as a result of the way the agriculturists read the work, the idea that Jean Rivard could have been a capitalist ceased to even cross people's minds. And yet, a capitalist is just what he is.

At the beginning of the work, the narrator tends to emphasize Jean's poverty and his meagre inheritance: 'His inheritance was, all in all, no more than 50 louis' (3). Jean describes himself as 'a young man without a fortune' (11) or 'poor' (22). But 50 louis is still a fair sum. It is the equivalent of more than three years' salary for a hired worker, since Pierre Gagnon is hired to work – and what work! – for 15 louis a year, including board and lodging. To take another example, for 10 louis Jean buys six months' worth of food and supplies. Therefore, two men could live on fifty louis for two-and-a-half years. Moreover, Gustave Charmenil, always vacillating and seeking to justify his procrastination, cannot help but envy him this inheritance: 'I must confess to you frankly that, had I not already done two years' articling, and especially if like you, I had 50 louis at my disposal, I too would perhaps take to the woods' (35).

But no matter what the relative size of the starting capital (at the end of each part of the work, the narrator and Jean Rivard tend to more readily recognize the importance of this inheritance [161, 365]), the key thing is to make it grow, something Jean Rivard accomplishes admirably. His courage, perseverance, and especially his hard work ensure a phenomenal return on this initial capital. After seven years, his property is worth 1000 louis (234); after fifteen years, 4000 to 5000 louis (339) – an average yearly appreciation of forty percent. It is evident that work alone is not responsible for this remarkable growth. His property has increased in value well beyond the improvements Jean could have made to it: it is a capital gain. Like any fortunate capitalist, Jean Rivard plays the odds, and a good part of his wealth comes from timely investments. The narrator is well aware of this, and when Jean writes to Gustave, 'I will become rich, beyond my wildest dreams' (219), it is because a village is being built on his land and he is starting up various new businesses (pearl ash, flour mill, sawmill, general store). The narrator quickly adds:

Jean Rivard was not what one would call a speculator; he did not seek wealth by impoverishing others. But when he thought about his ageing mother, his nine brothers, and his two sisters, he felt justified in making the best of the opportunities offered to him, which, in any case, were the result of his courage and hard work. (222–3)

The argument is somewhat specious. Being a speculator does not necessarily mean seeking to impoverish others; it is taking advantage of a rise in the market (and necessarily making others pay a higher price than one paid). Neither Jean's hard work nor his courage caused the road (and later the railroad) to be built at his doorstep; nor did they cause people to settle around him. He made a good choice of land, nothing more.[47] Others equally courageous and hard-working would never glimpse such wealth, even in their dreams. He is thus a speculator, and a disingenuous one at that, who takes the credit for a situation for which he has been only partly responsible. As a result, the reader is not surprised when, in the following sentence, the narrator (and Jean, the narrator simply reading Jean's thoughts) justifies this good luck as divine intervention. God favours the brave and the elect; there is nothing arbitrary about it, just simple justice: 'He also seemed to see the hand of Providence at work in the way events had unfolded' (223). In this way everything combines to justify his good fortune. If one devoutly does one's duty, one can, in good conscience, 'take full advantage of every opportunity' that arises, even if, objectively speaking, the accumulation of wealth is disproportionate.

However, if we wish to adhere to the logic of the book, can we consider a rapid increase in wealth abnormal? Even excluding the benevolent intervention of Providence, the novel postulates – in complete conformity with capitalist ideology – a productivity that is peculiar to capital. The dollar can be multiplied by two, ten, or eighty (when 50 louis become 4000), depending on the circumstances, in the same way that a seed planted in the soil can benefit from optimal growing conditions and produce a high yield. This is natural. 'This is what a 50-louis inheritance had yielded, in less than two years, with the help of intelligence and hard work!' (161), exclaims the narrator. It is the inheritance that 'produces,' that yields a profit. Hard work and intelligence contribute to this yield; they 'help' it along, but they can by no means 'create' it. The structure of the sentence thus clearly asserts capital's innate potential for growth; its ability to produce (or to reproduce itself) can often be astounding.

That Jean Rivard is also the perfect example of the capitalist spirit is clear from certain less-developed aspects in the novel that contribute to its overall meaning. He can hire men, either to clear land or to help till the soil, and benefit from their work: in short, profit from the surplus value generated by the work force. The numbers are easily calculated. 'Clearing, fencing and sowing' cost £3.10 an acre, according to Gérin-

Lajoie himself (162, note). If we assume that Pierre Gagnon does half of the work (which, given his strength and experience, is a conservative estimate), for clearing and sowing half of 35 *arpents* (or 30 acres, the *arpent* being equal to 0.844 acres) for two years, his salary could have been calculated as follows: 15 × £3.10 = £46.50. However, he is paid only £30 (15 louis) a year, and even then he does not actually receive his wages but is credited with them by his master. But that does not include his other tasks: he is quite happy to be 'Minister of the Interior' (the cook), and he also takes on odd jobs (building crude furniture, repairing things), which are of enormous benefit to his employer. Pierre Gagnon is therefore a godsend; he is the most noteworthy of the workers in the novel, who have only the sweat of their brow to sell. However, besides Gagnon, there is also Lachance (the same calculations could be made for the production of potash, which he is in charge of), then, after their departure, all the other anonymous workers, since 'Jean Rivard had managed without difficulty to hire other lumberjacks' (185). When the narrator visits him at the end of the book, they often talk about these men who take orders from Jean Rivard (326), whom he keeps pace with (334) and supervises (336). Jean Rivard is a great leader: 'under his skilful direction, work was done with remarkable speed and regularity' (186). A prosperous employer, Jean Rivard is also, in the finest tradition of free enterprise, a supporter of the competitive spirit. He constantly stimulates his fellow citizens to 'emulate' (259) one another, kindling that 'commendable spirit of competition' (260) that, in his opinion, is the motive force of progress.

It comes as no surprise, therefore, that at the beginning of the book, a 'shrewd American' clearly understands this young man, and considers him one of his own calibre, a practitioner of the virtues of his race. At the end of a 'long conversation,' Arnold offers him a deal (59). This merchant, a typical American wheeler-dealer, buys Jean's potash on mutually beneficial terms.

Although Jean Rivard can be considered an exemplary capitalist, he does not, contrary to the standard caricature of the capitalist, become an exploiter of his fellow citizens. The whole of the second part of the diptych focuses on the protagonist's involvement in civic affairs; he tirelessly devotes himself to serving his neighbours and ensuring the progress of his community. As both the unofficial leader of the township by popular demand and an elected officer holding the positions of magistrate, captain of the militia, school commissioner, mayor, and MP, he constantly works for the common good. There is no contradiction between his private career and his public service. On the contrary, the two are inextricably linked. Tocqueville had, on many occasions, already pointed out this constant in American democracy: self-confident individuals living in liberty and equality do not hesitate to join forces to obtain what is beyond their individual reach. 'There is nothing that the human will despairs of achieving by the collective power of individuals acting freely.'[48] Individuals unite out of self-interest. This soon becomes a habit and an acquired taste.[49]

Like the Americans, then, Jean takes all sorts of initiatives. Considered the de facto leader of the township, he receives many visitors, and to each of them he advocates the value of work, courage, personal initiative, and cooperation. He establishes businesses with his brothers and sets up an 'association,' whose goal is to help found local businesses and factories. The character traits that ensure his personal wealth apply directly to the common good: 'Jean brought to the administration of municipal affairs the same orderliness and farsightedness that he used in running his own private affairs' (257). Personal success is thus the best guarantee of collective prosperity, both because the 'personal zeal ... of enlightened citizens' (347) brings about work and prosperity, and because individuals who have become rich concern themselves with the community. Jean states the principle for everyone: 'I consider myself to be independently wealthy, and hence I can devote part of my time to public administration, which I consider my duty' (331).

Thus, at the end of the book, Jean Rivard's village is rich and beautiful. These adjectives recur in the words of all those who describe it. M. Lacasse, greeting the new MP, speaks of 'the rich and beautiful parish of Rivardville' (305); from the balcony of his host's house, the narrator observes 'the rich and fair village of Rivardville' (316–17). Here everything radiates 'prosperity and cleanliness' (317). Jean Rivard's prophecy has thus been fulfilled: he has made himself and everyone around him wealthy. His future father-in-law, M. Routhier, had realized this when he took up in his own way the summary offered in the paratext ('a poor young man'):

Our neighbour is fortunate ... to have a son such as this. He is what you might call a courageous young man. I wish every parish could come up with just fifty such men: *the country would become rich* in no time, and our daughters would be sure of making good marriages. (58; my italics)

The wealth and prosperity of a nation depend on personal initiative, which guarantees individual happiness (good marriages, happy mothers) and the collective welfare.

Jean Rivard's plot, then, is indeed very simple. It focuses completely on the destiny of a young man who becomes rich in the first part of the novel and in the second ensures the prosperity of his small republic by applying to public service the skills that have proved so successful in building his personal fortune.

The American Intertext

'Rags to riches': a poor yet virtuous and brave young man works relentlessly and achieves fortune and honours. Five years before Horatio Alger's first success (*Ragged Dick*, 1867), Gérin-Lajoie had outlined the topos.

A narrative so steeped in American values prompts the following question: Had this Quebec writer read American authors? Had Gérin-Lajoie added literary knowledge to his personal experience of the United States? We have seen that he visited the United States on two occasions, the second trip being a six-month study period. The journal (written in English) of this second trip has been lost, as has the 'in-depth study of American institutions'[50] that Gérin-Lajoie had written. The loss of these works obliges us to resort to informed conjectures.

Thus, it is safe to suppose that, in order to study the 'political, social, religious, commercial, and industrial life of the American people,'[51] Gérin-Lajoie must have read several books to supplement his own observations. Add to this the fact that he was an insatiable reader, as his *Mémoires* and his own son attest.[52] He ended up as a librarian in Parliament, and, as he was able to read as much as he wanted, 'his life's dream, the dream of almost all young people who love studying and literature,'[53] came true. Therefore, Gérin-Lajoie must have read the work of American authors, especially since he unfailingly admired certain American historical figures, especially George Washington.[54] Furthermore, he was responsible for putting together the second volume of the *Parliamentary Library Catalogue* (*Catalogue de la Bibliothèque du Parlement*), which was devoted to 'works relating to America.'[55] Consultation of this catalogue reveals how rich were the library's holdings on the United States, especially the state of Massachusetts, and how many works it housed by American writers or by writers who were interested in the United States (Volney, Tocqueville, Martineau).[56] These were extensive resources that Gérin-Lajoie knew inside out and that he could exploit at will.

Unfortunately, in his personal letters Gérin-Lajoie gives scanty information about his specific readings. One must rely on the testimony of his work. On the one hand, *Jean Rivard* is teeming with all sorts of quotations or literary allusions, either explicit or thinly veiled. Authors from all backgrounds march together in this procession: the holy books and folksongs, sociologists and historians, the ancient classics (Homer, Cicero, Virgil, Horace) and French classics (Molière, La Fontaine, Racine, Boileau, Fénelon), philosophers in the literary sense (Voltaire, Montesquieu) and in the literal sense (Plato, Aristotle, Leibniz), the great Romantics (Mme de Staël, Chateaubriand, Bernardin de Saint-Pierre, Lamartine, Hugo) and the illustrious unknowns (Reybaud, Léonard, Pellico, de Bornier, Mannechet). However, Gérin-Lajoie rarely quotes American writers. This does not mean that they are not present, but drawing them out of the shadows involves conjecture and hypothesis. These hypotheses allow for some fascinating insights.

It seems that two authors are most prominent in the text – Benjamin Franklin and Ralph Waldo Emerson – both of whose works were available in the Parliamentary Library. Gérin-Lajoie quotes Franklin twice in the first edition of *Jean Rivard, Economist*. First in the epigraph:

Agriculture, the only honest occupation in which man receives real growth from the seeds he entrusted to the land, thanks to a sort of continuous miracle of God's hand in his favour in return for an innocent life and virtuous toil. (*Le Foyer canadien*, 2, 1864, 15)

Next, at the end of Chapter 18: 'Seeing this, I remember Franklin's words: we are ruined by the eyes of others' (249). These two quotations were to disappear in the second edition of the novel. Yet, although his name is erased from the text, Franklin is still present within it. Indeed, Chapter 4 of the Last Part of *Jean Rivard*, called 'The Secrets of Success – Important Revelations,' can be considered a paraphrase of one of Franklin's best-known compositions, the true epitome of the American spirit: *The Way to Wealth*.

For a quarter of a century, between 1732 and 1757, Benjamin Franklin had published an almanac, *Poor Richard's Almanac*, which had ensured his fame and fortune. This educational tool overflowed with proverbs, maxims, and aphorisms that Franklin reworked in 1757 into a coherent harangue. Father Abraham, an old man, is asked for advice, and he shares the secrets of affluence and prosperity with his audience, constantly quoting 'poor Richard.' This text, which was no doubt the first American guide to wealth and happiness, enjoyed a wide circulation in America, England, and France. It was a huge popular success, and offprints of parts of it were distributed by clergymen and nobles, or posted in public places. It has been said that 'it has been published more times than bibliographers can count, translated into all Western languages and many Oriental ones, and become, in short, the handbook of creative industry in all countries where wealth is sought.'[57] Many French translations appeared, in accordance with Franklin's great reputation in France. It bore three different titles in French: *Le moyen de s'enrichir* (Dubourg edition of *Franklin's Works*, 1773), *La science du bonhomme Richard* (Quétant edition, 1774, 1778, 1794, 1795), and *Le chemin de la fortune* (Castéra edition, 1798). The Quebec avatar of this popular work was entitled 'Les secrets du succès.' A Quebec avatar, indeed, because the kinship is astoundingly close. Just as Jean Rivard tells the narrator, who is eager to learn, that he will 'categorically and ... clearly' (333) explain the laws of success, so, in the same way, Father Abraham informs the onlookers who solicit his advice: 'If you would have my advice, I will give it to you in short; for "A word to the wise is enough," as poor Richard says' (BF, 94).[58] A series of recommendations follows in the same order for both authors, except for Franklin's word of introduction ('God helps them that help themselves'), which becomes Gérin-Lajoie's concluding line ('Aide-toi, le ciel t'aidera'). The principal way to become rich[59] is to work. 'Diligence,' 'industry,' Franklin repeats; 'work, work,' echoes Gérin-Lajoie. 'Early to bed and early to rise' (BF, 95) - 'from sunset to sundown' (333). One must rise early, work, and above all not waste a minute. Both authors place great emphasis on the lunacy of wasting precious time: 'Not one minute did I waste ... one of the great scourges of our Canadian countryside, is the wasting of time ... the mistake ... of wasting precious time every day ... I rise early, throughout the year' (334-6), Gérin-Lajoie repeats. Franklin had already said: 'Let us then up and be doing ... He that riseth late must trot all day, and shall scarce overtake his business at night ... If time be of all things the most precious, wasting time must be the biggest prodigality' (BF, 95-6).

But work must be backed up by 'close supervision, order, and thrift' (336) - 'With our industry we must likewise be steady, settled and careful, and oversee our own affairs with our own eyes' (BF, 97). Both authors mean by this primarily the supervision of employees. To this

Paratext and Plot 91

end Jean Rivard states: 'I supervise my men, I apply myself to getting the most out of their work' (336). Franklin says: 'The eye of the master will do more work than both his hands ... Not to oversee workmen, is to leave them your purse open' (*BF*, 97). However, this order implies that their full attention must always be paid to all aspects of their enterprises. Gérin-Lajoie immediately goes on to speak of the necessity of avoiding debt and useless spending, while Franklin had devoted a third section to the same recommendations: the need for saving, the importance of avoiding expense, especially on useless or luxury items, and, finally, the great danger of debt. Gérin-Lajoie sets aside a separate section to advocate keeping a journal of operations, which is only a corollary of the close supervision emphasized again and again by Franklin: 'Keep thy shop, and thy shop will keep thee' (*BF*, 97). Finally, they each conclude by underlining the importance, despite everything, of a benevolent Providence.

The two authors thus see the 'road to fortune' in much the same way, with the same steps to follow and the same obstacles to overcome, giving the same advice in the same order. The style is different, however: Jean Rivard is a notability, proud of his success and rather sententious, while Father Abraham, an old man, relates an almanac composer's aphorisms and therefore uses language that is popular, full of imagery, and 'homespun' as Americans would say. But even so, there are many stylistic analogies: 'never let anyone else do that which I can do myself' (338) – 'If you would have a faithful servant, and one that you like, serve yourself' (*BF*, 97); 'Never put off till tomorrow what you can do today' (338) – 'Never leave that till tomorrow, which you can do to-day' (*BF*, 96); 'I avoid as much as I can small useless expenditures which seem like nothing, but which by the end of the year come to a tidy sum' (338) – 'You may think, perhaps, that a little tea, or a little punch now and then, diet a little more costly, clothes a little finer, and a little entertainment now and then, can be no great matter; but remember, Many a little makes a mickle. Beware of little expenses' (*BF*, 98).

Franklin's advice is admittedly not original; he is the first, moreover, to admit that his words are 'the gleanings that I made of the sense of all ages and nations' (*BF*, 103). It is quite possible therefore that Gérin-Lajoie could independently have developed the same recipes for success. However, the composition of the two discourses makes a direct relationship between Franklin and Gérin-Lajoie more than likely.

Emerson's influence is more subtle and conjectural, but perhaps deeper and more crucial. It emerges both from some overlapping of their lives and from a remarkable thematic kinship. But first a word about the American author.

Emerson, poet and essayist, is one of the most extraordinary phenomena of American literature. A difficult writer and tortuous thinker, he was nonetheless one of the most popular literary lecturers at a time when lecturers were very much in vogue. He was famous in New England from the time of his first lecture at Harvard in 1837, entitled 'The American Scholar,' a true declaration of American intellectual independence. Between 1833 and 1881, he delivered more than 1469 lectures in America; in the 1850s and 1860s he gave between 48 and 60 lectures a year, most of which took place during the lecture season (November to March).[60] He was so popular and his lectures were so well attended that he had to implore the newspapers not to report them. The misplaced kindness of the newspapers prejudiced his success:

I am exceedingly vexed by finding in your paper, this morning, precisely such a report of one of my lectures, as I wrote to you a fortnight since to entreat you to defend me from. I wrote, at the same time, to the other newspapers, & they have all kindly respected my request, & abstained. My lectures are written to be read as lectures in different places, & then to be reported by myself. Tomorrow, I was to have read this very lecture in Salem, & your reporter does all he can to kill the thing to every hearer, by putting him in possession beforehand of the words of each statement that struck him, as nearly as he could copy them. Abuse me, & welcome, but do not transcribe me. Now that your reporter has broken the line, I cannot expect the *Traveller*, & other journals to respect it, for it is a thing of concert. Defend me, another time.[61]

Emerson was not only sought after in the United States, he was also very well known in England and France, especially by writers and thinkers. From the early 1840s, Edgar Quinet and Jules Michelet quoted and commented on him; in 1846, Daniel Stern (the Countess of Agoult) dedicated a book to him in which he was hailed as the personification of new American literature.[62] His renown in France continued to grow, and finally, toward the end of his life, he was elected to the Académie des sciences morales et politiques.[63]

It so happened that this famous man delivered an original lecture series in Boston while Gérin-Lajoie was there. Gérin-Lajoie arrived in Boston on 9 September 1851 and stayed there for six months.[64] From 22 December 1851 to 26 January 1852, Emerson gave these lectures, each of which was repeated in the neighbouring cities. For example, Emerson was in Boston on 22 December 1851, in Gloucester on the 24th, in Worcester on the 25th, in Boston on the 29th, in Lawrence on the 31st, in Woburn on 1 January 1852, in Boston on the 5th, the following days in Lawrence and Gloucester, the 8th in Salem and Harvard, the 9th in South Reading, in Boston on the 12th, in Dorchester on the 14th, and so on.[65] Every other day, on average, he addressed a large audience, particularly in the Boston area, but also in New Hampshire or in New York State (twelve lectures, 2–20 February 1852, in the latter state, for example). In short, he was impossible to miss. Emerson was a real whirlwind, making headlines and drawing large audiences. He was everywhere. He had the reputation of being an original thinker, a leading American, an eminent speaker. It is hardly likely that a Quebec intellectual on a study trip, with free time on his hands, eager to perfect his English, curious about Boston's intellectual life, himself a lecturer and the organizer of lectures at the Institut canadien a few years before, could be indifferent to such a phenomenon. It is quite plausible that the opposite was true: Gérin-Lajoie probably made a point of hearing Emerson.[66]

It also happens that Gérin-Lajoie had another chance to hear Emerson on his return to Montreal on 15 March 1852. Emerson arrived in Montreal on 15 April 1852, and gave six lectures in the Bonsecours Hall from April 19 to 24. These were reported by *La Minerve*, for which Gérin-Lajoie had been a journalist in the late 1840s and for which he would become a correspondent a few months later, and where he had been replaced by his friend Raphaël Bellemare: 'Mr. Emerson, the famous writer and lecturer invited by the Mercantile Library Association, draws a great crowd of people every evening in the hall of the Bonsecours Market,' reported *La Minerve*.[67] Montreal's English newspapers, for their part, hailed the event the most fulsomely: 'one of the largest and most intelligent audiences we ever saw assembled in Montreal';[68] 'one of the largest and most respectable audiences we have ever seen collected together in this city to hear a lecture';[69] 'there has been during the past evenings an unprecedented rushing to hear the lectures of this gentleman';[70] 'the most brilliant and effective lectures that have ever been given in this city ... the vast multitudes that have every evening attended the course';[71] 'never before has a lecturer had such audiences here. Night after night have crowds of the most intelligent people greeted him with enthusiasm. The interest, far from abating – as is usual in such cases – has been constantly increasing.'[72]

So both in Boston and Montreal, at a time when he was fascinated by the United States, Gérin-Lajoie had the opportunity to hear one of the most eminent American writers and thinkers of the time. It is likely that he seized this opportunity.[73]

If so, what did he hear? A series of lectures, a complete course as Emerson was wont to compose, dealing with the *Conduct of Life*. In Boston, the six lectures are respectively called 'Fate,' 'Power,' 'Wealth,' 'Economy,' 'Culture,' and 'Worship.' In Montreal, 'Power,' 'Wealth,' 'Economy,' and 'Culture' were delivered again, between 'England' and 'New England.' The *Conduct of Life* series was to be published in 1860, two years before *Jean Rivard*, whose protagonist seems to incarnate magnificently this lesson in conduct, as the following elements show.

The first lecture, 'Fate,' is a true tribute to man's energy and power. In the first part, Emerson identifies the limits placed on us by nature and life; this is called destiny. Man's power is physically, intellectually, and morally limited. Emerson uses the image of a circle that surrounds man and whose contours he must learn to recognize. This said, however, man is blessed with such powers of thought and will that fate can be considered as a reality that thought and strong will have not yet penetrated. 'A man's fortunes are the fruit of his character' (*RWE*, 41).[74] Man is so powerful that there comes a time when there is no conflict between necessity and freedom, between destiny and happiness: they are indistinguishable. 'A man will see his character emitted in the events that seem to meet, but which exude from and accompany him. Events expand with the character' (*RWE*, 42). One thinks of Jean Rivard, who, fatherless and at a loss, gets a grip on himself and builds a universe in his own way; a Jean Rivard who is blessed with good fortune but who in fact creates that fortune. Jean Rivard comes to mind even more readily because the example Emerson uses is precisely that of determined and vigorous men, founders of cities:

Hence in each town there is some man who is, in his brain and performance, an explanation of the tillage, production, factories, banks, churches, ways of living and society of that town ... We know in Massachusetts who built New Bedford, who built Lynn, Lowell, Lawrence, Clinton, Fitchburg, Holyoke, Portland, and many another noisy mart. Each of these men, if they were transparent, would seem to you not so much men as walking cities, and wherever you put them they would build one. (*RWE*, 42–3)

In the same way, Jean Rivard is transparent, from his first words in the novel. He dreams of his republic and then makes it a reality; he is a personification of that republic.

Emerson's second lecture, 'Power,' deals with this enthusiastic vision of human power. The essay is a tribute to power, to vitality, to that excess of energy that drives people to make the world in their own image and to leave their mark. Although it can be brutal and excessive, this power is good and, in the last analysis, in harmony with goodness, because it is life. Furthermore, in most cases, as Tocqueville pointed out and Jean Rivard's life proved, it contributes to public welfare: "Tis not very rare, the coincidence of sharp private and political practice with public spirit and good neighborhood' (*RWE*, 66). The key to success is to concentrate one's energy, to eliminate anything that might dissipate it, and to persevere if one lacks this vitality. The same strength is therefore displayed, but less concentrated in time. These are precisely Jean Rivard's characteristics: 'I have worked almost incessantly ... the goal of every step I took was to improve my property ... I did not waste one moment ... I always aimed for success' (333–4).

The third lecture, 'Wealth,' is a spirited apologia for wealth, and a glowing justification of its moral value. Emerson's thesis is unambiguous: man's destiny is to be rich. This is normal, natural, and good. 'It is of no use to argue the wants down: the philosophers have laid the greatness of man in making his wants few, but will a man content himself with a hut and a handful of dried pease? He is born to be rich' (*RWE*, 88). The road to wealth is to apply one's intelligence to nature, to make it yield its riches, and to count only on oneself. Individualism and self-reliance are the keys. The example to follow, as was the case with Volney, Tocqueville, and Parent, is English:

The strong race is strong on these terms. The Saxons are the merchants of the world; now, for a thousand years, the leading race, and by nothing more than their quality of personal independence, and in its special modification, pecuniary independence ... The English are prosperous and peaceable, with their habit of considering that every man must take care of himself and has himself to thank if he does not attain and improve his position in society. (*RWE*, 90)

And the best regime, liberalism, is one that allows to become rich those who deserve and know how to be rich. 'In a free and just commonwealth, property rushes from the idle and the imbecile to the industrious, brave and persevering' (*RWE*, 106). Wealth is just and good, indispensable to culture and to civilization. It must be productive, however, and systematic: 'Some men are born to own, and can animate all their possessions ... They should own who can administer, not they who hoard and conceal' (*RWE*, 97). Emerson finishes his presentation by offering countless specific recommendations, à la Franklin.

The next three lectures, 'Culture,' 'Behavior,' and 'Worship' mainly serve to qualify and moderate these enthusiastic expressions of triumphant individualism. They temper and confirm at the same time. For example, culture counterbalances the search for power and wealth as an instrument of power – 'the antidotes against this organic egotism' (*RWE*, 139). However, its function is to balance and channel it, not to dull it. Therefore, in a child's education, all activities must fulfil an educational need. All the same, these activities must have only one goal: to be 'lessons in the act of power, which it is his main business to learn' (*RWE*, 143). In the same way, man's behaviour must conform to certain norms, which Emerson rapidly reduces to his basic principles: individualism, self-reliance and inner power. 'The basis of good manners is self-reliance' (*RWE*, 186); 'manners impress as they indicate real power' (*RWE*, 189). Even the lecture on worship says little about religion or faith, but a lot about our innate moral sense and desirable human qualities: sincerity, self-reliance, honest work, wisdom. There is even a tribute to work and a lesson on political economy. 'The way to mend the bad world is to create the right world' (*RWE*, 224), Emerson declares, and he immediately gives economic laws as an example: the real way to defeat foreign competitors is neither by war nor tariffs, but by work.

Therefore, Emerson is constantly bringing his audience and readers back to the heart of his personal credo, the same credo Jean Rivard will follow: belief in oneself, boldness, defiance of convention, independence, energetic application, refusal to bow to difficulties, use of wealth and power to one's advantage and to the good of the community. In a word, self-reliance: 'Trust thyself: every heart vibrates to that iron string.'[75]

Gérin-Lajoie seems to have long pondered these appeals from the 'first philosopher of the American spirit'[76] in order to create his character. On a largely uninhabited continent, to a population with no commercial traditions, no wealth, no contacts, without its own state, with no marketable education, what better advice indeed could be given than that of Franklin and Emerson, taken up in the context of a simple and convincing plot: roll up your sleeves and make your own fortune. Imitate Jean Rivard, the American.

3

Intertextuality I: Jean Rivard's Library

The author's readings that I have examined in the previous chapter are somewhat conjectural. However, those of his novelistic hero are not. Jean Rivard's real status may well be a suitable subject of discussion – is he a farmer and tiller of the soil, as he has been traditionally viewed by the critics, or a producer and an industrialist, a capitalist visionary and an American pioneer, as I perceive him and have previously described him? Nevertheless, unanimous agreement could easily be reached about at least one of this character's traits: he is an exemplary reader. The first and possibly the greatest reader among the characters in Quebec literature, he precedes by a whole century the well-known fictional readers found in the works of Hubert Aquin and Réjean Ducharme. Should Jean Rivard be seen as a settler? Is he not rather the fictional reader whose reading gives us insights into the various meanings that run through and shape the novel he inhabits? Hence it is important to examine what he reads.

An Exemplary Reader, a Remarkable Library

Undeniably, Jean Rivard has no equal as a reader. Witness his quite extraordinary library, unmatched in nineteenth-century Quebec literature. Indeed, according to Laurent Mailhot, in Quebec, 'before the middle of this century, fictional libraries were almost as wanting as real libraries.'[1] The latter, of course, were practically nonexistent. Private libraries were extremely rare. In the nineteenth century there were scarcely any to be found; later on, according to Laurent Mailhot again, they were limited more often than not to *Le petit catéchisme*, the *Almanach*, and Eaton's catalogue. Moreover, even institutions owned hardly any books in the first third of the nineteenth century: students copied out in longhand the most important passages in the few books available. As for public libraries open to all, none were yet in existence. Indeed, one of Gérin-Lajoie's lectures at the Institut canadien in 1847 focused precisely on the urgent need to organize public libraries.[2] The Institut canadien itself was, of course, founded in part to fill this need; the young Quebec intellectuals of the time were poor, and French books were expensive and rare. Individually, people could not afford books; an association, however, by pooling the meagre resources of its members could manage to buy a few volumes or subscribe to periodicals; individuals could then borrow them from the association's library. It was thus taken for granted that it was virtually impossible for the great majority of people to purchase books, let alone build a comprehensive collection. Moreover, even the associations' buying power was limited. They did, however, receive volumes as donations from dignitaries. For example, this was the case at the Institut canadien with Prince Napoleon: the December 1861 number of *Le Pays* takes stock of the very valuable collection that he sent from France to thank the members of the Institut canadien for their warm reception a few months before.

Given that real library collections were so meagre, it comes as no surprise to find that the contents of fictional libraries are likewise extremely small and miserly. Fiction in this case does not compensate for the disappointments of reality. Furthermore, when an interesting library happens to be mentioned in a literary work of the nineteenth century, we are usually informed immediately that it has been subjected to merciless ecclesiastical censorship. As early as 1846 Chauveau presents us with a heroine who is reading, but he wastes no time making it quite clear that the book in her hands is one of the few to have survived a clerical book-burning: 'The book from which she was reading was one of the few to escape the bonfire on which almost all of M. Guérin's library had been thrown, by the decision of the parish priest.'[3] So fictional libraries are rare, or else are expurgated at the first opportunity.

Jean Rivard's library, however, is an exception to the rule. It is large, relatively expensive (50 louis, or *double* the initial cost of his land), occupies 'a whole section of the wall' (328) in a fairly large room; with its five hundred volumes it is the envy of his visitor, the narrator. Built at a time when public libraries were still a rare phenomenon, this private collection is something of a miracle. It reflects the image of its owner who, even though he has a family and is kept busy as a landowner, businessman, and industrialist, has responsibilities as school trustee, mayor, leader of the township, and adviser to all, nevertheless still manages to read 'an hour or two' every day, even taking a book with him when going to work in the fields. What is more, he does not leaf through his books absent-mindedly. He has read every book in his library and has even read some of them 'as many as three or four times' (330). That amounts to almost a book a week over a period of fifteen years, a rate that would do credit to many a professor or other professional reader. Furthermore, this reading program takes no account of the 'political news-sheets,' nor does it include 'papers devoted to agriculture, education, and industry, nor for that matter purely literary anthologies' (350) to which he subscribes. It does not account either for the time devoted to writing, for 'never did Jean Rivard let a day go by without writing. He regularly kept a journal of his operations and noted with meticulous care his observations' (40).

Jean Rivard, the Reader indeed! At least as much as if not more than the *Pioneer* or *Economist*! Maurice Blanchot's apt term comes to mind here: there is no *'désoeuvrement'*[4] in this novel. There is never any lack of work to do, it goes without saying, but no lack of works to read, either. Books are everywhere. They always accompany the protagonist. Just as Jean Rivard never stops working, so books are never at rest: they always answer the call; they are constantly shaping the meaning of the host novel.

The presence of such a library and of such a reader in a nineteenth-century Quebec novel never ceases to amaze and fascinate. *Jean Rivard* certainly has a profuse intertextuality, as has been shown to some extent in the previous chapters of this study. Even when reading the novel inattentively, one cannot help being impressed by the number of allusions, references, and quotations Gérin-Lajoie offers his reader. But the presence of books in the book and particularly of a fictional library obviously constitutes a level of intertextuality that is more than just the literary awareness of an omniscient narrator who makes generous use of quotations. The abundance of books *in the diegesis* constitutes another indication of the astonishing modernity of this novel. It is patently obvious that books are different from other fictional objects, even in a novel that sets out to create realistic effects, and that a library is not a neutral place, a simple habitat like any other fictional space. Books are signs or carriers of signs, literally holding all kinds of meanings in high concentrations.

Of course, a fictional library does not have an absolute value. With its two senses of a place where books are stored and a collection of these same books, a library can be just a mausoleum like the ancient one in Westminster Abbey described by Washington Irving: 'a kind of literary catacomb, where authors, like mummies, are piously entombed, and left to blacken and moulder in dusty oblivion.'[5] It may also just be a lifeless, unused space, like Jay Gatsby's library, which had probably been transported in its entirety from some European ruin, according to the Fitzgerald novel's narrator, and where each book represents a step in the hero's climb to a precarious position at the top of the social ladder. In that novel, one of Gatsby's guests, sobering up in the high Gothic library, exclaims:

'They're real ... Absolutely real – have pages and everything. I thought they'd be a nice durable cardboard. Matter of fact, they're absolutely real. Pages and – Here! Lemme show you.'

He snatched the book from me and replaced it hastily on its shelf, muttering that if one brick was removed the whole library was liable to collapse.[6]

The fictional library, however, can also be the scene of romantic meetings such as in *Le Rouge et le Noir*, or even the source of dangerous books, poison for the mind (*Emma Bovary*)[7] or for both mind and body, such as the monastic library imagined by Umberto Eco (*The Name of the Rose*).[8] It can also prove to be the scene of incredible adventures, both physical and intellectual, such as those of the young Sartre in *Les mots*.

Compared with these libraries, Jean Rivard's is fairly down-to-earth. It is, however, both as a fictional space and as a collection of works, at the very heart of his enterprise. The place is his office as well as his library, the nerve centre of his household, where he plans his activities and takes stock of them; this room opens directly onto the outside and nature, where Jean Rivard's activities are concentrated, and it is located right next to his dining room. This position enables him to 'readily command his household,' as Montaigne, the owner of another famous library, used to do.[9] In all probability the places of physical and intellectual nourishment are located intentionally side by side. This library is thus where Jean Rivard works and thinks, the real centre of his world, his command post, a space of his own between his family and the outside world. Jean Rivard not only 'runs his business' from his library but as much as possible lives his life there:

I spend most of my leisure hours in this room. I am generally here from five to seven in the morning, especially in winter. It is here that I sit up with my wife and children when we have no visitors or only close friends. We read, talk, write in the company of these great geniuses whose works fill the shelves of my library. I have spent many delightful hours here. (330)

His library is not just a physical space; it is also, because of its collection of books, a centre of knowledge of an entirely practical kind. The narrator gives an enthusiastic description of both the place and the collection:

The room containing Jean Rivard's library was rather large and looked on to the garden. It directly adjoined the dining room.
  'This room,' he said, 'serves both as an office and a library. I carry out my business affairs here, receive people who come to consult me, and keep my journal and my accounts. Here, too, I keep my small collection of books.'
  Saying this, Jean Rivard opened a large armoire covering a whole section of the wall and showed me four or five hundred volumes carefully arranged on the shelves.
  I have always loved books. And to find, this far from the city, such a large number of volumes all together like this was for me both a surprise and a joy.
  I could not restrain my curiosity and stepped forward immediately to acquaint myself with the authors.
  At the top, there was an excellent edition of the Bible and several choice works on theology and religion. Then came the principal Greek, Latin, and French classics. Next, there were about thirty works on history and politics, in particular histories of France, England, the United States, and Canada. Beside these were several small elementary treatises on the physical and natural sciences, and on the arts and trades. But the largest number of volumes concerned agriculture, Jean Rivard's favourite branch of study. There were special works on all aspects of that science: agricultural chemistry, fertilizers, drainage, stockbreeding, gardening, fruit trees, etc. On the lower shelves were some encyclopedias and language dictionaries and works on law, and the Statutes of Canada that Jean Rivard received in his capacity as justice of the peace.
  'I envy you your library, you know,' I told him. 'In this collection of five hundred volumes you have managed to bring together everything needed not only for an education but for the entertainment and enrichment of the mind as well.' (328–9)

It is quite obvious that this treasure trove the protagonist presents with false modesty (and opens theatrically!) is not the arbitrary result of some kind of bibliomania, that is, a simple determination to own books and accumulate an impressive library. In fact, Jean Rivard explains to the narrator how carefully he selects his books, since he has gradually built up his collection over the years. There is no rubbish in this collection, no concern with adornment, no desire to impress visitors or business acquaintances at little cost (the armoire is kept shut); nor do the books lose their individuality because of their number or their proximity to others on the same shelf (as in some personal libraries where the arrangement of books on the shelves is often dictated by format and appearance). Only good books are kept here, carefully arranged according to their content in descending order from the absolute (the Bible) down to practical knowledge and fragmented information (dictionaries), with all the intermediary stages of culture ('the classics') and learning ('history and politics') in between. These books are a spendid demonstration of how earnest and transparent Jean Rivard is, and of his personal quest for knowledge that will guide him in his life and in his undertakings. If the fictional book or library, as Philippe Hamon points out very appropriately, 'always represents a nexus of norms, the intrusion of value systems into the text, axiology, and ideology in concentrated form, condensed evaluations,'[10] it does seem that the global meaning of Jean Rivard's library is the pragmatism of the protagonist, that is, his will to succeed in his endeavours by accumulating effective guides for action.

In this rich and diversified library, four books occupy a special place. Jean Rivard points out to the narrator these 'four rather old and battered volumes standing, on one side, in a corner':

'You haven't looked at these books' he said to me, 'and yet they are by no means the least interesting.'
Opening them I saw they were: *Robinson Crusoe, The Adventures of Don Quixote, La vie de Napoléon,* and *The Imitation of Christ.*
'These are my first friends, my first working companions. I look after them carefully. Robinson Crusoe taught me to be industrious, Napoleon to be active and courageous, Don Quixote made me laugh in my moments of despair. *The Imitation of Christ* taught me submission to the will of God.' (330)

These 'old and battered friends' and 'working companions' have not stood up to being put to work as well as their still-vigorous owner. This is probably because they have been used a lot and in more ways than one, in spite of the single lesson that Jean Rivard draws from each of them.

Intertextuality I: Jean Rivard's Library 103

The other books, those with no title of their own, which are lost in the list of their collective subject matter, are not mentioned elsewhere in the diegesis. These four books, however, are clearly emphasized: they have a title, a personality, and a function in the plot.[11] Two of them in particular are very important in the novel. For even though Jean Rivard takes all four with him when he leaves Grandpré, he does not make equal use of them in the woods.

The Imitation of Christ is certainly less important than the others. When the narrator presents these books for the first time, he quickly disposes of the religious book in a single sentence; '*The Imitation of Christ* was the book for Sundays and holidays. The three others were for weekday reading' (42). Most of the time Jean is bored to death on Sundays and holidays; it is when he is not busy that he finds 'his isolation the heaviest to bear,' 'his solitude becomes an exile, his cabin a tomb' (45). Nothing can then distract him from his despondency, not even the valiant efforts of his hired hand, Pierre Gagnon, let alone this book, which is associated with his loved one, Louise Routhier, and reminds him of her. When they had parted, the young lovers had exchanged as gifts the most precious love tokens of the time: devotional objects. Jean gave Louise a 'small rosary of coral beads blessed by Our Holy Father the Pope,' so that she could recite ten Hail Marys every day for him, and Louise gave him 'a little *Imitation of Christ* she had already used, which only made it more appealing in the eyes of its recipient; she made him promise to read a few pages of it, at least on Sundays, since in the forest, where he would live in isolation, he would be deprived of the opportunity to worship God in his temple' (28).

Thus, this book came to represent boredom both through its association with the heavy burden of an inactive day and its connection with his absent lover. Reading it has to replace the Sunday mass. It only makes more painful the absence of this weekly gathering, a social event that was the high point of the week for French Canadians of the time. As a replacement for the mass, it proves, therefore, to be totally inadequate, not only for Jean, in fact, but also for Louise, who, after her marriage, would like to go to mass every Sunday:

In vain had Jean Rivard read to his Louise the finest chapters of *The Imitation of Christ*, that precious little book which she herself had given him long ago as a souvenir and which he kept religiously. He had still seen in her pretty eyes, to which tears seemed to come involuntarily, that she felt a deep sadness, and he had resolved to do all in his power to remedy it. (194–5)

In short, while the other three volumes succeed admirably, each within its own sphere, this one is totally ineffective.

This ineffectiveness seems to be due to three factors. First, it is less a book than an object, it is less a carrier of signs (which is an appropriate definition of a book) than a sign itself. It is, in fact, the sign of an absence, even of a double absence: it stands for the mass and it symbolizes the beloved woman left behind. It is, therefore, an object, but an object defined by an absence; in a way it represents the presence of an absence. Thus the mere sight of it could only trigger feelings of emptiness and nostalgia. The second reason for its ineffectiveness is that it is a precious object 'religiously kept'; it is a relic not really meant for actual use. In this case, possession matters more than consumption: it is more important as a precious object than as a book to be read. Finally, perhaps the deepest reason why reading this book never has any consequence is that it is linked to an obligation. Three of the books Jean Rivard takes with him by choice, thus letting us anticipate his answer to the famous question: What books would you take with you to a desert island? *The Imitation*, however, has been imposed on him. Louise makes him promise to read from it 'at least every Sunday.' Jean will have to read from it out of an emotional obligation that immediately overlaps and is reinforced by his religious duty (it replaces the mass). He will not overdo it, however, reading only a few pages, and Pierre Gagnon never asks him to read on.

The other books, by contrast, are read out of interest, for pleasure, and on a daily basis. They are read two hours a day during the first year and often more than that, 'late into the night' (42). These readings are taken up and extended throughout the day by Pierre Gagnon who repeats, often word for word, what he has heard the night before, reliving the episodes or playing the parts. *The Imitation*, like the boredom it causes, is limited to a few pages every Sunday. There will be no further references to *The Imitation* elsewhere in the novel other than the two cases already mentioned, of which the first, as we have seen, cannot be considered meaningful.

It can thus be said that this book, like the woman who has given it to Jean Rivard, quickly drops out of the picture. As Louise Routhier soon ceases to preoccupy the hero after their marriage, this book has very little significance in his life. When the protagonist informs the narrator that *The Imitation* has taught him 'resignation to the will of God,' what the reader had probably only suspected becomes clear: the lesson to be drawn from this book is an empty one. Jean Rivard has never had to resign himself to anything, nothing unpleasant has ever interrupted his steady climb, no setbacks have ever affected his career as a pioneer and economist; in short, he has always come out of his struggles victorious. The teachings of this book have, therefore, always remained abstract and irrelevant: they have been the inescapable expression of orthodoxy but are without any subjective significance.

The Adventures of Don Quixote de la Mancha is mentioned more frequently in the work, but its significance also remains somewhat limited. The work has, it seems, but one function: to amuse. But even on this humour Jean Rivard imposes strict limits. Pierre Gagnon enjoys calling himself Sancho Panza, but 'out of respect for his master' he does not dare call Jean, Don Quixote. Furthermore, when he ventures a well-meant analogy between Louise Routhier and 'the beautiful Dulcinea of Toboso,' Jean reacts sharply:

Pierre, I do not like jokes of this kind. Do not profane in this way the name of my Louise. Call her all the poetic or historic names you like, but do not liken her to the coarse, stupid lover of Don Quixote. (51)

There is no ambiguity in this rebuff. Moreover, it is the only time Jean Rivard's mood changes abruptly, and these are the only harsh words he utters in the course of the novel. His rejection of the analogy is therefore peremptory. Louise is no Dulcinea, and consequently there is no way Jean can be Don Quixote. The meanings that modern critics have read into the work of Cervantes are unknown to Jean Rivard. For him, the Knight of the Mournful Countenance is neither a pilgrim in search of the absolute nor a knight pursuing an ideal, any more than he embodies the tragic sense of life. For the down-to-earth Jean Rivard, Don Quixote is merely a comic figure, at best a jester, good for making people laugh as a temporary distraction from real, concrete things such as work and success. Thus, contrary to all literary or historical logic, Pierre will remain Sancho Panza; he will accompany, however, not an unrealistic knight, but rather a quintessentially concrete hero, the Emperor Napoleon, the only name suitable for his master. Indeed, Jean Rivard will never refuse to be called either Napoleon or Robinson Crusoe.

Robinson Crusoe and Napoleon are, thus, the only fully accepted 'friends' of Jean Rivard and the only fictional and historical equivalents considered worthy of his destiny. They transpose and metaphorically extend his adventure each in its turn, but in contrasting ways.

Robinson Crusoe, Homo Oeconomicus

Travel Narrative and Novel

The fact that the most famous travel narrative of modern times, *Robinson Crusoe*, is the favourite work of a protagonist who puts down firm roots is not the least of the ideological paradoxes in *Jean Rivard*. Robinson Crusoe, who defies his father's prohibitions by going to sea and not returning home for thirty-five years, and who immediately embarks on another adventure, this time in the other direction, toward the East, although he is over sixty years old, seems at first glance an unusual model for a pioneer. When one of the goals an author sets himself is to fight against the emigration of his people to another country, it may indeed seem paradoxical that he attaches such importance to the account of a traveller sailing the South Seas. Defoe's novel would seem more appropriately found in the baggage of an adventurer on his way to the California gold-mines, like so many of Jean Rivard's contemporaries.

In fact, *Robinson Crusoe* is not an isolated phenomenon in the novel. Gérin-Lajoie seems to have a weakness for travel accounts. Jean Rivard takes *Robinson Crusoe* with him when he leaves for the forest, but the second winter he also takes an anthology entitled *Voyages autour du monde et dans les mers polaires* (130), which he has borrowed from M. Lacasse or from Father Leblanc. Gérin-Lajoie's protagonist has therefore a pronounced fondness for travel accounts. Pierre Gagnon and, in the second winter, the young settlers who gather at Jean Rivard's place for reading sessions also share this taste. So does Antonine, Gustave Charmenil's very serious-minded young lady-friend. He writes to Jean Rivard:

You may have heard that young ladies can read nothing but novels. You are wrong. Antonine is not as good at mathematics as Mme du Châtelet was, but she reads history, and even works on the sciences, philosophy, religion, travel, etc. (268–9).

Why this fascination for travel narratives? The novel itself provides some answers. Travel accounts stimulate the imagination and spark enthusiasm. Jean Rivard's young neighbours react strongly to his readings:

These accounts of perilous adventures, horrible sufferings, unheard-of hardships, held an extraordinary interest for the imagination of our young pioneers. (130)

Travel accounts have an adventurous and heroic content. By their exoticism, their distance in time or space, and their portrayal of protagonists of uncommon mettle, they are escapist dreams and provide strong emotions bursting into the existence of the readers or listeners condemned to lead dull, ordinary lives. They embody somehow the values of a rich, imaginary universe. They offer, in short, the characteristics of fiction, yet they are real at the same time: in sum *they are not novels*.[12] They thus have the advantage of escaping the moral disfavour in which novels were held at the time by serious littérateurs and moralists.

The contrast between travel accounts and novels is very clear in Gustave's letter quoted above. Antonine, that model young lady, does not read novels. She reads serious works, among which Gustave does not hesitate to include travel accounts, immediately after religious works. His list of Antonine's reading continues with Fénelon's *Traité sur l'éducation des filles* (269). Travel accounts are thus positioned between religion and education in this list, as if, following the example of religion, they were endowed with high moral value, and, like educational treatises, their role were to teach, all the while arousing enthusiasm and stimulating interest. The travel narrative, in short, is a work that is exciting yet serious, fascinating but rewarding and educational, bringing together irreconcilable opposites.

On the basis of the diatribes against the novel genre found elsewhere in the work or in the paratext, it can also be postulated that the distinction between the travel narrative and the novel should not be seen solely in terms of the former's truth or educational value. Travel accounts also enjoy the advantage of recounting adventures, but these *have no love interest*. Women are by definition resolutely excluded from them. Their world is a male preserve: the hero, who goes in search of glory, knowledge, adventure, or fortune, but never to find a heroine, makes the most painful sacrifices and succeeds, of course, since he lives to tell the tale.

It thus becomes understandable why the *Voyages autour du monde* was the book lent by M. Lacasse, a man 'with a great store of good sense' (18), unless it was a loan from Father Leblanc, the priest at Grandpré, an 'indispensable adviser' (6), sought after for his wisdom and his experience. It would be unlike either of them to recommend frivolous books that could be harmful to naïve young readers and listeners. Finally, it is likewise understandable why, in the novel *Charles Guérin* cited above, one of the few books rescued from the book-burning decreed by the priest should be a travel account. The book that Louise Guérin is reading is the story of a 'young English sailor ... on a desert island' (perhaps *Robinson Crusoe*?).[13] In the clergy's thinking, it is apparently preferable to read an adventure story, which preaches courage and energy, even at the risk of awakening atavistic nomadic tendencies, than a novel, which may arouse interest in a love adventure, love being a passion that is uncontrollable by definition. In any event, curiously enough, in *Jean Rivard* these travel narratives do not encourage their readers to go off in search of adventure. Jean Rivard, a practical man, uses these readings to teach his listeners geography or astronomy. The travel account, therefore, does not necessarily incite anyone to travel around the world; it broadens horizons while teaching lessons in heroism.

In this way the paradox of a travel narrative being the favourite book of a Canadian pioneer is more apparent than real. The travel account does teach, but in a pleasant way. It entertains while stressing the importance of certain virtues that are indispensable to the success of any career. It does not present the moral dangers of novels, yet it is just as interesting. It does not enervate its readers by depicting easy social conquests; it incites them to confront nature and triumph over it. In the case of *Robinson Crusoe* in particular, it must be admitted that, while the work is a travel account, it is also and above all, in its best-known part, a marvellous story about settling into a space and taking possession of it. This account constitutes, therefore, a striking *mise-en-abyme* of the Canadian pioneer's adventure, taking it up in an exotic, heroic mode.

Robinson Crusoe and Jean Rivard: A Similar Fate, Similar Values

Jean-Jacques Rousseau, whose *Émile* professed a teacher's hatred for all books, made an exception only for *Robinson Crusoe*. He considered this book 'the most appropriate treatise on natural education,' the only book that teaches everything that books are capable of teaching. Émile, therefore, has to read it until 'his head is spinning,' until he believes he is Crusoe himself.[14]

For Gérin-Lajoie, Daniel Defoe's novel does not serve thus as an encyclopedia of all practical knowledge. Ultimately the English traveller has nothing to teach Canadian settlers: 'Thunderation, boss!' Pierre Gagnon *often said*, 'Robinson Crusoe and Friday were ninnies by the side of us' (98; my italics). Where strength, skilfulness, and enthusiasm for work are concerned, Jean Rivard and Pierre Gagnon are second to none. For them Robinson Crusoe is not a role model; his situation is simply analogous to their own. 'The story of Robinson Crusoe, stranded on his desert island and obliged to extract his means of subsistence from nature alone without any human help, bore a resemblance to that of our pioneers, which Pierre Gagnon easily grasped' (42). Crusoe is a mirror reflecting them and their situation – the wilderness of the Eastern Townships is an exact counterpart of the desert island.[15] He also reflects the values of their universe: individualism and independence, resourcefulness and courage.

Other analogies, which are not expressed openly by Pierre Gagnon but perhaps do not escape his notice, may be drawn between *Robinson Crusoe* and Jean Rivard's adventure. In more ways than one, Jean Rivard can recognize himself in the shipwrecked Englishman who, as many economists and critics have observed,[16] exemplifies that economic individualism that was to become the hallmark of nineteenth-century America. Robinson Crusoe's desert island as well as Jean Rivard's uninhabited forest provide the place and the opportunity for an individual to realize his potential in a context of absolute economic, social, and intellectual freedom. The shipwrecked sailor and the pioneer must be self-sufficient, do everything, and succeed in everything. There are, therefore, a good number of parallels between the two protagonists.

Robinson Crusoe, like Jean Rivard, is educated, but his education is useless. Jean's education 'did not provide him with any means of subsistence' (4); as for Robinson Crusoe, 'being ... not bred to any trade' (*RC*, 3),[17] he does not know what to do. His family, just like those around Jean, would like him to become a lawyer: 'My father, who was very ancient, had given me a competent share of learning ... and designed me for the law' (*RC*, 3). After hesitating for as much as a year (far longer than Jean), he decides nevertheless to break away from his family and his milieu, disregard his father's tears (in Jean's case it was his mother's), and, at the age of nineteen, exactly the same age as Jean Rivard, go in search of adventure. He will take longer than Jean Rivard to settle in his territory, although his first voyages along the coast of Africa and to Brazil can be considered as the equivalent of Jean Rivard's first exploratory trip: he is getting his hand in. Like Jean, he very soon meets people who will help him throughout his life. These are not servants, the likes of Xury, Friday, and the shipwrecked Spaniards who become his devoted labourers – the equivalent of Pierre Gagnon, Lachance, or Jean's other hired men. On the contrary, they are people of his own rank, often older and established, who, like the Lacasses, the

'Honourable' Smiths, and the Arnolds of Gérin-Lajoie's novel, encourage Crusoe, help him or do business with him that is profitable to both parties. That is what happens with the first English captain, who in a way adopts him, turns him into a sailor and a merchant, and enables him to amass £300, a sum that will be the basis of his fortune. He is helped by the captain's widow, who scrupulously keeps his money in trust for thirty-five years. The same is true of the Portuguese captain who rescues him off the coast of Africa (Crusoe had been a slave for two years and was fleeing Morocco), helps him in many ways, and remains his incorruptible trustee during his long absence, despite every indication that he is dead. He is likewise assisted by his Brazilian associates, who manage his properties, reap profits from them, and give him a scrupulous accounting of his assets upon his return twenty-eight years later. Crusoe's associates, like Jean's, are thus honest, skilful, helpful, and ready to give him credit, because they recognize the merit of the young man standing before them.

But it is mainly on his island that Crusoe resembles Jean Rivard. Like Jean, he is a capitalist at the outset; in other words, his adventure starts with a capital, which he will make yield a profit. Jean, as we have seen, has a capital at his disposal, and it would not be cynical to consider that it is his father's death that brings this capitalist to life. Indeed, his 50 louis inheritance enables him to buy land and tools, to hire labour, and to borrow money. It may well be wondered what would have become of Jean Rivard if his father had not died, if he had not been left this capital. The answer given in the novel is clear: he would have been a struggling, penniless lawyer, like Gustave Charmenil. Crusoe likewise inherits everything in the wrecked ship. He comes into all his companions' goods, which they had accumulated on the ship of life. In this case the cliché ceases to be a metaphor. During the first thirteen days Crusoe returns eleven times to the wreck; each time he prepares a raft, loads it, and brings it back to his shelter after countless difficulties, which brings to mind Jean's hard trips with his supplies from Lacasseville. Finally Crusoe notes: 'I had the biggest magazine of all kinds now that was ever laid up, I believe, for one man.' (*RC*, 35) He even adds: 'I had brought away all that one pair of hands could well be supposed capable to bring; though I believe verily, had the calm weather held, I should have brought away the whole ship, piece by piece' (*RC*, 36). This appropriation gives way to a comic passage, like many others in which religion and business sense go hand in hand. Robinson finds in the wreck a bag filled with coins, a discovery that in the circumstances is admittedly less useful than that of the smallest plank or nail. He then delivers a lovely sermon ('O drug! what art thou good for'). But, reconsidering, he takes the bag anyway ('However, upon second thoughts, I took it away' [*RC*, 36]), even risking drowning with his 'useless' drug, since this time he must swim to shore. Money is money, no matter the circumstances.

Thus, with a good stock of provisions, Crusoe settles in, enlarges his cave (his shelter is a 'storehouse' before it is a dwelling), and, as Jean Rivard 'the merchant' contemplates with the soul of a shopkeeper his maple-sugar loaves (50), enjoys looking at his goods: 'It was a great pleasure to me to see all my goods in such order, and especially to find my stock of all necessaries so great' (*RC*, 43).

This legacy, this inherited capital, is, therefore, of great importance. It creates a situation that led Ian Watt to note that, for *homo oeconomicus*, solitude (the disappearance of family and friends) is a blessing rather than a tragedy: it is the necessary prelude to success.[18] The inheritance gives rise to both protagonists' adventures and guarantees their success. In particular, it allows the reader to realize that they are brilliant managers and very skilful capitalists. Rather than squander their assets, they put them to work and thus ensure a life of comfort for themselves. Just as Jean Rivard, at the end of the novel, responds to the narrator's compliments by stressing the importance of his '50 louis inheritance' (365), so Robinson in his *Further Adventures* will point out to the shipwrecked Spaniards, who marvel at everything he has accomplished on his island, that it would have all been impossible but for his original capital: 'The supplies I had providentially thrown into my hands, by the unexpected driving of the ship on shore, was such a help as would have encouraged any creature in the world to have applied himself as I had done' (*RC*, 246–7).

Humility is, no doubt, required of him, but it is not certain that 'any creature' would have applied himself as diligently as Robinson Crusoe. 'I was not idle' is a phrase that recurs constantly like a refrain to underscore his various labours. He works without respite. His Caribbean island is not a paradise in the sun suitable for *dolce far niente*; on the contrary it is a vast building site. He exploits its resources and subdues it. As soon as he is washed ashore, the sole survivor of the wreck with no hope of being rescued in the near future, he does not waste time lamenting. Tears are no consolation, inactivity is depressing, while busyness works wonders: 'This [his solitude] forced tears to my eyes again; but as there was little relief in that, I resolved ... It was in vain to sit still and wish for what was not to be had; and this extremity roused my application' (RC, 31). 'To sit still' is for Crusoe a real affliction. Jean feels depressed on high days and holidays, and Crusoe feels unhappy when he is not working: 'Sitting still, which to me especially was the unhappiest part of life' (RC, 303).

The need to be on the move, to be active, to be involved in business, to organize, and to be *productive*, is characteristic of the two protagonists. This need is at the heart of the merchant and capitalist mentality. One example among many: in his *Further Adventures*, after stops at his island, and then in Brazil and Madagascar, Crusoe is abandoned in Bengal by an angry crew. He spends some time there, then one of his fellow countrymen pays him a visit and makes him a proposal:

Here we are posted, you by accident, and I by my own choice, in a part of the world very remote from our own country; but it is in a country where, by us, who understand trade and business, a great deal of money is to be got. If you will put one thousand pounds to my one thousand pounds, we will hire a ship here, the first we can get to our minds; you shall be captain, I'll be merchant, and we'll go a trading voyage to China; for what should we stand still for? The whole world is in motion, rolling round and round; all the creatures of God, heavenly bodies and earthly, are busy and diligent; why should we be idle? There are no drones in the world but men; why should we be of that number? (RC, 301)

'What should we stand still for? The whole world is in motion.' Let us compare these words with Étienne Parent's invitation to his fellow countrymen to compete with the English speakers who are merchants par excellence:

Gentlemen, are we, indeed, living in a century and in circumstances such that we can afford to let things be, let things go? We are in a world constantly in motion, always restless, ever in a whirl. We will be worn down and crushed if we do not busy ourselves, too ... Dominion over the world has been given to movement, activity, and the live, constant action of man over matter.[19]

The same idea is repeated almost word for word.

Crusoe's response to his fellow countryman's invitation is disarmingly simple: 'I liked his proposal very well.' Six more years of trading in the Orient follow (he is now almost seventy), and he completes a trip from China all the way to Europe by caravan. Crusoe, like Jean Rivard, does not work just to ensure his well-being and his security (he is by now very rich, just as Jean Rivard is well off at the end of the novel); work for both of them is a fundamental need, a physiological necessity, which they have to satisfy in order to be happy.

Thus work fascinates Crusoe. On his island he sensuously describes his tools and his various jobs, for example all the necessary stages in bread-making, from ploughing the land to cooking the dough (*RC*, 73-6). Like Jean, he has banished the word 'discouragement' from his vocabulary. All of his tasks, at least during the first few months, are long and tedious, but there is no stopping him. He needs a plank wide enough to make a shelf in his storage room. This will take him forty-two days to make, since he must remove from a large tree, using nothing but his axe, everything he does not want to keep, thus illustrating unknowingly the humorous definition of sculpture. 'Anyone may judge the labor of my hands in such a piece of work; but labor and patience carried me through that, and many other things ... with patience and labor I got through everything that my circumstances made necessary to me to do' (*RC*, 71).

Not everyone has the same qualities, however. When Crusoe returns to his island which, under his direction and influence, has become a flourishing colony, he notices that the settlers have not all been equally successful. His observations find their inspiration in Solomon's thoughts and in the very passage that served as an epigraph to *Jean Rivard, the Pioneer*. There is an interesting twist, however. Whereas Gérin-Lajoie quotes 'The *thoughts* of a strong, hard-working man always produce abundance; but every slothful man is poor' (1), Defoe prefers 'Solomon's words ... that the diligent *hand* maketh rich' (*RC*, 231). The hand rather than the thought, in the image of this eminently practical man. His conclusion is the same, however: 'The diligent lived well and comfortably, and the slothful hard and beggardly; and so, I believe, generally speaking, it is all over the world' (*RC*, 231).

The work of the diligent man, whether it be Crusoe or Jean, is not sporadic and impulsive like that criticized by Volney; it is rational and methodical. Once an undertaking has been well thought out and decided, it is carried out, no matter what difficulties arise: 'I seldom gave anything over without accomplishing it, when once I had it in my head to begin it' (*RC*, 103). This practical, calculating mentality is what most distinguishes Crusoe. Even if he is alone on his island, he arranges his life in a very rigorous way. When he keeps his diary, it is not to leave a record for someone ('I was likely to have but few heirs' [*RC*, 41]) but, rather like Jean, out of 'a habit of reasoning and carefully calculating all of [his] affairs,' in order not to proceed 'like the blind man who has nobody to guide him' (338, 339):

> As I observed before, I found pens, ink and paper, and ... while my ink lasted, I kept things very exact ... I now began to consider seriously my condition, and the circumstances I was reduced to; and I drew up the state of my affairs in writing. (*RC*, 41)

> And now it was that I began to keep a journal of every day's employment. (*RC*, 43)

His diary, like Jean Rivard's, enables him to 'search his soul' (339); every day he takes stock, both morally and financially. With him, then, self-analysis works like a balance sheet: 'And I stated very impartially, like debtor and creditor, the comforts I enjoyed against the miseries I suffered' (*RC*, 42). The accounting exercise thus becomes salutary in itself, for assets can always be found, no matter what the situation is; accounting is a moral lesson. It teaches us that there is always some reason to rejoice: 'We may always find ... something to comfort ourselves from, and to set, in the description of good and evil, on the credit side of the account' (*RC*, 42). Life, in short, is an 'account,' and both protagonists have bookkeeping in their blood, without having ever learned it; they calculate incessantly and with genuine interest.

Every day, indeed, Crusoe marks a notch in his post, but this is a rough-and-ready practice, which anyone can do. He feels, furthermore, the need for a strict timetable:

> I began my third year; and though I have not given the reader the trouble of so particular an account of my works this year as the first, yet in general it may be observed, that I was seldom idle, but having regularly divided my time according to the several daily employments that were before me. (70)

Every day Crusoe devotes a few moments to prayer (three times a day), three hours to hunting in the morning, several hours to preparing and storing food, and four hours in the evening to one particular job. He keeps a detailed account of everything he does, everything he owns, everything that comes from the wreck: quantity, weight, condition, use. Each page of his narrative entails its own array of figures and various statistics: the number of goats or of turtles, the number of days spent or miles covered, the quantity of corn or grapes, the area and productivity

Intertextuality I: Jean Rivard's Library 115

of his fields. When Crusoe returns to his island after an eight-year absence, he brings back supplies for his 'settlers,' the other shipwrecked Spaniards, Portuguese, and English who arrive unexpectedly at the very end of his stay. 'My cargo, as near as I can recollect, for I have not kept account of the particulars' (RC, 194), he tells us before giving a detailed, tightly-written, half-page description of his varied cargo. In other words, even when he does not note everything down, he remembers it all: a rigorous inventory is stored in his memory. It therefore comes as no surprise that, like Jean Rivard, he ends the account of each of his adventures with a precise, systematic balance sheet.

Orderly, careful, and attentive to everything, Crusoe builds an estate for himself and maintains it meticulously. He has his castle, a real impregnable fortress, but also his country home in the middle of the island, a large store of supplies in a cave elsewhere, a secret enclosure to protect young goats from theft by natives, a boat on the other side of the island, hiding places for powder, and provisions scattered all over the place; everything is checked regularly, kept up, well preserved, ready to be used at any time.

This diligence and application are admirable in themselves, but they stand out even more when contrasted with others' weaknesses. Jean Rivard, embodying the English pole of the antithesis established by Volney, will be contrasted with the bad French-Canadian settler, who is idle and lacks both foresight and practical sense. Crusoe, though alone on his island, is also contrasted with unproductive Latins. On a neighbouring island there are sixteen Spaniards and Portuguese living in a state of poverty, abandonment, and despair despite their numbers. Crusoe finds a way to save them and bring them back to his island as subjects. In the course of conversations with him, they will compare themselves unfavourably with the Englishman:

He ran on then in remarks upon all the little improvements I had made in my solitude; my unwearied application, as he called it; and how I had made a condition, which in its circumstances was at first much worse than theirs, a thousand times more happy than theirs was, even now when they were all together. He told me it was remarkable that Englishmen had a greater presence of mind, in their distress, than any people that ever he met with; that their unhappy nation and the Portuguese were the worst men in the world to struggle with misfortunes; for that their first step in dangers, after the common efforts were over, was to despair, lie down under it, and die, without rousing their thoughts up to proper remedies for escape. (RC, 246)

Crusoe, out of humility, then stresses his starting capital.

'Seignior,' says the Spaniard, 'had we poor Spaniards been in your case, we should never have got half those things out of the ship, as you did: nay,' says he, 'we should never have found means to have got the raft on shore without boat or sail; and how much less should we have done if any of us had been alone!' (RC, 247)

The moral is clear. It is, as we have seen in the first chapter, that of Volney and Tocqueville, Parent and Gérin-Lajoie: the Englishman manages on his own by using his practical intelligence, while the Latin is more often than not ineffectual. It would seem logical to conclude from *Robinson Crusoe* that the French should be added to the list of Latins who are easily discouraged. Indeed, when Crusoe returns to his island eight years later, he has an opportunity to save travellers whose vessel has caught fire: 'It was a French merchant ship of three hundred tons homebound from Quebec, in the river of Canada' (RC, 196).[20] Crusoe marvels at the untimely reactions of the French, their extravagant excesses, the total unleashing of emotions, even by an old priest who 'was the worst ... the priest was gone stark mad' (RC, 198). This even goes beyond the expression of joy by Friday, the 'savage,' when he had saved his father:

... and it was but a very few that were composed and serious in their joy.
  Perhaps, also, the case may have some addition to it from the particular circumstances of that nation they belonged to; I mean the French, whose temper is allowed to be more volatile, more passionate, and more sprightly, and their spirits more fluid than in other nations. I am not philosopher enough to determine the cause; but nothing I had ever seen before came up to it. (198)

It is obvious that such Frenchmen, being intemperate and volatile, would have reacted even less well to misfortune and misery than the Spanish and the Portuguese.
  This practical sense and reserve of the English (or of those who, like Jean Rivard, imitate them) explain, therefore, their success in life. This behaviour, however, is also the source of a certain coldness of character, since being 'composed and serious in their joy' is their ideal. Crusoe goes into great detail when he is dealing with transactions, accounts, and various activities, but he is resolutely silent when it comes to his emotional life. Back in England, after twenty-eight years on his island and thirty-five years away, rich beyond his wildest dreams, he settles

down and dismisses his emotional, conjugal, and family life in half a sentence:

> In the mean time, I in part settled myself here; for, first of all, I married, and that not either to my disadvantage or dissatisfaction, and had three children, two sons and one daughter; but my wife dying, and my nephew coming home with good success from a voyage to Spain, my inclination to go abroad, and his importunity, prevailed, and engaged me to go in his ship. (RC, 185)

In the same sentence he has become a husband and a father, a widower and a bachelor! He will have a few warmer words for his wife in *Further Adventures*, but she dies very conveniently a few pages into the novel. And when he praises her, he uses a resolutely commercial and pragmatic vocabulary that says a lot about where his real interests lie:

> It is not my *business* here to write an elegy upon my wife ... She was, in a few words, the stay of all my *affairs*, the centre of all my *entreprises*, the *engine* that, by her *prudence*, reduced me to that happy *compass* I was in. (RC, 192; my italics)

But praise is still recognition of worth, even when clothed in the language of finance. Louise Routhier, as we know, becomes nothing but a silent shadow in the *Economist*, and Jean Rivard, when asked to reveal the secrets of his success, does not even mention his wife – 'Out of considerateness, no doubt,' ventures the narrator, who, for his part, counts her as 'one of his most important *secrets*' (340). I would say, rather, that he fails to mention her out of egotism and an awareness of his own worth and self-sufficiency. Jean would have succeeded with or without Louise Routhier: his recipe for success is something he carries within himself.

Jean remains a good father and a good husband, it goes without saying, just as Crusoe no doubt loves his ephemeral wife. The coldness in each of them is, however, real. In a society geared to capitalist values they both embody the tendency to replace truly personal relationships with contractual ones: contracts signed or promises given matter more than an intersubjective relationship. Jean therefore signs contracts with the Honourable Smith, with Pierre Gagnon, with Lachance, with M. Lacasse, with Arnold; he makes tacit contracts with his brothers before becoming the partner of one or the other. Finally, he contracts his marriage in a notary's office before solemnizing it in church: marriage is first and foremost a contract; as for his wife, she has, as we have seen, a book value before being a spouse. This unromantic conception of wife and marriage should be compared with Defoe's. When five English sailors select native wives for themselves on Crusoe's island, the first man to choose picks the ugliest, oldest woman of the lot: 'and she proved to be the best wife of all the parcel' (RC, 229), notes Crusoe, using his merchant's vocabulary.

However, Jean Rivard does not carry coldness and pragmatism as far as Crusoe. The latter tends to think of people in terms of their usefulness to him. For example, he is very pleased to have a companion on his island after twenty-five years of solitude. Yet his first concern is to make Friday useful: 'I was greatly delighted with him, and made it my business to teach him everything that was proper to make him useful, handy, and helpful' (RC, 128). A practical and industrious man's first duty (his 'business') is to ensure that his subordinates are kept busy: they are only valuable if they are 'useful, handy, and helpful.' Friday will thus always be 'my man Friday.' In other words, after being rescued by Crusoe, he has sworn to be a devoted slave, becoming his master's chattel, with no name, identity, or status aside from those bestowed by his master. 'And first, I let him know his name should be Friday, which was the day I saved his life ... I likewise taught him to say Master; and let him know that was to be my name' (RC, 126). Nonetheless, Crusoe does show affection for Friday, in a condescending, paternalistic way, as the demiurge might love one of his creatures. Xury's fate is not as pleasant. This young boy accompanies Crusoe when he escapes from Morocco at the beginning of the novel: 'Xury, if you will be faithful to me, I'll make you a great man ...' (RC, 15). The boy swears his loyalty and proves it many times during their flight. Despite this, Crusoe sells him at the first opportunity, to the first possible buyer, in fact – the Portuguese captain who picks them up off the coast of Africa. Crusoe's only expression of regret comes three years later when he has become a planter in Brazil:

However, we began to increase, and our land began to come into order; so that the third year we planted some tobacco, and made each of us a large piece of ground ready for planting canes in the year to come: but we both wanted help; and now I found, more than before, I had done wrong in parting with my boy Xury. (RC, 22–3)

The 'wrong' he had done was neither moral nor religious. He had simply made a commercial mistake, a bad business deal. There is a labour shortage in Brazil, and a devoted slave would be of considerable value. Indeed, it is in order to solve this labour problem that Robinson Crusoe embarks on the voyage that ends when he is stranded on his famous island. Readers are wont to forget that he was shipwrecked on his way to Africa to take on a cargo of 'black gold.'

Crusoe is calculating and pragmatic right from the first steps he takes in the business world, and so he remains at the end of his life. He never refuses a potentially profitable transaction. In his *Further Adventures*, he is alone in China with an associate and a young servant he claims to like very much. When Crusoe's nephew abandoned him in Bengal, he had left him this young man as a companion. This servant offers to go to Japan and the Philippines with the ship and bring back the fruits of his voyage to England (while Robinson returns over land by caravan): 'I was really loath to part with him; but considering the prospect of advantage, which really was considerable, and that he was a young fellow as likely to do well in it as any I knew, I inclined to let him go' (RC, 321). Though 'loath to part' with his servant, he cannot resist a bargain. The 'prospect of advantage' outweighs all other considerations, even though he is old, alone in the world, in a faraway country, on the other side of the globe from his home, and already rich beyond his wildest dreams. How can he resist the possibility of a profit, especially a considerable one?

Jean Rivard does not take the capitalist genius quite so far. However, his relationship with Pierre Gagnon is always characterized by a suspect condescension and a calculating spirit: people generally seem to matter to him less than their practical value. Once he is married, Louise Routhier progressively disappears as a woman and wife, and becomes a pale copy of her husband's organizing genius. Jean meticulously regulates his republic's future, just as he determines his children's education and their future (*Le Foyer canadien* 2, 1864), and arranges, or tries to arrange, his own brothers' and sisters' lives. 'And what have you done with your two sisters?' (362), the narrator asks at the very end of the novel, using a turn of phrase that accurately represents his state of mind by the end of his guided tour of this very special town. Jean Rivard does as he pleases: he treats people as objects, just like Robinson on his island.

In short, if *Robinson Crusoe* holds so important a place in *Jean Rivard*, it is not because Gérin-Lajoie has a weakness for travel novels, although this might be a small factor. This great realistic novel is the vehicle for an ideology, that of early capitalism and its norms of behaviour, an ideology with which Gérin-Lajoie's protagonist identifies completely. Jean Rivard and Robinson Crusoe are young, isolated, left to their personal initiative after having broken away from their native environment. Indeed, I think it is important to emphasize that the two novels are works of severance. At first, Jean 'would not think of defying the widespread prejudice' in favour of the bar and against manual labour. Father Leblanc encourages him to break away from the ideas of his surroundings: 'Be the first, my young friend, to challenge this harmful prejudice' (13). Jean does so, but must endure his mother's tears and the sneers and derision of his family. Crusoe and Jean both exhibit a passion for productive work and disgust for idleness, a need for order, and an acquisitiveness that ensure their fortunes. They both keep rigorous accounts – without ever having learned how – of their belongings and activities; bookkeeping is for them a pleasure and a religious duty. Jean spontaneously speaks of 'examining his conscience' before his balance sheet at the end of every day, and Crusoe instinctively uses an economic vocabulary to describe his spiritual life. They both make their capital grow with the help of associates. Thus their wealth grows out of proportion to their own input: Jean quickly becomes rich through land speculation, and Robinson Crusoe's land in Brazil continues to make a profit, even in his absence. They are capitalists, somewhat cold, stiff, and rigid (a very Calvinist rigidity); devout, but with a surface devoutness that is not adverse to profit and seeks to help others, not through charity but, in accordance with economic liberalism, by giving others an opportunity to help themselves. They profit from the surplus value provided by the work force (Jean Rivard more than Crusoe) while maintaining a friendly but above all condescending relationship with their subordinates.

Jean Rivard is thus a replica of Robinson Crusoe who instructs us about the values and preoccupations of the Canadian pioneer. He also provides an essentially economic outline of Jean Rivard's adventure: how to transform an uninhabited area – the forest in the New World or a desert island – into a prosperous space.

It could also be stated that, by analogy with the British sailor's adventure, a heroic dimension is conferred on a historical enterprise – settlement – that Gérin-Lajoie's contemporaries considered mundane and without prestige. This heroic significance, however, is more fully taken on by another intertextual element: the presence of the Napoleonic myth.

Napoleon: The Conqueror, the 'Self-Made Man,' the Liberal

It may seem a bit surprising that a Canadian pioneer in 1843 would pack a history of Napoleon in his bags, but its inclusion is less surprising than that of a travel narrative. Napoleon was a dominating presence in the nineteenth century, as a military genius who had terrified all the Western nations, changed the face of Europe, liquidated the ancien régime and created modern nations. He was also hailed as a genius at organization who profoundly changed all European institutions and fashioned modern France in particular. Napoleon was a constant cultural and historical reference because he dominated the century. It is easy to understand why an educated young man like Jean Rivard, an exceptional pioneer, would be attracted to this figure and be delighted by his fascinating destiny.

However, although Napoleon was a constant reference in the nineteenth century, he was an ambiguous one, both intrinsically and in Gérin-Lajoie's novel. 'Napoleon taught me to be active and courageous,' Jean Rivard reveals to his visitor, the narrator. But Napoleon also teaches many other things, because the various meanings he represents could not possibly be covered by this one-dimensional interpretation. This historical figure's intrusion in the novel is even far less innocent than other intertextual elements, and for two reasons. First, Napoleon is accompanied by a multiple discourse that is profoundly polarized and at times cacophonous. Second, in French Canada, especially in 1862, to give a place of honour to Napoleon in a literary work was also a way of taking sides in a complex ideological debate. Thus, Napoleon's significance and his diegetic and discursive value in this novel are difficult to determine because they remain ambiguous. Yet this very ambiguity enables us to establish the richness of this intertextual element.

Napoleon, a Constant Analogue

Let us begin by indicating Napoleon's importance in the novel. He is undeniably the protagonist's most constant analogue. From the start of his adventure, even before he begins reading the biography of Napoleon, Jean chooses military analogies. In his first letter to Gustave Charmenil, he announces: 'I am moving out in a week, lock, stock, and barrel [*avec armes et bagages*]' (27). His adventure is seen as a campaign, an expedition that, like any military operation, requires heroic qualities. We have seen in Chapter 2 of this study that Jean Rivard is already a hero by virtue of his rigorous resolution. Like the already mythical hero to whom he will soon be compared, he is blessed with an energy and a remarkable speaking talent that galvanizes his audience. Napoleon before his troops or Jean Rivard before his family: the effect is the same.

'The energy and air of resolution with which he said those two words silenced those who laughed and in a way electrified his young listeners' (23). The military imagery becomes more clear in the following pages as the narrator offers a comparative description of the type of courage that Jean Rivard's venture demands:

> By boldly venturing into the forest to live far from all society and devoting himself to the most difficult work, Jean Rivard showed extraordinary courage. Military bravery, that ardour that manifests itself from time to time before the enemy on a battlefield, is far inferior, in my opinion, to that calm, cold bravery, that constant courage that is stimulated neither by honours, distinctions, nor human glory, but by the sole sentiment of duty and the noble ambition to do things properly. (29–30)

Next there is an allegorical description of the diverse phases of land-clearing, a description that emphasizes the violent, conflicting (and thus *personalized*, as is every battle) aspect of that work. Jean launches into a hand-to-hand battle with true gigantic enemies:

> Our lumberjacks began by examining the trees they intended to destroy, in order to determine the direction in which they were leaning; because every tree, even the proudest, tends to lean a little, and it is in this direction it must fall. From dawn until dusk, our two pioneers made the forest resound with the sound of that useful instrument that might with good reason be considered the emblem and the tool of civilization. The frightened birds fled these once peaceful retreats. When a huge hundred-foot-tall tree, cut to the heart by the murderous blade of steel, appeared to be about to yield, there was a second of solemn silence, followed by a terrific crash as the colossal tree fell. A muted roar was heard from the ground.
> Just as in the world of politics, finance, commerce, or industry, the fall of a great figure results in the ruin of a multitude of lesser characters, so the fall of a great tree destroys a number of weaker trees, some of which are decapitated or broken in the middle, others completely uprooted.
> Our pioneers had barely given their felled enemy a look of superb satisfaction when they set to cutting it up. In a few seconds, the tree was stripped of its branches and cut into many pieces that lay scattered on the ground, awaiting the agonies of the fire.
> And the same work started again every day. (33–4)

Thus, in the mind of both the protagonist and the narrator, certain elements of the Napoleonic analogy preceded the actual reading of

Napoleon's life. Land-clearing is a war, the pioneers launch a campaign, their work demands courage superior to that of a soldier, theirs is the victory of civilization and of new values over gigantism and inertia, a victory made concrete by the final purification ('the agonies of the fire'). When Jean Rivard starts reading the *Histoire populaire de Napoléon*,[21] this analogy is filled out, particularly through the extension this story finds in Pierre Gagnon's memory and imagination. 'This man, like many others of his class, possessed a fantastic memory,' and Jean Rivard was often surprised to hear him repeat almost word for word, in the middle of their land-clearing work, long passages he had read to him the night before' (42–3). Pierre Gagnon thus decides to call his master 'Emperor,' a status Jean will keep, in his eyes, until the end of the work. 'You will always be my emperor as before' (213), he assures him, even when he no longer works for Jean, showing the same attachment to his master as the most faithful *grognard* (veteran) toward Napoleon. It is above all Pierre Gagnon who maintains the metaphoric transposition of Jean's life throughout the novel:

They were both armed for war, marching together against the common enemy; that enemy was the forest surrounding them, through which the two valiant warriors must clear a way. Our pioneers' work was nothing short of bloody battles; every evening they would count the number of dead and discuss the next day's campaign plan. The dead were the trees felled throughout the day; the tallest were the generals and officers, the shrubs were merely canon fodder. (43)

In Pierre's mind, the transposition is constant and, moreover, is not limited to land-clearing.

When Jean Rivard builds his first house, 'Pierre Gagnon's imagination was fired up at the sight of such progress, and historical recollections crowded into his memory. The house that was being built was nothing less than the Emperor's Palace; it was Fontainebleau or the Luxembourg being decorated to receive Empress Marie-Louise' (154). When Pierre Gagnon must battle bullies in order to go and vote, his cry of victory bursts forth: 'I am voting for Jean Rivard! and long live the Emperor!' (303). Indeed, his Napoleonic fervour can be excited at any given moment. At the end of the chapter in which Jean Rivard is presented as the legislator and the builder of a future utopian town, he exclaims: 'I was certain ... that you would do as much as the great Napoleon. Now that you have no more enemies to battle, you will give a kingdom to each of your brothers' (224). And on the last page of the novel, it is once again Pierre Gagnon who establishes the ultimate parallel. Not only has

Jean Rivard led the true life of Napoleon, waging war, always victorious, against the forest, building, establishing, and administering the new town and the whole township, he has also led the life of which Napoleon *dreamed*. Addressing the narrator, Pierre finishes extolling his Emperor as follows:

Finally, sir, since you are a lawyer, I suppose that you have read the story of Napoleon, and that you know what he said: if I were not Emperor, I would like to be a justice of the peace in a village. Ah! Our master did not miss the mark; he has been a justice of the peace for a long time, and will be as long as he lives. (367)

From beginning to end, Jean Rivard's life is thus lived under the influence of the Napoleonic epic, thanks to Pierre Gagnon. However, the verve of the 'brigadier' (*passim*) is inspired by the master's *reading*, and is maintained by rereadings or constant allusions to them:

Then, turning toward Pierre with a smile: 'It's the opening of the Italian campaign,' he said. 'In recognition of your past service, I name you leader of the brigade; Lachance will be under your command, and you will receive your orders directly from me. Moreover, I will not stray far from you, and you will always find me wherever honour and victory lead.'

'Hurray! and forward march,' cried Pierre Gagnon, who was fond of this kind of joke. (68)

Although Jean Rivard maintains his critical distance (that of a 'joke') and sometimes protests for appearances' sake, he accepts his hired man's flattering associations: 'Without wishing to contradict Pierre Gagnon, I scarcely resemble the great Napoleon, but I am of his opinion that ...' (190), he writes to Gustave Charmenil. When the narrator asks for the secrets of his success, he quite naturally compares his incessant work to that of a military leader:

I did not waste an instant. I was on my feet more than ten hours a day, working the earth, felling trees, sowing, reaping, hoeing, harvesting, building, coming and going, supervising everything, giving directions like a general who pushes his army through obstacles and danger, always aiming for victory. (333-4)

This parallel is also constantly being made by the narrator, who repeatedly takes up some elements of the comparison. The burning of the felled trees is 'the fire of Moscow' (71); the stumps blackened by the fire on the battlefield are 'ghosts' with 'gloomy heads' (74); Jean does 'fierce battle with the trees in the forest' (156); he 'resolutely wages war against the forest' (156); he has 'a campaign strategy ... drawn up long ago' (184). The narrator is quick to use the same technique of denial and affirmation that Jean Rivard uses in his letter to Gustave Charmenil or when he is 'joking.' The association with Napoleon is rejected or criticized only to be immediately confirmed and reinforced. 'Although he did not have Napoleon's immense genius, Jean Rivard seemed to have the same confidence in his star' (151): If Jean Rivard is less Napoleonic in one way, then he is sure to be more so in another. Moreover, by and large the narrator is not far from thinking, like Pierre Gagnon, that not only does Jean Rivard have Napoleon's qualities, but he is far superior to him by virtue of the effects of his actions. The 'Moscow fire' in the township of Bristol, for example, produces riches rather than destroys them: 'One had caused many families to be miserable and poor ... the other was to bring prosperity and happiness to the labourer's cabin' (71). Pierre Gagnon finds himself judging Napoleon along the same lines:

'I do not mean to scorn Napoleon,' he added, 'but I believe that if he had done as you have rather than going around turning all the countries upside-down and killing people right and left, his life would not have ended so sadly. (224)

and regretting that Napoleon was not a pioneer like them:

Thunderation! I would like to have seen him felling trees; I think it would have made a great fire. (224)

We have thus come full circle: the transposition has been reversed. Land-clearing naturally brings to mind images of battles, war, violent confrontation. (Moreover, Jean's prophetic dream imposed these images.) For this militaristic campaign, the *Histoire populaire de Napoléon* offers a prestigious historical analogue: the wars waged by Napoleon. The extension of this campaign (the founding and administration of a township) confirms the validity of this analogue: Jean Rivard also has the administrative talents of the Emperor. And, in a reversal of the comparison, the most fervent propagandist for this association dreams of a pioneering Napoleon: the Emperor is tranferred to the township of Bristol.

Today's reader may well find this analogy clearly hyperbolic (and Gérin-Lajoie had his reasons for choosing the most coarse and 'primitive' character in the novel to draw this analogy, which he could then validate by other means), but it is nonetheless a constant. What should we think of it?

Right from the start, we must recognize the simplicity and effectiveness of the military comparison: it conforms to the internal demands of the simple comparison. Between war and land-clearing there is an obvious, close relationship that is structurally indispensable to a realistic comparison. In both cases, striking and cutting down are involved, as are advancing, destroying, burning, and occupying. The physical activities closely resemble each other, and the logical link must have been inescapable for Gérin-Lajoie, especially since he himself was fascinated by the military spirit, as is shown by his activities at Nicolet College.[22] Once this military analogue of land-clearing had been adopted, the image of Napoleon was naturally inevitable. For this there were historical, literary, and specifically Canadian reasons.

Napoleon's Century

The historical reasons are related to Napoleon's presence throughout the century. Jean Tulard notes: 'There is a Napoleonic age just as there was an age of Louis XIV.'[23] Or, as Victor Hugo said:

Toujours Napoléon, éblouissant et sombre
Sur le seuil du siècle est debout.[24]

Very modern in his skill at public relations, Napoleon, from his first campaigns, was careful to build and spread his image; he was well served by a patriotic press, which he subsequently controlled, and by the vehicles of popular culture like images and songs. He was also well served by a truly remarkable career that would fascinate anyone. This unimaginable life quickly became a legend of mythical dimensions. 'In 1821, the myth is definitively established, combining many facets: the young hero, the master of the world, the exile. Three images that Napoleon himself created and imposed on his contemporaries, then on posterity. A succesful creation.'[25] Yet it was successful because it had an objective basis that ensured its validity despite all criticism, and because it had an element of mystery that guaranteed its longevity. Gérin-Lajoie, as a man of his century, could not escape this fascination.

As a writer and intellectual, brought up on the French Romantics, he was even more susceptible to this Napoleonic fervour. Of the authors he read, Chateaubriand, Lamartine, and especially Balzac and Hugo, were obsessed by Napoleon. The literary myth prolonged and deepened the popular image and at the same time, because of the renown of the writers in question, extended it in unexpected directions. Gérin-Lajoie, who had read Madame de Staël, Chateaubriand, and Lamartine, as is evident from his novel (81, 112, 123, 179, 198, 224 ...), does not retain from these authors the tyrannical image of Napoleon, even less that of the Corrupter and the Megalomaniac. For him Napoleon is definitely not the scourge of modern times, the gravedigger of the Revolution and of individual freedoms, a new Attila, a ridiculous Nero, a Tamerlane, or a Genghis Khan.[26] On the contrary, Napoleon is the Hero and the Giant; Gérin-Lajoie could certainly take up Victor Hugo's lines as his own:

I am one of those people who, with all qualifications made and accepted, fully and definitively admire Napoleon; I acquit and crown him in the judgment of history. He is criticized for what makes him a man; the rest springs from the archangel and the giant.[27]

And one could say of *Jean Rivard* what many others, without exaggeration, have said of Balzac's *Comédie humaine*: Napoleon is a constant presence therein:

Does not the *Comédie humaine* deserve the title of 'comédie napoléonienne'? There is indeed scarcely a Balzac novel that does not contain at least one reference to Napoleon ... One might almost think that Napoleon is the central character of this fresco with the other characters playing minor roles.[28]

In the *Comédie humaine*, Napoleon holds a place of exceptional importance, at least equal to that which Stendhal granted him in his work. The Emperor rarely makes a personal appearance; yet he is everywhere, in the evolution of individual destinies as well as in the general orientation of minds and of France. Even characters who had no relationship with him have been marked by him.[29]

Thus, Gérin-Lajoie joined, perhaps consciously, the ranks of all the writers who contemplated Napoleon's genius. He might even have borrowed the image of a wood-cutting Napoleon from Chateaubriand, who presented it negatively ('France's generations were periodically felled like trees in a forest; every year 80 000 young people were cut down')[30] or from Victor Hugo, in whose work it often recurred:

> Quand ce grand ouvrier, qui savait comme on fonde,
> Eut, à coups de cognée, à peu près fait le monde
> Selon le songe qu'il rêvait ...[31]

A dream, then a new world to be built with great blows of an axe: such is Jean Rivard's fate as well. The metaphor, however, is reversed in Victor Hugo, who was always fond of striking contrasts, and the lumberjack is cut down in his turn:

> L'empereur était là, debout, qui regardait.
> Il était comme un arbre en proie à la cognée.
> Sur ce géant, grandeur jusqu'alors épargnée,
> Le malheur, bûcheron sinistre, était monté;
> Et lui, chêne vivant, par la hache insulté,
> Tressaillait sous le sceptre aux lugubres revanches,
> Il regardait tomber autour de lui ses branches.[32]

For Gérin-Lajoie, there is no such fateful reversal. In his work, the great Romantic poet's occasional metaphor becomes an obsessive, constantly glorifying image.

Gérin-Lajoie's nationality is no doubt partly responsible. In French Canada, Napoleon seemed to enjoy a particular fervour, which further explains his presence in the novel. In the absence of an overall study of the subject that would be the counterpart of Marcel Trudel's *Voltaire*,[33] it is difficult to get a precise idea of the Napoleonic myth's hold over French Canada, but there are accounts that enable us to state that it was considerable. Ringuet assures us that, even in the twentieth century, French Canadians showed a real passion for the Emperor:

One would think that only the France of the Crown and the Church had a place in French Canadians' hearts. Indeed, all they remember of the French Revolution is the guillotine. However, our people have a true passion for Napoleon. They are mad about his legend. I do not know whether this is still the case; but then, there were very few homes in French Canada that did not have a print recalling the Napoleonic epic. Canadians who go to France visit the Invalides, like everyone else, but they bring with them a devotion that goes beyond the tourist's simple curiosity.[34]

This devotion was even greater at the beginning of the nineteenth century, when Napoleon could incarnate the hope for revenge for French Canadians. In his *Mémoires*, Philippe Aubert de Gaspé writes of the hatred of English speakers for Napoleon, whom they saw as the true Antichrist,[35] and of the difficulty his fellow citizens encountered in expressing their admiration for the Emperor: 'It was not even permissible to admire the brilliant achievements of this prodigious man, whose only equals, if he had not surpassed them, were Alexander and Caesar.'[36] Even a staunch royalist like Gaspé's father, who considered Napoleon a usurper, gave him credit for his 'great military genius,' even if it meant being called 'French' and 'bad subject'[37] by the English governor of Quebec. Governor Craig's fear accurately expressed what Napoleon could incarnate for French Canadians at the turn of the century when he described the 'gang of unprincipled lawyers and notaries' who waged war against him in the Assembly:

They have no property, and have nothing to lose and everything to gain from a change resulting from their intrigues or the confusion that they could cause in the province. These men have gradually become more audacious as they have considered French power more solidly established by Napoleon's success in Europe. This is evident. The general opinion of everyone you talk to on this subject is that they are trying to prepare the way for a shift in allegiance and a return to the French regime ... Unfortunately the minds of the masses have been poisoned; they await this event, they talk about it in secret conversations. I have been assured that a song is being circulated in which Napoleon is named as the man who will expel the English.[38]

Thus, in a general way, even after the fall of the Empire, the evocation of Napoleon was linked to the glorification of patriotism. To speak of Napoleon and to recognize his genius and conquests was to assert one's race and nation against the English. In his 4 May 1827 interview, Goethe commented on Béranger's *Souvenirs du peuple*, which had contributed to immortalizing and idealizing the Napoleonic legend:

What is more, in his political songs, Béranger has shown himself to be a benefactor to his nation. After the allies' invasion, the French found in him the best spokesman of their oppressed feelings. He lifted their spirits by evoking many memories of glorious feats of arms under the Emperor, whose memory still lives in every village and whose great qualities are loved by the poet, without his wanting the despotism of his reign to continue.[39]

What was true of the French was even more true of French Canadians, twice conquered in a way, with no glorious past (except in their dreams and by association with France) and with no concrete hope of independence. The compensatory power of Napoleon's glory could be truly intoxicating.

It is undeniable that the legend was present and effective in French Canada. As a last piece of evidence, I will cite one of Gérin-Lajoie's contemporaries. At the very end of *Charles Guérin*, Pierre Guérin tells his brother and sister about his adventurous life. On his arrival in France in 1830, he finds himself penniless after having deserted his ship. He and his companion then buy a magic lantern and travel across France as 'strolling players.'[40] The first story he tells is that of Napoleon: 'It was a fine sight to see me tell about the battles of the Empire and repeat the sublime words of the little corporal, or the tales of *Bluebeard* or *Little Red Riding Hood*.'[41] The passage is revealing. In 1853 a French-Canadian novelist assumed that the story of Napoleon was so well known in Canada that one of his characters could even tell it to the French. What is more, this story, although very recent, has joined the category of ageless tales or folklore: stories that we all know but all retell each other, for the pleasure of a good story and to recognize ourselves, to confirm our life and being.

This being said, however, the significance of this great historical figure in *Jean Rivard* remains to be explained. The contextual reasons for Napoleon's presence in Gérin-Lajoie's novel reveal some of the richness of this intertextual element but do not really make its significance clear. To sing the praises of Napoleon at the beginning of the century (at the time described by Gaspé) was literally a form of subversion; to make the Emperor the constant analogue of a protagonist in 1862 implies something else on an ideological level. In this novel, it seems to me that Napoleon is the sign of a threefold ideological discourse: a heroicization of settlement presented as a campaign of reconquest; an exaltation of will at the service of the mystique of personal success; and an implicit glorification of liberalism and secularization. Each of these aspects will be examined in turn.

Clearing the Land or Waging War

As I have stressed in the previous chapter, settlement was an objective widely shared by all ideological tendencies in Quebec society in the middle of the last century. Whether ultramontanes or liberals, conservatives or reformists, federalists or annexationists,[42] members of the Quebec Board of Trade or physiocrats, all approved of the development and occupation of the ecumen. Taken in its wider sense of exploitation of unproductive lands by populating them and by introducing all forms of industry (industry in Étienne Parent's sense), colonization readily met with general approval. It was, according to general opinion, the real vocation of North America: these virgin lands had to be populated and surrender their resources. Gabriel Dussault, inquiring into the meaning of this surprising 'Holy Alliance,' which brought together the interests of such different groups, stresses the conquering aspect of settlement for French Canadians.

> Simply put, this project was presented as essentially a *utopia of reconquest by a perfectly legal and peaceful strategy of expansion and territorial occupation*. If people got so worked up when it was evoked, it is because it was the dream of a lost homeland that had to be recovered.[43]

Settlement ensured the reversal, one century later, of the disaster of the Plains of Abraham by occupying the territory, surrounding the English, and gradually smothering them. Dussault emphasizes the catalytic role of Rameau de Saint-Père's book, *La France aux colonies*,[44] in the realization that this reconquest was possible. This book, written without the author's setting foot in the country but composed after patient and rigorous research on Canadian geography and demography, was published in 1859 and was received 'with an enthusiasm, an excitement, and a recognition unparallelled in the history of Franco-Canadian relations.'[45]

There has been a concerted effort to turn Rameau into an agriculturist,[46] and there is no doubt that, in some pages of his work, this patriot and fervent Catholic warns the French-Canadian people against American materialism. But Gabriel Dussault is right to recall that the essential aspect of this remarkable book, which was unanimously approved by people of all the ideological tendencies in French Canada, is altogether different:

> On the other hand, there is a point that Rameau stresses throughout his book and that, with a great deal of statistical evidence, comes almost as a revelation: it is the surprising demographic progress of French Canadians, their capacity for expansion and consequently *a kind of reconquest* that is in progress *just one cen-*

tury after the Conquest ... It is in this immediate context of reconquest – and not in some agrarian mystique or in some physiocratic economic theory – that Rameau regularly locates settlement.

... Moreover, that is the way his message is understood in Quebec.[47]

Rameau furthered the influence of his book by a triumphant visit the following year.[48]

Thus, at the time of *Jean Rivard*'s genesis, settlement was not perceived as a last resort or fall-back solution and even less as a spiritual isolation sheltered from the vicissitudes of the century; settlement, then, was seen as *an act of conquest*, which the author Gérin-Lajoie quite naturally associated with the great conquering figure of Napoleon. I have not been able to determine whether Gérin-Lajoie had read Rameau's work. Everyone around him was talking about it, however, and in literature that often amounts to the same thing. Some of Gérin-Lajoie's closest friends were among Rameau's first acquaintances in Canada. In fact, his brother-in-law, Henri Parent, who was studying in Paris, personally delivered some documents that Rameau had requested of the historian Garneau and was 'the first link in this long chain' of Canadian friendships.[49] Étienne Parent received the first copy of *La France aux colonies* and he lent it to journalists so that they could comment on it;[50] in June 1860, Rameau was welcomed in Quebec by Étienne Parent, Father Ferland and Father Casgrain and in Montreal by Loranger (a close friend of Gérin-Lajoie), who asked the distinguished visitor to give a lecture (23 October 1860).[51] Thus, all those with whom Gérin-Lajoie had family ties or bonds of friendship found themselves drawn into the French author's sphere of influence. Moreover, these links were long maintained. Étienne Parent was Rameau's most faithful correspondent and the affection that the latter felt for him was apparent during his second trip to North America in 1888:

We did not arrive in Montreal until midnight, but regardless of the late hour, my old friend Parent's grandson was waiting for us at the train station and took us off to meet his family. There I found all of Étienne Parent's descendants who welcomed me with the same affection that the grandfather had shown me in 1860, almost twenty-nine years earlier. But he is no longer here with us![52]

It is therefore likely that Rameau exerted some influence – at least through third parties – on Gérin-Lajoie, who, in his novel, demonstrates exactly the same concerns: ensuring the progress of settlement and preventing emigration to the United States. Rameau continually comes back to the same idea in his travel notes, his correspondence, and his conversations with his French-Canadian friends: French Canadians must occupy the land, not let themselves be surrounded and smothered by immigrants from the British Isles, but on the contrary displace them and drive them out by the strength of numbers and the irresistible spread of the 'oil stain.'[53] It is especially important to be the first to arrive in order to get the best land. It is obvious that in his view a war is being waged and the survival of the nation is at stake.

Gérin-Lajoie deserves credit for proposing an exemplary historical analogue of this war in a literary work. But this new Napoleonic war has the advantage of being waged without bloodshed, without even confronting the true enemy. It is sufficient to borrow the enemy's strategy and to present him with a *fait accompli* in terms of both numbers and position. Therefore, it does not seem an exaggeration to assert that in a metaphorical sense each blow of the axe directed against a 'giant of the forest' is aimed in fact at the English. The figure of Napoleon in *Jean Rivard* is the favoured vehicle for a conquering ideology. And in 1862, as throughout the First Empire at the beginning of the century, the enemy is the English.

Success!

Simultaneously the figure of Napoleon also conveys an ideology that in this study, to simplify, I have characterized as American, that is, a triumphant exaltation of the individual and of personal success. Napoleon's dazzling career is the prime model of success and inspires a profound admiration. The Romantic hero, who is often a misfit, is sustained by it, as is the obscure Canadian official. 'Romantic heroes [those of Balzac, Stendhal, and, let us add, Gérin-Lajoie] henceforth take Napoleon as their model ... What are the reasons for this fascination? The phenomenon of a mind-boggling rise to power, an obscure second lieutenant becoming Charlemagne's heir.'[54] According to Balzac and Stendhal, Napoleon is 'the most prodigious professor of energy';[55] for Julien Sorel, he is the most 'renowned example of a go-getter.'[56] Jean Tulard rightly stresses this fundamental aspect of the Napoleonic myth:

Napoleon was the stuff the Romantics' dreams were made on; he was the model on which they fashioned themselves ... His will and intelligence made Napoleon the symbol of individual energy. René Huyghe has accurately observed that the only philosophical system developed under the First Empire was that of Maine de Biran. The individual, he said, can know himself only as a life-force that functions on will power. This was involuntarily giving the best image of Napoleon, the exaltation of the self in action ... The affirmation of the individual is the lesson that the Romantics drew from the Napoleonic adventure.[57]

What Balzac found fascinating in Napoleon was his will power, that 'will of steel' ... a will that is the source of all forms of power. When Corralis [in *Autre étude de femme*] said that 'Napoleon was all-powerful because that is what he set out to achieve,' he summarized Balzac's philosophy ... Will and energy, all that is inseparable from a new ideology of which Stendhal made himself the prophet and which Barrès glorified at the end of the century. Napoleon is truly the father of individualism for a whole literary trend. Therein lies the explanation of the fascination that the myth exerts from the Romantics to the Déracinés.[58]

Thus, Napoleon was the most illustrious representative of the sovereign power of a bold and strong-willed individual. Moreover, his entire era glorified personal advancement. It was the epoch when 'sergeants became princes, postilions became kings, and archduchesses married adventurers,'[59] as Victor Hugo put it. 'What fine times they were!' exclaims one of Balzac's characters. 'Colonels were promoted to generals in the twinkling of an eye; generals to marshals of France, and marshals to kings ... Finally, sappers who knew how to read became great nobles just the same ... Keep in mind that, since every soldier stood a chance of acceding to a throne, provided he showed himself worthy of it, a corporal in the Guards was something of an oddity.'[60] Napoleon is therefore the figure par excellence of those other 'fine times,' Canadian in this case, in which the pioneer is 'promoted' to emperor and the fatherless nineteen-year-old 'accedes to' a republic of his own.

This interpretation of the Napoleonic myth, which is indispensable in understanding *Jean Rivard*, has been particularly emphasized by Ralph Waldo Emerson, a remarkable writer of rare insight. Emerson, the Sage of Concord, travelled frequently throughout the United States and Europe, as was shown in Chapter 2; he was well-versed in every country's literature and was better acquainted than anybody with his own era, at once a strong presence in his own century and yet remote in the tranquillity of his haven in Concord. He had quite an unusual opinion of Napoleon. According to him, Napoleon was clearly the 'prophet' of capitalism, the exemplary representative of the commercial mind. It is at this point, it seems to me, that Jean Rivard's ana-

Intertextuality I: Jean Rivard's Library 135

logue takes on its full meaning for the novel and that intertextuality sheds extraordinary light on Gérin-Lajoie's work. In a lecture read in January 1848 in London – among Napoleon's actual enemies – Emerson seemed to be taking malicious pleasure in making the Emperor the model for his hereditary adversaries in areas that were most authentically theirs:

The class of business men in America, in England, in France and throughout Europe; the class of industry and skill. Napoleon is its representative. The instinct of active, brave, able men, throughout the middle class everywhere, has pointed out Napoleon as the incarnate Democrat. He had their virtues, and their vices; above all, he had their spirit or aim. That tendency is material, pointing at a sensual success and employing the richest and most various means to that end; conversant with mechanical powers, highly intellectual, widely and accurately learned and skilfull, but subordinating all intellectual and spiritual forces into means to a material success. *To be the rich man, is the end.* 'God has granted,' says the Koran, 'to every people a prophet in its own tongue.' Paris and London and New York, the spirit of commerce, of money and material power, were also to have their prophet; and Bonaparte was qualified and sent ... I call Napoleon the agent or attorney of the middle class of modern society; of the throng who fill the markets, shops, counting houses, manufactories, ships of the modern world, aiming to be rich.[61]

'To every people a prophet in its own tongue' – The reader must appreciate Emerson's subtle irony. In London, New York, or Paris (or even in Montreal or Rivardville), everyone speaks but one language, that of business. Capitalists are a single people, regardless of geopolitical divisions, because they have a single goal: wealth. Napoleon, in Emerson's mind, is quite detached from his military role; he is not the model general but rather the model captain of industry. Paradoxically, this exceptional man was what he was because he practised, in exemplary fashion, quite standard virtues. Emerson expresses the paradox thus:

We can not, in the universal imbecility, indecision and indolence of men, sufficiently congratulate ourselves on this strong and ready actor, who took occasion by the beard, and showed us how much may be accomplished by the mere force of such virtues as all men possess in less degrees; namely, by punctuality, by personal attention, by courage and thoroughness ... I should cite him, in his earlier years, as a model of prudence.[62]

These virtues are the very ones that Jean Rivard practises and proposes as recipes for his success at the end of the novel. Punctuality refers to avoiding 'one of the great plagues of rural Canada ... wasting time' (334); personal attention is 'careful surveillance' (336); as for courage, 'Napoleon taught me to be active and courageous' (330); thoroughness is meticulousness and 'order' (336); and, finally, prudence permeates Jean Rivard's every word and deed. In short, reading Emerson's essay devoted to Napoleon is to discover in every line a description of the qualities and temperament of Gérin-Lajoie's protagonist. The exemplary capitalist, Jean Rivard, who has been described in the second chapter of this study, thus finds in Napoleon his nearest equivalent and his protective, if not eponymous, model.

Liberalism on Quebec Soil

Finally, there is a third ideological dimension in this Napoleonic intertext, which is more difficult to draw out as well as more debatable than the first two, but seems to me sufficiently present to justify a few hypotheses. The ambiguities of the Napoleonic myth and the contradictions that his image conveyed have already been mentioned. Historians have often treated this problem. Jean Tulard, for instance, in the conclusion of his study, stresses these multiple contradictions, at once social, political, religious, and moral. Is Napoleon the strong man who consolidated bourgeois France or the democrat, the faithful friend of the people? The champion of the libertarian principles of 1789 or the paragon of authoritarian regimes? The persecutor of the Pope (excommunicated by Pius VII) or the restorer of the Church and of the clergy? The consummate go-getter or the little corporal who aroused the most unselfish devotion? Historians may well hesitate. To these ambiguities of the legendary figure are added those of his descendants.

Jean Rivard was published in 1862, just a few months after the visit to Canada of an influential member of the imperial family. In the wake of Prince Napoleon's Canadian tour and in the context of the debate surrounding this visit, Gérin-Lajoie published a work that gave the figure of Napoleon a choice position. On one hand, since Napoleon and his descendants were especially topical during the months that Gérin-Lajoie was writing his work, it may be assumed that he was influenced by a contemporary event and as a result was inclined to make great use of Napoleon's image in his novel. On the other hand, since Prince Napoleon's visit had given new and vigorous life to the debate between liberals and conservatives, it may be presumed that the use of Napoleon at that precise moment was a way – a symbolic, strictly literary way – of taking up a position in this ideological debate. Specific information about the Prince's trip and its repercussions enables us to shed some light on this aspect of Gérin-Lajoie's novel.

In January 1860 the Pope's temporal sovereignty over the Papal States came under attack. On 19 January 1860, he published an encyclical to the entire Church calling for prayers and above all answering Napoleon III's suggestion that he abandon his States. Pius IX reminded the Emperor that he had made a commitment to protect the Pope and that on Judgment Day he would have to answer for his actions. This encyclical was obviously read out in Canada, accompanied by explanatory pastoral letters from Canadian bishops. In the clergy's circular (19 March 1860), which accompanied the 'pastoral instruction of the Bishop of Montreal on the independence and the inviolability of the Papal States,'[63] Bishop Bourget answered in plain language the fourth question he raised, 'Who are the enemies of the Papacy in France?' Napoleon III was the enemy since he was untrue to his word and ungrateful, because he owed everything to Providence. The Bishop then reminded his priests that Napoleon I had stripped Pius VII of his temporal power. Napoleon III was doing the same, and he would no doubt end up like his uncle, alone and dispossessed. Once again, on 31 May 1860, in a 'pastoral to the clergy,' Bishop Bourget referred to the affront to papal authority (this time following the appearance of articles in *Le Pays*) and issued a pastoral letter to his priests on the excommunication of those who had invaded the Papal States.[64]

Thus, in the early 1860s, the Napoleonic family was rather poorly regarded in Canadian religious circles: the Pope's problems evoked an emotional response in all of Quebec's pulpits, and these problems were in large part attributed to the French Emperor. It was at this moment that one of the members of the imperial family chose to visit Canada.[65]

Prince Napoleon was Jérôme Bonaparte's second son, therefore Napoleon I's nephew and Napoleon III's cousin; he had close ties to the latter and was his designated successor. On one level, he represents all the glory of this illustrious family, who then occupied the throne of France. But Napoleon Joseph Charles Paul was also the 'Red Prince,' who at that time embodied one of the poles of Napoleon I's conflicting legacy: the liberal and democratic pole (Napoleon, the liberal sovereign, always on the people's side, who had safeguarded the achievements of the Revolution). Thus, when Prince Napoleon visited Montreal and Quebec, from

11 to 17 September 1861 (he had, like all French visitors in those days, previously made a lengthy visit to the United States, which was the true purpose of his trip), he was preceded by his reputation as a red, anticlerical freethinker, who had furthermore married the excommunicated King Victor-Emmanuel II's daughter. Therefore, he was the black sheep of conservative ultramontane Catholics in France, who had forewarned their Canadian correspondents. Moreover, on 1 March 1861, on the eve of his departure for America, he had delivered a sensational speech against the Papal States to the French Senate. What sort of reception should be given to a person who, with his large retinue, could not possibly go unnoticed, who moreover represented France, but who was a fierce adversary of Pius IX and of the Pope's temporal power?

If *Le Pays*, the organ of the Institut canadien, which had been condemned by Bishop Bourget since 1858, is to be believed, Prince Napoleon got a very bad reception, because the clergy had prohibited the people from displaying their joy:

The poor turn-out of the Canadian people to honour a man who knows how to encourage a taste for knowledge and study was a very unjustifiable prejudice, a very unfortunate incident of national rudeness. ...

Just as the inhospitable aloofness of last September was justified on the grounds that the Prince had insulted the Pope, so rumours are being spread today that he sent only *impious* books. Always lies in the name of religion.

... There are people today and even more than we think, who *privately admit that it was wrong* to have a hostile attitude ... Secretly they say: 'It is a shame that *they prohibited us from going to greet him!*'[66]

Were the people truly prevented from welcoming the Prince? Admittedly, they were encouraged to stay away from him, but with limited success. The Prince himself and Maurice Sand, who was accompanying him, emphasized the people's enthusiastic welcome. The Prince was visibly delighted by the Canadians' disobedience of their priests' instructions and by the uneasiness of the clergy, torn between hostility and the duties of protocol:

Half of the people came to see me in my hotel in Quebec or signed the visitors' book. It was a genuine procession, attesting to a great liking for France, all the more so since the people gave me a warm welcome despite the clergy, who said

Intertextuality I: Jean Rivard's Library   139

many unkind things about me and wanted to prevent any demonstrations ... I visited Laval University ... It is run entirely by the clergy. The priests, the bishop (replacing the archbishop who is in his second childhood), the rector, the vicar-general, and the professors, welcomed me with uneasiness and obvious embarrassment. I examined everything in detail.[67]

'Great hostility of the clergy toward me,' he noted later on,[68] or, again: 'The Catholic clergy is very influential and very violent; the periodical press in Lower Canada is mainly in its hands; its editorial policy is much the same as our *Univers*, and is written in unreadable French. The clergy's attitude here is very different from what it is in the United States. In the United States, the priests are modest, devoted, and liberal, because they have no power; here they are already more arrogant and violent because they have more power and influence.'[69]

The clergy, therefore, was hostile but it did not completely succeed in preventing the people from warmly welcoming the Prince. It is very difficult to get an accurate idea of the scope of the welcome, as all the witnesses are content to use vague expressions ('a considerable crowd,' 'numerous citizens,' etc.). The only journalist to quote numbers is the one from the *Quebec Mercury*, who mentions about 200 people, most of them English-speaking, on the Grand Trunk wharf for the arrival of the Prince in Quebec:

A contemporary says that the persons who were on the wharf, at the landing on the city side, were principally French Canadians. Our reporter thinks this a mistake, and that there were more of English-speaking persons than French.[70]

Some of the people may have stayed away as *Le Pays* asserted, but the number of French Canadians who disobeyed the clergy surprised both French and English observers. Étienne Parent told his correspondent Rameau, who was 'surprised by the cordial reception that the French Canadians gave Prince Louis-Napoleon': 'Even if he had been worse than you describe him, he would have been received with pleasure among us, in his role as a French prince. It was France that we saluted and cheered in him.'[71] An English-speaking journalist, seeking to explain this phenomenon, used the same argument as Étienne Parent:

The Herald, speaking of his cordial reception, remarks 'that the Prince's quality as a Frenchman and member of the present royal family of France, does more in French Canada to secure his popularity, than his marriage into the family of the excommunicated Victor Emmanuel, and his speeches in favour of the *déchéance* from temporal power of his Highness the Pope, do to create disfavour for him in Catholic Canada.'[72]

Thus, despite his bad reputation, despite the Canadian clergy's hostility, Prince Napoleon was fairly well received. It was as ambiguous a welcome as could be wished. A French prince was acclaimed, but a prince who was liberal and anticlerical. The clergy, who always encouraged nationalist feelings as a means of resisting anglicization and ultimately Protestantism, found itself in the unenviable position where this attachment to France benefited an enemy of the Church. The people themselves had to choose between two values: loyalty to the language and to the motherland or faithfulness to the Pope and the Church. It seems that some people stayed away, thus demonstrating their hostility toward Prince Napoleon (or at least their docility to the Church).

But the decision to stay home or to go and cheer evidently does not have the same import as deciding whether to represent a historical character in a novel. The good Quebec middle class had only two options: to go or not to go and greet the Prince. The novelist had many possibilities before him, as the intertext by definition is unlimited. His choice becomes all the more significant in that he had an immense repertory at his disposal and from it he selected this figure. It so happens that this figure is ambiguous, and the decision to use him in these precise circumstances risked placing the novelist in one ideological camp, that of *L'Avenir*, *Le Pays*, and the Institut canadien (which had given a warm address to the Prince). In all likelihood, Gérin-Lajoie was well aware of all the consequences of this intertextual choice.

In the precise context of this historical moment (1860 to 1862), the Napoleonic saga, rich in ambiguous and contrasting meanings, as we have seen above, conveyed especially one very limited significance, that of red liberalism. Napoleon or the Napoleons are depicted as adversaries of the Pope, virulent anticlericals, the incarnation of secular forces struggling against the Church. From spring 1860, in all the churches in Quebec, Napoleon and his descendants were being represented as enemies of the Pope in France and Italy and as the primary cause for his loss of temporal power. Since at that very time the clergy was blackening Napoleon's reputation, the fact that the novelist brought him into play was not a neutral act. The exaltation of Napoleon in a context where ultramontanes and conservatives were portraying him in a negative light certainly enabled the reader to precisely situate

Intertextuality I: Jean Rivard's Library   141

Gérin-Lajoie on the political chessboard: distinctly leftist, on the liberal and anticlerical side.

This statement may seem surprising since it is difficult to imagine the steady, prudent Gérin-Lajoie in the camp of Dessaulles, Papineau, or Dorion.[73] Without going as far as placing him in the radical camp, it must be recognized nonetheless that the Napoleonic intertext leads to this similarity. This is confirmed by a careful reading of the novel, where real religious sentiments are found (as they are in the Red Prince's notebooks), but where there prevails a liberal and republican spirit that resolutely relegates the clergy to its own realm, thus ensuring harmonious relations between the political leader (Jean Rivard) and the spiritual leader (Octave Doucet).[74] This is also confirmed by a parallel reading of this work and the Reds'[75] program as summarized, for example, in the January 1851 issue of *L'Avenir*. Is *Jean Rivard* a red novel? It is certainly a far cry from the interpretation that the nationalist conservatives, headed by Monsignor Camille Roy, tried to impose on it in the late nineteenth and early twentieth centuries, an interpretation that critics have been content to reproduce ever since.

To this analysis of certain elements of *Jean Rivard*'s rich intertextuality, it is possible to object that the work does not actually realize the meanings conveyed by the intertext. For instance, in the novel, Jean Rivard is compared to Napoleon for his military valour or administrative skills, but he is not explicitly compared for his capitalist spirit or liberal ideology. He is compared to Robinson Crusoe for his resourcefulness and energy, not for his capitalist genius. This is only partly true and does not constitute a crucial objection. These meanings necessarily accompany the intertext, whether one likes it or not. Integrating an element into a literary work, be it word, image, symbol, or theme, means accepting the whole range of that element's meanings. The writer chooses a word for a particular reason, but this word is accompanied by all its various connotative values, a true aura that influences the meaning of the work and indeed gives it its richness. What is true about any word is all the more true about an element that has been carefully considered, which is the case with this kind of intertext, where the author deliberately seeks an evocative analogue in his own cultural tradition. Moreover, in a very real sense, intertextuality defines itself by the coexistence of many discourses – complementary or independent, individual or parallel, interdependent or conflicting (monologic or dialogical) – in a single intratextual space. Each of these discourses conveys many virtualities that the analyst must bring out. When Gérin-Lajoie decided to give Napoleon important stature in his novel, his choice was laden with meanings, not just in an absolute sense, but also because it was linked to specific historical circumstances. It is important, then, to clarify this meaning.

Through this interpretative work, Gérin-Lajoie's novel can be to some extent rehabilitated, and, in particular, attention can be drawn to its surprising modernity. There are very few Quebec novels that attach such importance to books and to a fictional library, with all the ambiguities and the richness, at once semantic and diegetic, that this entails. It is perhaps this diegetic plan that is the most surprising. André Belleau indicated that Quebec novels were 'saturated with literary references,'[76] but that these references more often than not had a discursive, enunciative function (to enrich a description, enhance a situation, embellish the discourse); very rarely did they have a diegetic function. They were not integrated 'into the very framework of the story':[77]

According to the data that I have collected – but it would be better to undertake a methodical search – the function of literary references in most Quebec novels remains essentially discursive and enunciative ... What is involved here is not so much French (and European) literature in its intertextual relationship with our own, but rather the formal conditions of integration of all literature and even of all culture into the text of the Quebec novel. The impossibility of making a writer, a book, a reading experience into truly diegetic performers while Quebec novels are saturated with literary references – Ducharme, for example – refers us, in my opinion, to the concrete status of literature in Quebec society.[78]

This 'concrete status,' in Belleau's mind, is one of decoration or of a knick-knack.

André Belleau is no doubt right in the case of the contemporary Quebec novels he cites, but not at all in the case of several nineteenth-century novels (let us remember the 'diegetic performance' of *Le petit Albert* in *L'influence d'un livre*), and certainly not for *Jean Rivard*. Admittedly, the books read by the hero have a discursive function in the novel: they continually serve to fill out a scene, to authenticate a discourse. But they are also deeply integrated into the protagonist's adventure. Jean Rivard becomes, literally, the protagonists of these books – Crusoe or Napoleon. These readings mark, accompany, and mould him: in short they make him what he is. The protagonist here literally becomes one with his library. This library is his private space and his cocoon. It is also his

Intertextuality I: Jean Rivard's Library 143

synecdoche, in both senses of this figure of speech. Jean Rivard always carries a part of it with him, and each part is fashioned in his own image. Or as Baudrillard's definition puts it: 'The collection is made up of a succession of terms, but the final term in the collection is the collector.'[79] Thus, Jean Rivard's library represents his true ethopoeia, portraying him completely, shaping him and guiding his action.

Finally, we realize that this kind of intertextuality (a book within a book) is based on an illusion. The book is read in the host book, but in reality it encompasses its host. What expected to swallow is itself swallowed. The book that is read structures the host story as a whole and serves as a model for it. The heroes of the books that are read are models for the protagonist of the host book, and in the final analysis the books that are read are models for the writer of the host book. The protagonist and the writer reproduce the model in the books they have read. Jean Rivard becomes every inch a Robinson Crusoe and a Napoleon; Gérin-Lajoie rewrites the story of their success in all its aspects.

But the author could not have realized that in proceeding in this manner he was paradoxically undermining the very basis of his venture. Indeed, Gérin-Lajoie could not have imagined – the practice of literature was less sibylline in his day, less indebted to literary casuists of every stripe – that the mise-en-abyme concealed a basic ambiguity and constituted an insoluble paradox. The mise-en-abyme can give an extension, a scope, a value, and an importance to the story; at the same time it subverts the realism of the narrative by attracting attention to its literariness, by recalling its composition and its materiality. The more Crusoe and Napoleon are exploited, the more Jean Rivard identifies himself with them, the less Gérin-Lajoie succeeds in convincing us that his text is a 'true life narrative.' His work becomes more and more 'literary.'

Nevertheless there remain the various meanings of the books that are read. They may well subvert the primary intention of the host book (to convince the reader of some reality), but they inform it with their riches and enable the contemporary reader to imagine something of the complex polysemy of this work that has been said to be univocal and dismissed as a banal thesis novel.

4

Intertextuality II: *Jean Rivard* as a Utopia

The intertextual richness of *Jean Rivard*, of which some glimpses were provided in the previous chapter, is not limited to the striking issue of its fictional library. It is no doubt appropriate to acknowledge Philippe Sollers' now classic description of intertextuality, echoed in the Introduction to this study: 'Every text is situated at the meeting-point of several texts, which it rereads, accentuates, condenses, displaces, and deepens at the same time.'[1] The expression 'several texts' can refer to all of the very different texts quoted by an author, 'the pieces taken from different textual organisms,'[2] which he then transplants, integrates into his own work, and structures to suit his own purposes. Gérin-Lajoie, for example, quotes abundantly, drawing his quotations from all kinds of sources. The term can also refer to a clearly defined network of texts, a family of works that form the real circle of an author's enterprise, although he does not necessarily acknowledge them explicitly. Without thinking about it, without intending to do so – or without stating it – the author produces a work that fits obviously and neatly into a very precise literary tradition. Such appears to be the case with *Jean Rivard*: a remarkable avatar of a proven genre, an extremely American incarnation of a millenarian inspiration, a work that, in short, is at the meeting-point of a rich, utopian intertextuality.

Utopia in the Nineteenth Century

The nineteenth century is truly the century of utopias. Curiously, a historian of the genre, Raymond Trousson, has expressed amazement at the scarcity of utopian *narratives* during the first half of the century:

Intertextuality II: *Jean Rivard* as a Utopia 145

Those who remember the number and diversity of eighteenth-century utopias cannot fail to be struck by the scarcity, at least of literary utopias, in the first half of the nineteenth century.[3]

This opinion, however, is not universally shared. Two critics who are perhaps the best historians of the utopian genre at present express a contrary opinion: 'The eighteenth century probably produced as many utopian texts as the sixteenth and seventeenth put together, and the nineteenth quintupled that number.'[4] No doubt, the distinction must be made between utopian narratives and works of utopian inspiration. The latter, which have been an important trend in modern thought since the Renaissance, reach their peak, as it were, in the nineteenth century. The great utopians of the century, such as Robert Owen, Karl Marx, Charles Fourier, Claude Henri de Saint-Simon, Étienne Cabet, Edward Bellamy, can easily compete with the great names of other glorious historical periods of utopias: Plato during antiquity; More, Rabelais, and Bacon during the Renaissance; Foigny, Vairasse, and Cyrano in the seventeenth century; Morelly, Mercier, and Restif de La Bretonne in the eighteenth century. In fact, the profound changes brought about by the Industrial Revolution encouraged utopian thought in two contrasting but complementary ways and gave it extraordinary vigour. On one hand, the Promethean illusion of having conquered nature and being able to create a new world through technology stimulates the creative imagination of several thinkers:

In this new world of falling water, burning coal, and whirring machinery, utopia was born again. It is easy to see why this should have happened, and why about two-thirds of our utopias should have been written in the nineteenth century. The world was being visibly made over; and it was possible to conceive of a different order of things without escaping to the other side of the earth. There were political changes, and the monarchic state was tempered by republicanism; there were industrial changes, and two hungry mouths were born where one could feed before; and there were social changes – the strata of society shifted and 'faulted.'[5]

On the other hand, the alarming discovery of a new affliction (the proletariat) and of a radical dehumanization (reification) on a gigantic scale makes people strive to achieve a better world, a world of justice and truth. Therefore, the number of utopias, which are both extremely critical of the prevailing order and enthusiastic about the possibilities offered by the new discoveries, increased in the nineteenth century. But, above all, and this is what distinguishes this century from previous eras, the written utopia is henceforth put into practice. Works are put to work. There is a succession of attempts to establish utopias; practical endeavours and organizations with numerous cellular outgrowths make utopias an important social movement in terms of both the number of adherents and the scale of the resources mobilized.

A distinctive feature of this movement is that the originators and theorists are European (particularly English, French, and German), whereas their favoured country is America. Some examples may serve to illustrate the extent of the movement. Thus Robert Owen, emboldened by his success as a philanthropic industrialist in Manchester and in Lanarkshire, bought 30 000 acres (including nineteen farms, orchards, vineyards, and a well-constructed village) in Indiana in 1824, so as to found New Harmony, a community that was to inspire all the American utopias of the nineteenth century. It was called *New* Harmony because previously the property had belonged to a community of unmarried Pentecostals (led by a German, George Rapp), who between 1814 and 1824 had constructed this utopia and named it Harmony. New Harmony, like all utopias, had a tendency to proliferate. For example, one of its members, Joseph Warren, subsequently founded Utopia in Cincinnati and Modern Times on Long Island. Previously, in 1774, Ann Lee and the Shakers, utopian working people from Manchester, had settled in Albany, New York, in 1774. Around 1850, the group, which relied exclusively on recruitment because celibacy was compulsory, had 6000 members in eighteen villages. In 1847 Étienne Cabet bought 100 000 acres of land in Texas and then the town of Nauvoo, Illinois; the old master himself left for his American Icaria at the end of 1848, after having sent two contingents of the faithful ahead of him. In 1856 he died disillusioned in New Orleans, but his disciples proliferated afterwards. Charles Fourier's numerous disciples, after his death in 1837, followed Victor Considérant to America and established several short-lived communities, of which the most prosperous and long-lasting were the North American Phalanx, in New Jersey, the Wisconsin Phalanx, and, no doubt the best known, Brook Farm in Massachusetts, where intellectuals and writers from New England, including Nathaniel Hawthorne and Margaret Fuller, used to meet. Finally, between 1841 and 1858, Fourier alone inspired more than forty American utopian communities, the first of the 2 985 984 phalansteries he had dreamed of creating!

Thus, all were attracted to America: the followers of Owen to New

Harmony (Indiana), Yellow Springs (Ohio) and Nashoba (Tennessee); Fourierists to Red Bank (New Jersey), Brook Farm (Massachusetts), Wisconsin, Ohio, and New York State; Icarians to Texas, Nauvoo (Illinois), Cheltenham (Missouri), and Corning (Iowa); and all the religious utopian communities of which the most conspicuous were the Shakers (New York), the Zoarists (Ohio), the Amana (Iowa), and the Perfectionists (New York). America itself was, from the start, a utopian project: the Puritans, who established a commonwealth in Plymouth, were the first of a long series of visionaries who fled Europe to reconstruct society on fresh foundations in Arcadia. The movement expanded in the nineteenth century. In 1840 Emerson could exclaim in a letter to Thomas Carlyle: 'We are all a little wild here with numberless projects of social reform. Not a reading man but has a draft of a new community in his waistcoat pocket.'[6] In short, they all vied with each other in dreaming. None of this comes as any surprise.

America offered immense space, vast, inexpensive expanses of land for establishing communities; it offered isolation, far from the corrupting influences of old Europe; it offered the enormous agricultural and industrial potential of a young continent, destined to enjoy exciting expansion; finally, it offered freedom, that is, political freedom, freedom of conscience, and freedom of association. In short, there was a feeling in America of a new beginning, a new life, a *different* life, which is the very definition of utopia. The map of America was dotted with precise plans for utopian settlements. A specialist on the question notes: 'A map of America showing only its utopian experiments from the mid 1600s until this moment would be remarkably full.'[7] There were about 130 such endeavours before the beginning of the Civil War. Thus, it is fair to say that the nineteenth century was one of the great centuries of utopias and that their realm was America.

It is in this context of a nineteenth century obsessed with utopias and of America as their homeland that *Jean Rivard* must be situated. A few commentators have already indicated (in a positive way, of course!) the utopian quality of the work, but without dwelling on it, without making it a fundamental component of the novel.[8] To me it is one of the most successful works of utopian literature. Would it come as any surprise to discover that Jean Rivard, the voracious reader described in the previous chapter, was created by a man who had taken *Les aventures de Télémaque* among his few belongings on his first trip to the United States?[9] This choice is laden with consequences, because Fénelon's work is not only a pleasant, educational novel, but it contains two of the most famous utopias in French literature: the *Bétique* (Book VII) and *Salente* (Books VII–X and XVII). Thus, while still a youth, to foster his American ambitions (or to console himself for his setbacks as a young, penniless traveller), Gérin-Lajoie chose a utopian work as a vade-mecum. Twenty years later, this particular inspiration resurfaced, and he wrote one of the few utopian novels of Quebec literature. It can even be said without hesitation that *Jean Rivard* is one of the best utopian novels of the century. Furthermore, anyone who takes the time to read some of the utopian writings of that century will even agree that, on a strictly literary level, it is one of the most successful utopian narratives in world literature. This can be determined after close examination of the novel, but first some considerations on the ambiguities of the notion of utopia and on the characteristics of the genre will make it easier to situate *Jean Rivard*.

The Ambiguities of the Notion of Utopia

'We hope that none of our readers will waste their time looking for the location of Rivardville on a map of the country,'[10] warns Gérin-Lajoie. Herman Melville, himself the author of a utopia, would have said: 'It is not down on any map; true places never are.'[11] Indeed, Rivardville cannot be found on a map because this city is a 'non-place,' a land to be found nowhere, according to the first meaning of the word utopia, a space that does not exist as such, except in the serious, reasoning imagination of its creator, the utopian writer. No one could possibly find Robinson Crusoe's island either, nor the New Atlantis (Francis Bacon) somewhere in the Pacific Ocean, nor the City of the Sun (Tommaso Campanella) in some plain in Ceylon, nor Christianopolis (Andreae), nor Ajao Island (Fontenelle). These lands, even when their precise location is given (Fontenelle), cannot be found, unless one ends up there by chance, as the narrator does in Rivardville. Rivardville is an island, in the same way that all the other places cherished by utopian writers are islands, whether marine or terrestrial. They are scattered across the map of America, often situated and described with precision, but unfindable unless one travels toward them laterally – a sideways journey that the utopian novel describes.

But the epithet 'utopian' is ambiguous. Indeed, the whole notion of utopia may well give rise to numerous ambiguities and create misinterpretations. These problems must first be cleared up.

The current perception of utopia as an impossible dream, as an ideal dreamed up by a visionary, must be dismissed from the outset. What

Intertextuality II: *Jean Rivard* as a Utopia 149

comes to mind is the jest of Édouard Montpetit, who considered two facts as undeniable signs that *Jean Rivard* was a utopia: the teacher was given a salary increase without asking for one, and the inhabitants of Rivardville reduced their tobacco consumption to improve the library![12] What Montpetit humorously pointed out in 1924 has since been repeated frequently and always in a negative light: *Jean Rivard* is fiction, an unrealistic vision of life (in the last analysis, unachievable), 'a dream world where the novelist's imagination bends reality to the requirements of his ideal.'[13] In short, it is a charming illusion.

At the other extreme, but still within the framework of the common meaning of the notion, it should not be thought that all the novel's documentary baggage contradicts the view that it is a utopia. The fact that there are figures, notes and convincing historical equivalents to Jean Rivard's life story – in short, 'proofs' of all kinds – does not make the work any less a utopia. On the contrary, all this scientific paraphernalia is an integral part of the genre.

Another ambiguity arises: it is not because the novel describes a paradise on Quebec soil that it can be called a utopia. Once again we are dealing with a popular meaning of the term: utopia as a place of perfection and bliss, the privative *u* being confused with or replaced by the Greek diphthong *eu*, signifying 'good.' Admittedly, in the 'Last Part' of the work, Rivardville is represented as a paradise. The narrator is amazed by one wonder after another ('I was amazed by all I had seen' [326]); he is not subject to the body's limitations ('Although I had been on my feet for more than four hours, I still did not feel at all tired' [326]); he has the impression he is living in a Garden of Eden ('The whole parish seemed to me like an immense garden' [343]), where even the boundaries of death are pushed back ('So people live long lives and hundred-year-old people are not rare' [353]). Thus, he exclaims with enthusiasm and delight: '"Happy man!" I exclaimed, "what more could you wish for?"' (330). According to him, the citizens of Rivardville inhabit a paradise on earth and are truly blessed.[14] But it is not this Eden-like dimension that makes the work utopian. In fact, as many theorists of the genre have emphasized, few people would like to live in most utopias. Or, to repeat Berdiaeff's jest in the epigraph of Aldous Huxley's *Brave New World*, the most famous of all dystopias: 'Utopias are feasible; the problem is how to stop them from being realized.'[15] The paradisiacal dimension appears in *Jean Rivard*, as will be seen later, but this is not a determining factor. Utopia is not to be confused with Cockaigne, or with Arcadia. Other elements characterize it much more distinctly.

Nor does *Jean Rivard* have to be considered a utopia simply because it is a novel expounding a thesis. Once again, that would involve accepting only the common pejorative sense of 'utopian.' It is certain that the thesis novel as a genre is based on an 'illusion' or on the fixed resolve to confuse different realms of things, a resolve that could be described as 'utopian': its purpose is pragmatic, its narrative promotes concrete action by potential readers. In terms of its aims, the thesis novel postulates at the outset that literature can have an effect on life, an assumption that is no doubt 'utopian.' As Susan Suleiman puts it: 'Recognize that the project of the fable as of all "exemplary" narratives, is utopian: to *modify* the actions of men (and of women) by telling them stories.'[16] Here again, the term utopian is used in the sense of unrealistic, the sense that is the least rich and the least interesting.

Finally, some readers who are more familiar with the author's life are perhaps tempted to confer utopian status on *Jean Rivard* immediately, in that they readily perceive everything conveyed in the narrative as compensating for the author's failings. According to this view, Jean Rivard lives Gérin-Lajoie's ideal life on all levels (physical, social, emotional, intellectual, and political), sublimating his disappointments, compensating for (and acknowledging) his feeling of powerlessness. Here the penniless lawyer and obscure civil servant, longing for the life of a gentleman farmer, the dreamy intellectual, who was also a member of a victimized group, gives free expression to his frustrated yearning for power. This character study of the typical utopian writer has been well explained by Raymond Ruyer:

> The combination in the utopian writer of a speculative mind and a power complex is of a very special kind. For their authors, utopias are dreams of empowerment and an Adlerian compensation for the congenital powerlessness of pure theory ... The author reforms the world in his mind through an intermediary, by dreaming of an increase in power for a class or for people in general. Chesterton maintains that the most democratic utopia is always, in reality, a picture of tyranny and a tyrant's dream, the tyrant being the utopian writer himself, who gives himself the satisfaction of organizing the world as he pleases. The speculative mind's power complex may also be revealed in its moralistic, preaching, and pedagogic aspects. There is something pedantic in the social utopia. The social art of the utopian writer seeks to 'put nature right,' which is, according to Bergson, the definition of pedantry ... Many minor utopian writers are the weak protesting against reality, because they cannot play a role to their liking, and they are seeking compensation for their

Intertextuality II: *Jean Rivard* as a Utopia 151

weakness. They improve their self-image by reforming the world in their minds.[17]

No doubt we could dwell on Gérin-Lajoie's character: a speculative mind with aesthetic gifts, who dreams of empowerment. But the picture, though as attractive as could be wished, would be as false as it is exaggerated. Georges Duveau, in particular, has severely criticized the way the utopian writer has been caricatured as a theoretician, a nonentity, a failure or a dreamer, as opposed to the man of action who is endowed with all the virtues. André Canivez, in his introduction to a collection of Georges Duveau's essays, rightly insists on this aspect of Duveau's thought:

Thus he often observes that pure utopian writers are relatively few and that many of them had been active socially and politically, as statesmen or revolutionaries, or on a more modest level, as magistrates, businessmen, diplomats, lawyers, clergy, writers, and publicists; that is why he could not subscribe to this view of utopias as a refuge for those who, for lack of knowledge, ambition, or courage, fail to satisfy their need for action in the harsh and unpredictable world of history.[18]

Duveau even proposes to reverse the relationship: intellectuals have a tendency to overvalue the man of action and to portray writers, in particular utopians, as full of frustrations. But that is a purely intellectual and gratuitous view of things. Is not the man of action himself often a failed author? In too much of a hurry to do painstaking, demanding work, he throws himself into exhilarating action:

The pages of history are cluttered with all the failures, the actors hissed off the stage, playwrights and vaudeville writers whose plays were rejected, painters who could not get their pictures exhibited in a famous salon, poets whose works were remaindered in the secondhand bookstores! Among the rebels of 1848 or the Communards of 1871 there were numerous actors who finally found at the barricades, in the bars or in the clubs, the applause they had vainly sought in the popular theatres of Belleville or Montrouge ... And, of course, a mediocre painter called Hitler cast a very dark shadow over our time. Philosophers and historians certainly envision writers as repressed men of action, but less frequently they envision men of action as frustrated authors or artists.[19]

According to Duveau, utopian writers are evenly divided among all of the character groups: the passionate (Fénelon, Auguste Comte, Plato, Saint-Simon), the phlegmatic (Robert Owen, Renan, William Godwin), the sanguine (Francis Bacon, Anatole France, Aldous Huxley, Jonathan Swift), the choleric (Diderot, Fourier, Proudhon, Rabelais, George Sand), and the sentimental (Rousseau, Robespierre). Therefore, he proposes to acknowledge the creation of utopias as a normal aspect of human existence in society, because it transcends eras, societies, and human types. In short, 'it appears as though the utopian function is fundamental to mankind and that the creation of utopias is like a solid attribute attached to consciousness.'[20] Thus, it is neither the author's biography nor his character that must be investigated if we are seeking a Quebec utopia in *Jean Rivard*. It is through an analysis of the work itself, in the light of the characteristics observable in the utopia as a particular genre, that it is possible to isolate the various elements that make this book a utopia. But first, let us seek a definition of the genre.

A Definition of Utopia

What is a utopia exactly? Some critics, perplexed by such a rich, heterogeneous corpus, are tempted to deny that any generalization or definition is possible:

What do utopias have in common? The answer is very little in detail, except, perhaps, for an almost universal dislike of lawyers, and there are even exceptions to that generalization.[21]

Even in terms of this jest, it must be acknowledged that *Jean Rivard* fits the general rule, since a remarkable distrust of the legal profession and of the litigiousness associated with it is evinced throughout the entire novel, which begins with Father Leblanc's speech against a career in law. Throughout his work Gérin-Lajoie presents Gustave Charmenil's tirades about the countless hardships of his profession, while at every opportunity he paints unflattering portraits of lawyers: during the election campaign, in which Jean Rivard's opponent was 'a wily, skilful young city lawyer, who solicited votes, not in the public interest, but in his own' (299); in Parliament, filled with 'smooth talkers' (*Le Foyer canadien* 2 [1864], 320); even in Rivardville, where Gendreau-le-Plaideux, who would have become a lawyer if he had had an education (286), embodies unadulterated contrariness and stupidity.

But a utopia is more than a suspicion of lawyers. The elimination of

Intertextuality II: *Jean Rivard* as a Utopia 153

controversy and of controversialists is only an effect of the utopian vision, which essentially is 'the description of a world built on different principles than those that govern the real world.'[22] According to Ruyer's excellent definition, utopia is 'a mental implementation of lateral possibilities':

Utopias must not be defined by their intentions, which are extremely varied, nor by their fabula. Their common principle, their essence, must be sought elsewhere. This essence is the use of the utopian method, the utopian mode. Just as, despite the immense variety of comedies or tragedies, there is an essence of the comic or the tragic, so, in spite of the variety of utopias and the heterogeneity of a genre that includes Plato, Cyrano de Bergerac, Morris, and Haldane, there is a utopian mode, which can be defined as a *mental implementation of lateral possibilities*.

By its nature, the utopian mode belongs to the realm of theory and speculation. But, whereas theory as such seeks knowledge of what exists, the utopian mode is an exercise or a game concerning possibilities lateral to reality. The intellect, in the utopian mode, becomes 'the power of concrete implementation'; it amuses itself by mentally trying out possibilities, which it sees as extending beyond what is real ... The transition from the utopian mode, from the utopian implementation to the actual utopia, occurs when the implementation of what is possible creates a whole new world. Utopia must at least create a miniature but complete world.[23]

The world it creates responds to a different logic and to different principles; it solves the multiple problems and inadequacies of the existing world. 'I had discovered a new world' (363), the narrator in *Jean Rivard* exclaims. This exclamation anticipates the phrase that Ernest Bloch later used as a definition of Utopia and its touchstone: *Incipit vita nova*.[24] 'Here, a new life begins' is what one might read when entering utopia's portal.

The utopian writer creates a world that corresponds to his ideal and is necessarily superior to the one that already exists. But utopia is not the only lateral possibility. Reflecting on the notion of utopia, J.C. Davis distinguishes with great precision between utopia and four other possible answers to the problem of an ideal society.[25] Historically, five answers, one of which is utopia, have been given to the problems of satisfying desires in the community, organizing harmony and contentment, and removing conflicts and hardships. First, there is Cockaigne, which is a fantasy for peasants and the poor; it is an integral part of the saturnalia and the banquet of fools; it is a medieval vision, but still widespread; it is an ideal society, in which everyone's appetites are satisfied, even the crudest; it is the country of abundance. Arcadia offers a less crude vision of abundance: nature is beneficent, appetites are more moderate, and man works, but all is moderation, ease, harmony, and natural comfort. In contrast to the first two visions, the commonwealth of moral perfection insists upon moral values. Since everyone is converted or of high moral character, the social order is necessarily perfect. To use some French examples, the commonwealth would be Rabelais' abbey of Thélème, and Arcadia would be the country of the cannibals in Montaigne. Finally, the fourth answer is the millennium. Upon his second coming, Christ will reign for a thousand years and saints will then live on earth: there will be absolute, collective, earthly perfection that will continue until the Last Judgment.

By comparison with these four distinctly different visions, utopia appears to be more realistic, moderate, and articulate; in short, feasible. It involves no idealization of nature, as in Cockaigne or Arcadia, no idealization of human nature (even under God's influence), as in the commonwealth or the millennium. Utopia assumes no radical change in man or in nature: nothing is changed, but everything is arranged, planned, and ordered. It is the idealization of organization; utopian writers essentially seek to reorganize society and its institutions. Thus, it has rightly been said that utopia aims more at order and stability than happiness. As a result, the majority of utopias impose a totalitarian discipline because individualism, pluralism, and anarchy are the primary threats to stability.

Utopia, like the other four forms of society briefly discussed, is based on a criticism of the existing order. Contemporary society is perceived as unsatisfactory because it does not fulfil the individual's aspirations, nor those of the community. The utopian writer, like other visionaries, presents his dream of an ideal society. However, it is not just a dreamlike fantasy; it is a normative project that 'conforms not only with what could be, but with what ought to be.'[26] The utopian writer, who is much closer to the scientist-inventor than to the dreamy, creative artist, offers, after study and contemplation, his solution to the enigma of human organization. Therefore, utopia is 'a combination of scientific reasoning, criticism, and fantasy.'[27] This very special fusion of criticism, reasoning, and fantasy explains the various characteristics of utopia. An analysis of *Jean Rivard* in the light of these characteristics will clarify them, as well as bring out some aspects of the novel that are too often ignored.

Jean Rivard as a Utopia

A utopia is, by definition, a critical work first. Even if there is no reference in a particular work to the world as it is, utopia is always an expression of dissatisfaction in terms of both genesis and ultimate purpose. The utopian writer, in imagining a new and different world, protests against the one at hand. He knows that readers will make the desired comparisons. Utopia is always a 'magic mirror which, by its own consummate beauty, reveals all the more clearly the ugliness, the injustice, and the maladjustment of the world in which we live.'[28] More often than not, however, the author takes it upon himself to provide the contrast and make it explicit. Robert L. Shurter, who has studied American nineteenth-century utopian novels, even proposes to use utopias as a barometer of social dissatisfaction in different time periods.

This critical function is crucial in *Jean Rivard*. The specific criticisms that Gérin-Lajoie expresses in his work are too numerous to discuss in detail. He attacks high society, speculators, fickle women, politicians, elections, frivolous youth, the idle, the improvident, the fainthearted, the state, education, reading, and so on. However, this kind of criticism can be found in other types of works of this period that are not utopias. It is not these specific criticisms that make the work utopian, but the narrative and diegetic techniques used to combine in a contemporary form the two worlds of the novel – the one being criticized and the one being proposed – thus respecting the bipolarity peculiar to the genre.

Gérin-Lajoie employs several distinct methods to contrast these two worlds. Two techniques are used in the narration: a curious, astonished narrator who is a newcomer and wants to tell of his discovery; and the epistolary form, which hands over the narrative to Gustave Charmenil and Jean Rivard, thus contrasting their parallel worlds directly, frequently, and on various subjects. In the diegesis, the protagonist basically breaks away from the first of these two worlds to build in the wilds his utopia, which he had first glimpsed in a dazzling dream. Structurally speaking, the division of the narrative into two books corresponds to 'a standard law of the genre.'[29] This division may assume two forms: first, evil is denounced, then the ideal society is described; or else the reader is led in the first book through an account that has indisputable narrative merits, then is presented with a second book, which is more theoretical and abstract, more like an essay, in which an attempt is made to complete the economic and social exposition begun in the first book. This second book continues to be strongly critical, since the systematic exposition of the new world constitutes, at least implicitly, an indictment of the existing order. Such is the case with Edward Bellamy, who is considered the most popular American utopian writer. After the enormous success achieved with *Looking Backward* (1888), he published *Equality*, a dry, economic treatise, literally killing himself over the work but obtaining a very modest success. The second of these two forms is also used by Gérin-Lajoie: the narrative quality of the first book and the clearly explanatory, didactic character of the second are unmistakable.

However, the critical dimension is only the foundation of a utopia. The purpose of the genre is not only to criticize the here and now, but also to construct a different world. Such is the case with *Jean Rivard*. The reader does not really become aware that he is dealing with a utopian work, or that all the criticism dispersed throughout the narrative corresponds to a particular logic, until he reaches the 'Last Part' of the novel. In this finale, the critical elements dispersed throughout the text take on a consistency and coherence that throw new light on the entire work. What was thought to be a diptych thus becomes, in reality, a triptych, and this third part gives the whole work its meaning.

That the work is a triptych despite a double title appears to be obvious enough. The 'Last Part,' subtitled 'Fifteen Years Later,' is separated, so to speak, from the *Economist* by the interlude of Jean Rivard's political career. In the second edition, the numbering of the chapters starts again with this part, thus giving it the same status as the two previous parts. It is presented in seven chapters, compared with the sixteen chapters in the *Economist*, and the twenty-five in *The Pioneer*. This is a rigorous progression, since each part has nine chapters fewer than the one before it. However, it is particularly because of the ambiguity of its subtitle that the Last Part acquires the status of a distinct section. The subtitle announces 'fifteen years later,' but fifteen years after what? The reader is inclined to believe it is fifteen years after the end of the preceding chapter. This is a false impression, even if the narrator is party to it by his use of precise stylistic turns of phrases. Indeed, when he learns that he is in Rivardville, he thinks: 'This reply reminded me of Jean Rivard, whom I had known by sight at the time when he was sitting as a member of the Legislative Assembly' (313). 'Reminded me ... at the time ...': the narrator seems to be dealing with a distant memory. But it is nothing of the sort. The adverb 'later' has led the reader astray, since Jean Rivard was a Member of Parliament for four years, until the previous year, a fairly recent 'time.' So, it is five years since Jean Rivard's election, which is related at the end of the previous chapter.

Intertextuality II: *Jean Rivard* as a Utopia   157

The question therefore remains: fifteen years after what? Fifteen years after he settled in the forest (with wife, house, and partially cleared land). The actual function of this chronology, which at first seems ambiguous and imprecise, appears to be to separate this part of the work from the previous one, giving it the status of an epilogue, a retrospective assessment. The three great stages in the protagonist's life are described in these three distinct parts: his taking to the forest and clearing the land (*The Pioneer*), the creation of a republic (*Economist*) and a glorious retrospective look at this recent, but heroic, past ('The Last Part'). It is only through this final part that the novel takes on its full meaning.

It is, in fact, in this epilogue that the narrator intervenes and becomes a character (and, as a result, an interdiegetic narrator) to see for himself what exists in Rivardville. Filled with wonder and convinced by his inspection of the place, he decides in the last lines of the novel to relate what he has witnessed: 'Do not be surprised if some day I take the liberty of writing your story at the risk of not being believed' (367). This story is the one the reader has been following since the beginning of the novel, but it started, as far as its history is concerned, in the last lines of the narrative. Therefore, the order of events as experienced by the protagonist is perfectly chronological; on the other hand, the order of the narrative is completely retrospective.

This introduction of the narrator into the diegesis borrows some of the commonplaces of the utopian genre, right down to stylistic details. First, the narrator must be a newcomer to the utopia. Since he is completely ignorant of this new world, he must make an extended visit and is more often than not accompanied by a guide, who explains in detail each of its aspects; in return, the narrator must give his narratee an explanatory account. This double explanatory level greatly reduces the narrative function of the narrator himself (telling the story), and stresses both his function as a witness (indicating his sources) and his communicative function (addressing his narratee directly). It imparts to utopian narratives a strong descriptive and demonstrative dimension, which largely explains why they are so static. This is exactly what happens in *Jean Rivard*. The narrator, a newcomer, is given as a guide none other than the leader of Rivardville, who is in the best position to explain everything to him and to show him all of the secrets of the place.

This stranger, who is on a trip, discovers the utopia entirely by chance. In fact, for all intents and purposes, there are only three ways of reaching the utopia: through a dream, through a temporal projection (often dreamed) into the past or into the future, or through a spatial projection (the generally accidental discovery of a previously unknown island or region when a journey is interrupted). A traveller, thrown off course by a fierce storm (as in Bacon's *New Atlantis*, in Andreae's *Christianopolis*, or in Cabet's *Voyage à Icarie*), is stranded and discovers the utopia. Thus the narrator of *Jean Rivard* testifies:

It was 1860. I had taken the train from Quebec to Montreal, travelling through the Eastern Townships, when, *in the middle of a dark night, during a driving rain storm*, one of the engines was *derailed* and the passengers were forced to *interrupt their trip* ... The next day, I got up at dawn, perfectly refreshed in mind and body; and desiring to look round the *place in which I had been stranded the night before*, I went out of the house. (313 and 315; my italics)

The Last Part starts with the metaphor of the thunderstorm and the shipwreck (he is 'stranded' on an unknown beach), introducing the utopian narrative as such.

During the first stage, the narrator visits a paradise on earth. The observation can first be made that he feels 'perfectly refreshed' after only a few hours' sleep: in utopia, the air is invigorating, the nights are serene, sleep is refreshing. His awakening is therefore agreeable, allowing him to be dazzled by a harmonious order:

What delicious coolness! My lungs seemed to swell with pleasure. Soon the sun rose in all its splendour and I could see a magnificent sight. A perfumed mist rose from the earth and combined with the rays of the rising sun. The air was calm, the noise of the mill could be heard and the workmen's axes and hammers resounded in the distance. The birds sang charmingly in the foliage of the trees. Their songs mingled with a rooster crowing, hens cackling, and, from time to time, a cow mooing or a dog barking.

The smell of roses and mignonette was rising from the garden and perfumed the air. Everywhere there was a feeling of calm, of cheerful serenity that enraptured the soul and lifted it heavenward. Never had I loved the countryside so much as on that day.

When, because of his profession, a man must live in a city, surrounded by the works of men, hearing only the voices of vanity and sordid self-interest, seeing only the deafening activity of business, and then is suddenly transported into a scene of rural tranquillity, his heart swells and his soul blossoms, so to speak, as they come into contact with nature, that source of greatness and mystery.

Recovering a little from my ecstasy, I looked around me. (315–16)

Intertextuality II: *Jean Rivard* as a Utopia 159

From this description, it can easily be seen that the narrator has enjoyed a paradisaic, religious, almost mystical experience; the vocabulary is insistent ('perfumed mist ... enraptured the soul and lifted it heavenward ... his soul blossoms ... that source of greatness and mystery ... ecstasy'), and the upward motion of the passage is sharply drawn. The exaltation results from the beauty of the moment, of course, but above all from the tranquillity (mentioned twice), purity, and serenity of the scene; everything is in harmony, in equilibrium. There is no dissonance in this symphony of visual, tactile, gustatory, and olfactory sensations.

This harmony is, of course, an essential component of the utopian world. Even work does not destroy the natural equilibrium; on the contrary, in a utopia, a solution is found to the relentless conflicts that rage elsewhere in the world of harsh reality. The sentence structure brings together and harmonizes two elements that are normally contradictory: calm and noise ('the air was calm, the noise of the mill could be heard'). The noise contributes to the calm. The parallelism of the sentences makes no distinction between human noises and natural sounds: 'the noise of the mill could be heard and the workmen's axes and hammers resounded ... The birds sang charmingly in the foliage of the trees.' The noise of work is thus harmonious; it is combined with natural noises. It does not destroy the calm atmosphere, but rather contributes to it through a sort of euphonious rhythm. *It is music*: this is the first impression of work, which is natural and exalted in the utopian environment.

The crucial aspects of this first viewing of the place (order, calmness, beauty, regularity) are repeated and amplified after a more detailed inspection. The narrator visits the farm, the village, and the surrounding countryside. The reader learns that the space in Rivardville fulfils the requirements of the genre. Everything is beautiful, pleasant, peaceful, and looks prosperous. But, above all, everything is orderly.

Indeed, the utopian passion for symmetry is given free rein under Jean Rivard's rule. His first house (155) was already a marvellous expression of this geometric rigour: for more than a year he had thought about the design of it, so he had 'planned it to perfection' (152). It formed a perfect square (30 feet by 30 feet), was 'perfectly well-lit,' had windows on all four sides, two symmetrical doors, one for each façade, a window in each of the two gables, and was divided into 'four rooms of equal size.' Even the height of the steps 'raised two feet from the ground' obeyed the even-number rule. That was the first house, but even though it was perfectly planned, it was replaced by an even better one: the more recent brick house that the narrator admires in 1860. He describes it for the reader's benefit: it has two floors, two gables, two elm trees to shade it, and whitewashed outbuildings, surrounded by trees in rows 'planted at intervals.' Two principles – the number could have been predicted – had governed its conception: convenience and healthfulness (326, 327). The domestic space must be functional to enable its occupants to be efficient and precise; it has to be salubrious (ventilation, fenestration) to ensure the well-being and thus the happiness of its occupants.

This house holds the central position in the utopia. The narrator can see everything from its balcony: 'On my right, I saw a long row of farmers' homes; on my left, the rich and pretty village of Rivardville' (316–17). The village itself is organized with a precision that is both mathematical and geometrical: 'approximately one hundred' houses on 'about ten perfectly regular' streets (317), which are carefully lined with various kinds of trees. It is easy to recognize Jean Rivard's hand in the village's symmetry. He has divided his own cleared land into 'six fields of equal size' (318), each in turn 'completely manured and fertilized' (319). To accompany these fifteen-acre fields are fifteen fine cows, four horses, thirty sheep, six pigs, and two apple trees: animals, trees, and space are organized according to the same rigorous rules (2, 4, 6, 15, and 30). There is a regularity about these numbers, in particular the number two. The reader, therefore, is not surprised to learn that the number of Jean Rivard's children increases 'every two years' (342)!

This will to plan nature, which is peculiar to the utopian writer, convinces Ruyer that, despite appearances, utopias are by definition opposed to nature, profoundly anti-vital. Accepting life with all its wild exuberance is out of the question: everything must be transformed, standardized, and organized. 'The two most constant characteristics of utopian worlds are symmetry and the unambiguous vigour of man's dominion over nature: the absence of weeds, harmful insects, gypsies, muddle, sordid negligence, and patchwork.'[30] Thus 'almost all of the utopian worlds are symmetrical, laid out with regularity, like an Italian or French garden.'[31] Indeed, at the end of his tour, the narrator exclaims: 'To me, the whole parish appeared to be like an immense garden' (343). Only 'turf,' 'a carpet of greenery,' and neatness are seen everywhere: the vegetation, like everything else, is kept under control to such an extent that the agricultural or rural dimension in *Jean Rivard* is even more unobtrusive in the Last Part than anywhere else in the novel. The narrator visits Jean Rivard's model farm and a small, agricultural town, but, paradoxically, this space takes on a fundamentally urban character since

Intertextuality II: *Jean Rivard* as a Utopia 161

man's dominion and his logician's will are evident everywhere. The meadows are carpets, the trees hedges, and the fields are squares cut out of the forest.

The regularity and orderliness the narrator observes in the homes, the village, and nature as a whole are obviously the work of Jean Rivard. His 'kingdom's' planned economy is quite consistent with the utopian pattern. The seventh chapter of the *Economist* is particularly revealing on this subject. Jean Rivard writes to Gustave Charmenil:

I am overwhelmed with work of all kinds. I can scarcely find a moment to write my friends. Aside from my work clearing the land, which continues apace, I have to direct to some extent the establishment of an entire village. I am busy from morning until night. Don't be surprised, my dear Gustave, if you hear it said one day that your friend Jean Rivard has founded a town. You are laughing, I am sure. It is a fact, however, that before long the vicinity of my cabin will be transformed into a well-populated, prosperous village. At the moment, I have just finished building a church. Everything is progressing around me: mills, shops, stores, all rising up as if by magic. (219)

Here, Jean Rivard 'directs,' 'founds,' builds, 'finishes.' He is in the centre of this feverish, creative activity ('around me ... the vicinity of my cabin'). He works and plans. He is very ambitious, but is aware of the obstacles and even dramatizes them through a fairly normal process of heroic self-enhancement. In the following chapter he will go into partnership with his brothers in various industries, 'more to have an excuse for *supervising and controlling their operation* than to gain any profit' (221; my italics). He will also be seen as the 'administrator of the family estate' (222) and, generally speaking, very happy because 'he will be able to exert *absolute control* over the settlement of the village' (223; my italics).

This absolute power is embodied in particular in the special attention he pays to town planning and architecture. Jean Rivard himself draws up the plan for his town and the shape of the dwellings:

He had indicated the streets, making them as broad and symmetrical as possible. He had marked the places to be occupied later by the school, the post office, the market, etc.

He had trees planted at intervals along the proposed streets, for he neglected nothing that could contribute to the fresh, cheerful appearance of his village.

He even went so far as to stipulate in his land grants that a house be such and such a size and such and such a distance from the road, that it be painted white and other *conditions that may seem childish, but that nonetheless exert a real influence on the progress of localities.* (223–4; my italics)

If that is 'childishness,' it is a frivolousness that Jean Rivard shares with all builders of utopias who are fascinated by the organization of space and convinced that psychological and social problems are, for the most part, caused by problems of architecture and town planning. Precise descriptions of their various towns abound.

This state intervention in the organization of space is only the most conspicuous exterior expression of political and social authoritarianism. Jean Rivard is an emperor, leader, president, king, or magistrate, mayor, Member of Parliament. The vocabulary, whether metaphoric or simply denotative, always emphasizes his authority, which, it should be added, has two characteristics: it is both charismatic and, paradoxically, democratic. Indeed, political and religious powers are frequently combined in utopias. Utopia is a totalizing vision: power is undivided. This is why, besides being a political leader, Jean Rivard assumes religious leadership to some extent. His prophetic qualities (he likes to talk with his neighbours about 'the future of their township: "Within ten years," he said enthusiastically, "within five years ..."' [132]); his warm, vibrant way of speaking, which exercises a 'magical effect' (132); his achievements, which a benevolent Providence ensures; his intelligence, perceptiveness, kindness, judgment; all these things give him a certain charisma. The novel, moreover, has a tendency to regard the places in which he lives as sacred: his house is built on a hill, like the churches in Grandpré and Rivardville; the church in Rivardville is built on his land; his house will be the priest's first home and the first place of worship in the new parish; a small stoup of holy water will always be found at its entrance, even when the priest has entered his presbytery. Therefore, his influence over the people comes as no surprise, especially since the novel emphasizes the genuine rapport between him and his friend the priest, Octave Doucet. His authority has something of the priesthood about it.

However, this leader seeks to govern by consensus and always manages to persuade people in the end, since harmony and social order are essential to utopia: unanimity is what most distinguishes it from harsh reality. Jean Rivard is by far the most aware of this:

Any unjust, frivolous opposition saddened him because he saw it as a source of

Intertextuality II: *Jean Rivard* as a Utopia 163

weakness. On the other hand, nothing gave him as much satisfaction as unanimity on any question.

'Unity is what makes societies strong,' he used to say constantly, 'just as it makes for the happiness of families.'

What he feared the most was discord breaking out in this small community, which had come into the forest looking for peace and happiness. (192)

This 'small community, which had come into the forest looking for peace and happiness,' is the precise definition of utopia in a few words. This definition applies equally to a forest, an island, a Renaissance château, or Mercier's Paris of 2440. Utopia means eliminating conflict, fighting against the disorder of nature or of human opponents and controlling happiness.

Gendreau-le-Plaideux is, of course, a secondary character who seems to contribute some disorder and disunity. Indeed, he constantly attempts to thwart Jean Rivard's plans and to question his every initiative. However, even this relentless opponent has his place in the utopia, which explains Jean Rivard's patience in dealing with him. If Ruyer is to be believed, such characters turn up more frequently from the middle of the nineteenth century. Utopias start to become places of boredom: everyone is too happy there. The absence of vices and passions results in a dull life, of which utopian writers readily see the disadvantages. 'Henceforth, in order to counteract and ridicule him, even the classic, convinced utopian writers, such as Morris and Wells, feel the need to introduce into their paradise on earth a malcontent, who grumbles about the boredom of paradise and expresses nostalgia for earth and hell.'[32] Thus this perpetual opponent, through his constant and absurd complaining, only further emphasizes the advantages of Rivardville and the outstanding qualities of its leader.

The immeasurable superiority of life in Rivardville is striking to an impartial observer like the narrator: it is superior in all domains, including work, which is exalted and, paradoxically, limited. Indeed, in all utopias, work is not only compulsory, but pleasant and profitable as well. The work day can be considerably reduced, since work is organized, intelligent, centred on the use of appropriate techniques, and all idleness is eliminated. So, while making work the first secret of his success, Jean Rivard can reveal to the narrator that he works only four or five hours a day, now that his utopia is established (331). This shortened day, which would delight all present-day trade unionists and greatly surprise many modern farmers, may appear to be unrealistic. However, it respects the requirements of the genre; in utopia, working days are never more than six hours long. Jean Rivard's four or five hours compare favourably with the four hours in Campanella's *The City of the Sun* and the six hours in More's *Utopia*.

The integration of the family into the workplace, the concept of the family as a unit of production, is another element of the utopian model. True, all kinds of families are found in utopias, and it must be recognized that the communist (Spartan) model predominates. Nevertheless, Jean Rivard's monogamous, patriarchal, almost self-sufficient family and his concept of marriage – in which the wife, in addition to her personal qualities, is an asset and a producer, delegated by her husband to the 'ministry of the Interior' (181), reproducing a microcosm of the collective order within the house (340–3) – correspond to the actual vision of the modern creator of the genre, Thomas More. In *Utopia*, the family is the social base, both a biological and economic entity. *Jean Rivard* follows this model. For example, in More, each family owns a large garden, which is tended with both pleasure and profit, while Jean Rivard and his wife have an extremely rich and diversified garden, which provides them with most of the family's food.

All of these elements, taken individually, admittedly have only a limited prominence. The family in *Jean Rivard* is only an idealized French-Canadian family of that period. It is usual for a family that owns land to have a vegetable garden, and Jean Rivard's is only a model one. A host has a natural tendency to show off his home; it is the visitor's duty, particularly when he is from the city, to go into raptures about the happiness and the salubrity of country life. It is natural for the founder of a town, especially if he becomes a local notability, to want to leave his mark and to control its development. However, each of these elements, insignificant in itself, is combined and associated with others and is integrated into a precise, narrative structure; the work as a whole then takes on a clearly utopian dimension. This is particularly true when the function of education in the novel is examined.

Utopia and Pedagogy: *Jean Rivard* **and Education**

The great importance given to education in *Jean Rivard* is quite representative of the utopian genre: every utopia has a precise vision of pedagogy. 'Whether it be Plato, Campanella, Saint-Just, or H.G. Wells, the utopian writer has been preoccupied for thousands of years with these hothouses in which "alphas" are raised, who ensure that the city is safeguarded.'[33] In fact, utopia is a place of structured life. The best way to ensure symmetry and uniformity is to educate according to a precise plan: uniform aspirations and a homogeneous vision of the world. As Ruyer points out,[34] once the educational mechanism is set in place and the system is regularly producing standardized graduates, it is almost as if the utopia can be considered perfect.

Certainly today the close links between political visions, utopian or otherwise, and educational programs may appear to be less obvious, because we are accustomed to considering compulsory education as 'normal' and the school environment as 'natural' (school as a natural place for a child!). However, reading a few utopias or referring to the relatively recent debates on compulsory education suffices to make us fully aware of what really is at stake. The school is *the* place for a utopia, that is, in the last analysis, for social control:

For a politician the masses are recalcitrant; therefore, his task is to educate them. A dual principle controls this *vicious circle* of power, which I call *educational utopia*, that is, the idea of *social reform by education*, the idea that it is possible to develop a man capable of a better society, or a better man capable of another society. The educational utopia is thus only another form of the political utopia; not only is the latter always accompanied by education, but it is pedagogic in itself; this we have known since Plato ... Utopia is a pipe-dream (dream is too appealing a term) that suppresses, transforms, and controls the individual in every function and at every stage of his development; it is an imaginary project (always for the future) to establish a social order, which is finally definitive and reassuring, in which all parts of society, having been formed in the same way, work automatically toward the same goal. If all states, socialist or otherwise, finally agree about educational planning, it is not by chance.[35]

It is in this precise context of an enterprise, which is essential to utopia, that the sensational beginning of the chapter Gérin-Lajoie devotes to education (Chapter 14 of the *Economist*) must be placed:

We have now come to the most critical, the most dangerous, and, at the same time, the most important and glorious chapter in Jean Rivard's whole career. We will see him win again in the face of the most formidable difficulties. After displaying outstanding intelligence and activity in the building of his own fortune and in the formation of an entire parish, his astonishing strength of character and dauntless moral courage will be put to use to establish schools in Rivardville. (280)

Following the example of Gilles Marcotte, it is easy enough to make fun of these pompous sentences:

The grandiose, the ever-noble, the heroic, and, inevitably, the bombastic take over. The novel continually suffers from the temptation to be epic, even when it seeks to be most humble and closest to reality, as with Gérin-Lajoie.[36]

But are Gérin-Lajoie's sentences simply the work of a clumsy writer who uses bombast and hyperbole, crude techniques which at that time were believed to be necessary, particularly if the goal was to arouse interest in a rather dry subject? It is understandable if readers feel ill at ease – all the more so because, on the surface, these assertions run counter to all plausibility and clearly appear exaggerated. The establishment of schools in Rivardville does not appear to be as 'critical,' 'dangerous,' 'important,' and 'glorious' as other stages in Jean Rivard's life. His initial decision to become a pioneer appears to be more critical; his choice of land and his agreements with various lenders seem more important; his entry into the forest and his Herculean labours for two winters appear to be more dangerous.

However, upon reflection, the justification for this preamble can be perceived more clearly. The narrator is not exaggerating, and his words must be taken literally. On one hand, since people at this time were extremely hostile toward education, it takes 'an astonishing strength of character and dauntless moral courage' to seek to establish schools, especially in a newly settled parish. Étienne Parent's testimony, which is easy to confirm, describes the true situation clearly enough: vigorous, general opposition, mistrust, hostility, and violence of the people; fear, prudence, timidity, discouragement, and silence from the notabilities.[37] What the narrator tells us of Jean Rivard's courage must be taken at face value. On the other hand, and above all, if we must take these hyperboles literally, it is because utopia and education are interconnected in the logic of the utopian world. The establishment of an educational system and the power subsequently exercised over it are essential to form and maintain a utopia. Jean Rivard's destiny, as the founder of a republic, and the destiny of the community are thus at stake here. Education is truly the 'lifeline' (280), not only for French Canadians, but also for this small community in the forest.

Intertextuality II: *Jean Rivard* as a Utopia 167

Moreover, the three quotations that head this chapter on education are revealing. It is known that Gérin-Lajoie is, relatively speaking, very restrained on this level. In his novel, only eleven of the forty-eight chapters have epigraphs. Chapter 14, however, has three, which are also voices that speak with authority:

God distinguished man from animals by giving him an intelligence capable of learning ... This intelligence needs to be taught, if it is to grow.   GENESIS

We can reform society through education and cure it of the evils which torment it.   PLATO

He who is the master of education can change the face of the world.   LEIBNIZ

The Word of God and two great philosophers are placed in a sequence that is both chronological and thematic. First, education is presented as being a divine institution, even if it means fabricating a biblical quotation for the sake of the demonstration. In fact, nothing that remotely resembles these two sentences can be found in Genesis. It does not matter, for all is fair; if the devil himself can quote scripture to suit his purpose, then a novelist, who does valuable work, must be allowed to extrapolate a little! What should be noted here, however, is not so much that Gérin-Lajoie takes surprising liberties with the Bible as that the origin of education is divine. God created man with intelligence, admittedly, but this intelligence remains incomplete, embryonic. It must not be left in this state; it needs to be taught. God himself ordered this need. To verse 28 onwards in the first account of creation ('Be fruitful, and multiply, and replenish the earth, and subdue it'), should now be added, according to Gérin-Lajoie, an apocryphal order: 'Be educated.' How unwelcome would be the person who, indifferent to this imperious voice ('This intelligence needs to be taught'), refused education.

Its absolute, imperative nature, as well as its basic or biological character (without education, intelligence remains undeveloped) are thus first established by divine commandment. The following two quotations confirm the usefulness of education. First, it has social benefits: education *reforms* and *cures society*. It also has individual and political advantages: education ensures world control. We are at the heart of utopian education as René Scherer understood it. Education is the key to social organization, and it is the source of power.

In light of these epigraphs, which reveal the inordinate importance attached to education (inordinate for today's reader, who is in a position to point out the limits of this panacea), the beginning of Chapter 14 loses something of the hyperbolic nature that Gilles Marcotte has criticized. Moreover, this beginning must be reread in conjunction with the previous chapter, a long letter from Jean Rivard to Gustave Charmenil, in which, for the first time in this novel, the question of education is tackled in an organized fashion. This letter is the true introduction to Chapter 14 and establishes clearly the context in which Jean Rivard is organizing his educational system. His argument is clear and simple. His goal is to establish a republic that is a model of progress and possesses all the necessary institutions: a political, eudemonic vision, which makes up '(his) whole ambition' (273). Unfortunately, one serious problem exists: the people's lack of public-spiritedness. This problem is understandable, since French Canadians, unlike the English, have had no apprenticeship in good citizenship. Education should compensate for it. If there is no tradition, then training must be provided for the people.

From the beginning, then, and without any ambiguity, education is associated with the political and social project to build a perfect republic, in short, a utopia. Chapter 13 in the *Economist* is lyrical and visionary, full of aspirations, and exclamations and constantly using the optative verb forms. Twice Jean Rivard exclaims, 'Oh! If I were king!' (276, 277), so as to imagine what sort of an educational system he would establish if only he had absolute power. He would like to have a monarchy and a republic, and be king but think up a republican project. Ideas jostle and contradict each other, but these details stop neither the hero nor the narrator. It is the educational system that matters to them, and this is set forth with consistency.

It should be noted first that these two chapters in the *Economist* clearly distinguish between education and agriculture, even further discrediting the thesis that this novel has an agriculturalist purpose. In this republic of the future, the model school and farm will exist side by side. The two must not be confused; the first is not dependent on the second. The model school's aim is to 'discover the individual aptitudes of each child, to distinguish those with more than ordinary ability, who will excel in careers requiring constant intellectual exercise' (277). 'The statesmen, legal experts, outstanding orators, inventors, in short geniuses' (277), who, otherwise, would remain uncultivated and would die without having used to the full their intelligence and talents, must be picked out in the country and among the children. The bright student would be directed toward 'some institution of higher education

Intertextuality II: *Jean Rivard* as a Utopia 169

where his intelligence could be developed to its full capacity' (277). These exceptional children are to be distinguished from the others, who are 'more particularly suited to the mechanical and industrial arts, to commerce and agriculture' (277; notice agriculture is in last place); they would also receive training adapted to their needs. For example, it is important for a farmer's son to acquire 'the knowledge necessary for the development of his intelligence and the special knowledge he needs for his profession as well' (277) so that he may become as competent in his field as a lawyer or a doctor in his.

This total, universal, relevant, and selective education is also intended for adults, particularly farmers who have long periods of leisure time in the winter. In their case, the main goal is to make them enlightened citizens, capable of judging political, administrative, commercial, and financial questions and able to vote with full knowledge of the facts (278). One hundred years in advance, Gérin-Lajoie suggests 'continuing education as a utopian model.'[38]

As far as its principles are concerned, Jean Rivard's educational plan follows Bishop Dupanloup's vision in every detail: the complete training of the individual (intellectual, disciplinary, religious, physical) regardless of his rank and abilities. In fact, 'in addition to reading and writing, grammar, arithmetic, line drawing, composition, the rudiments of history, geography, and the practical sciences like agriculture, geology, botany, etc.' (289–90) are taught in the model school in Rivardville. Adult education is provided by Sunday talks on all subjects: history, geography, discoveries in agriculture and in industry. Finally, the public examination at the end of the school year, which both the entire population and the superintendent of education follow 'with the greatest interest,' is not, it goes without saying, a ploughing competition, but rather a series of 'literary exercises' on various questions (295). Jean Rivard chose, hired, and trained the teacher who provides all the education ('He who is master of education can change the face of the world'). The teacher, in any case, is only an extension of Jean Rivard. A pedagogue at heart, Jean Rivard, who has already read to Pierre Gagnon and instructed his neighbours during his pioneer evenings, never misses a chance to 'instil' in his fellow citizens a few 'simple, practical notions' on all subjects (237). He never stops being a teacher and even personally attends to his children's education.

The enthusiastic, glorifying vision of education in these two chapters of the *Economist* is merely the high point of an uninterrupted discourse on this sensitive issue throughout the novel. The discourse is both positive and negative, because in a utopian world the educational project envisaged and described with such enthusiasm is necessarily accompanied by radical criticism of what actually exists. Vision and criticism are the two faces of utopia. Indeed, the criticism of education is constant and scathing in *Jean Rivard*. The novel begins by bitterly pointing out the weaknesses of the education available in Lower Canada. The hero's difficulties are admittedly caused by his father's death, which brings about a 'drastic change in the Rivard family's affairs' (3), but this death reveals only that Jean is ill prepared for life. At the age of nineteen, he does not know how to do anything: 'While the education he had received had developed his intellectual faculties, regrettably it provided him with no means of making a living' (4). What is worse, if he finishes his studies and does not become a priest, then 'after his course his position would be just as precarious, perhaps more so, than if he had never learned the first letters of the alphabet' (4). In the narrator's mind, it would be difficult to imagine a more defective education system: Jean Rivard finds himself, after completing his studies, unqualified, unemployable, lacking practical abilities, and worse off than the illiterate. Moreover, the moral and physical destitution of the poorly educated man is conveyed throughout the novel by the character of Gustave Charmenil, whose letters also stress the absurdities in the education of girls, which is centred on frivolousness and foolishness.

Thanks to his father's death, Jean Rivard succeeds in avoiding these pitfalls: he teaches himself the art of succeeding, choosing his models with care. He also carefully chooses his wife from a family that has not left 'uncultivated and useless' the abilities of a 'young girl endowed with intelligence, strength, and good health' (166). But at the end of the novel, in his discussion with the narrator, he has extremely harsh things to say about the absurdity of the general situation, which offers a pitiful future for young men and women who have received a long and useless 'education.'

Indeed, in the first edition, the education given in colleges and convents is criticized harshly in seven pages of the text. A whole chapter is devoted to the question ('Un dîner en famille,' *Le Foyer canadien* 2 [1864], 282–8), which was replaced in subsequent editions by this sentence: 'The conversation primarily centred on the type of education Jean Rivard proposed to give his children' (326). In the first edition it is not a conversation, but a monologue, not on the kind of education to give, but on the education to avoid. As is always the case in utopias, the narrator takes up the subject with a question:

Intertextuality II: *Jean Rivard* as a Utopia   171

In the course of the conversation, I took the opportunity to ask my host if he intended soon to send his son to college and his daughter to the convent.

His guide responds in minute detail in a precise, factual monologue that is a severe indictment of those institutions in which he himself had to suffer and that he dreads for his children.

There are three main grounds for his criticism of colleges. First, studies take a long time (few finish them) and are useless ('What will he have learned? How to decline *rosa, rosae,* to translate from and into Latin ... Where does all this get him?'). Second, colleges create habits of physical laziness: 'The complete idleness of the body during these years will perhaps have inspired in him an abiding horror of working with his hands. In that case, what can I do with him?' Third, these studies limit his horizons and restrict his choice of career to three in which there are no prospects:

On the other hand, if he finishes his studies and wants to take up one of the three professions, for which our top students are destined, his chances of failure and a life of poverty are still ten to one. Poor Gustave's letters frightened me.

As for convents, they are also subject to three criticisms. First, they should play only a temporary surrogate role: they should educate only those who may be corrupted by the example of a frivolous, dissolute family. Second, even so, convents instil the 'useless skills' of idle girls, such as embroidery, drawing, music, singing ... an 'education that is too elevated' in a young country. Third, they do not prepare girls for life and certainly not for marriage: 'sensible, young men' avoid these beauties who have no practical skills, and a lot of convent girls remain single for lack of a 'more solid, more rational education.'

Jean Rivard and his wife, therefore, take care to avoid these institutions. Their children receive basic training in the model school, which their parents complete by allowing them to use the family library and by drawing numerous lessons from daily tasks. However, if the son should later demonstrate superior talents and wish to do a 'regular course of study,' the father 'may' decide to send him to college, but with great reluctance, it seems.

These criticisms resemble others that were expressed at this time. Witness M. Wagnaer, in *Charles Guérin*, who rubs his hands in glee when he sees the two Guérin sons leaving for Quebec and an insecure profession: 'The mother was crazy enough to have her children study: that means that they will never come to anything.'[39] However, in *Jean Rivard*, these criticisms are combined with the positive vision, which has already been analysed, of constructing an educational utopia: the future school and education in this 'other world' that is the republic of Rivardville.

The commonplaces of utopian thought found in *Jean Rivard* are numerous and constant: a paradisaical atmosphere; spatial and political interventionism; benevolent yet firm authoritarianism; a passion for order, stability, and symmetry; attempts to standardize dwellings and minds; collective eudemonism; ardent proselytism by the guide and subsequently by the narrator; a clear tendency to self-sufficiency; fundamental hostility toward nature, which must submit to human control; a horror of waste and of useless luxury; the exaltation of intelligent work; the creation of a globalizing, universal education system. Together they build up a particular utopia, peculiarly American, while remaining French Canadian, both hybrid and original.

A 'Pure Laine' American Utopia

Jean Rivard is a profoundly American utopia by both its close relationship to the crucial works of nineteenth-century America and its down-to-earth pragmatism. It has often been pointed out[40] that the dominant theme of the nineteenth-century American novel, which most distinguishes it from the European novel of the same period, is undeniably the constant tendency to break away from established society and to seek an ideal community. The American novelists of the century searched for a reality tangential to society: 'The preoccupation with an ideal society constitutes an integral part of the American novelist's work.'[41]

Indeed, society does not have the same importance in America as in Europe. Institutions and social classes are not stratified and rigid. Society does not represent the only ambition and the sole destiny of the individual. In Europe, only one alternative exists: either conform, agree to play the social game and try to climb up the social ladder, like Balzac's Rastignac, or else criticize and propose social reforms, like Dickens. Balzac, an intuitive genius, could claim to be merely the secretary of society: 'French society was going to be the historian, I was to be only the secretary.'[42] In America, however, there was a third possibility, which was exploited in the classic novels of the nineteenth century: move away and form a new community.

Intertextuality II: *Jean Rivard* as a Utopia 173

This separation from established society, which was inconceivable in Europe, is not only possible, but it is glorified. The individual who moves away is right: it is the society he leaves that is wrong. The hero is not a dreamer, or a misfit, or an escapist like Chateaubriand's René. On the contrary, he immediately forms new ties and rebuilds a society, which he bases on democratic individualism. He recreates or rebuilds another community life, which is richer or more true: in the forests (Natty Bumppo), on a raft (Huckleberry Finn), on a whaler (Ishmael), in a community of the spirit (Hester Prynne).[43] This is not escapism at all, but a search for new, authentic values.

Certainly, when these American novels are compared with their European equivalents, they are unusually lightweight in terms of flesh-and-blood reality: they are romances rather than novels. It is quite remarkable that the terms used to criticize them at this level are exactly the same as those used by the detractors of *Jean Rivard*:

It can be admitted readily that in comparison with the social solidity observable in the novels of Dickens and Balzac, Hawthorne's and Melville's approach to society would indeed seem attenuated and tangential. They as well as Cooper and Twain would face the charge of being escapists, allegorists, day-dreamers, wishful thinkers, fantasy-mongers, romancers – they would in fact be called anything but novelists.[44]

It has been said of Gérin-Lajoie, too, that he was anything but a novelist. A dreamer, a utopian, and an idealist, Gérin-Lajoie is certainly all these things, but as such he is an authentic American writer of the nineteenth century.

But he is also a profound realist. Indeed, the great utopian writers have been considered great realists, more in step with their times than their down-to-earth contemporaries, because the latter were incapable of feeling the secret pulse, of sensing the latent forces of their time.

Paradoxically, the great utopians have been great realists. They have an extraordinary perception of the time and place in which they are writing and deliver themselves of penetrating reflections on socioeconomic, scientific, or emotional conditions of their moment in history ... The utopian often emerges as a man with a deeper understanding of his society than the hardheaded problem-solvers with their noses to the grindstones of the present, blind to potentiality.[45]

Jean Servier even believed that utopian writers not only had expressed the thought of a particular group, of a social class, but were also 'landmarks in the history of the West, signposting periods of crisis poorly perceived by their contemporaries and scarcely noticed by later historians.'[46] In short, they are realists in contact with the deep undercurrents of realism, far from the foamy surface. However perceptive Gérin-Lajoie may be on this level, on that of a more prosaic realism he is certainly a writer who is particularly anxious to give his utopia a concrete form, since he is aware of the fact that, if he hopes one day to see this social model realized, he must very clearly indicate the means of its historical creation, its 'axiological capital' and its geographical outlines. His wholly American pragmatism is used to realize a Quebec dream.

From this point of view, the relationship of Rivardville to history is typical. I do not mean history in the sense of the author's period or of the social conflicts in the 1860s. In this sense any utopia is inherently linked to history through its author, both because it criticizes and condemns the shortcomings of its time and because it aims to build a new future. That being said, it must instantly be stated that, paradoxically, the notion of history as *chronos*, temporality, succession in time, the transformation and flow of contingency, is fundamentally alien to the utopian dream. The theorists of the genre have often pointed this out: utopias, by definition, are ahistoric. On one hand, there is the here and now, changing and unstable, a sea of troubles; on the other, there is utopia, already established, organized, and static by definition, or rather anti-dialectical. It cannot be any other way; as everything in utopia is ordered, preconceived, and planned, any changes or modifications can only make for disturbance and disorder. Utopia's goal is to achieve a stable state, in short, to interrupt the course of history, to move beyond time. Utopia is resolutely outside of history. Moreover, on another level, utopia is ahistoric because it is never seen being developed, it simply *is*. Admittedly, the guide can vaguely evoke images of the early days, the legendary founder, the original crucial actions: for example, Utopus cutting off the isthmus to make Utopia an island. But all this remains extremely vague and indeterminate. In truth, utopia never *evolves*.

A practical person like Gérin-Lajoie cannot be content with pipedreams of this kind, nor would his century permit it. For the rational, positivist nineteenth century, it was no longer enough just to reach utopia by fortuitous means that had something of the adventure or the rite of passage about them. It was necessary to show precisely how the ideal state had been formed and not simply tell how the narrator had been stranded there. In short, 'reaching utopia' changes its meaning; it is no longer a question of a spatial or temporal journey, but a concrete problem of political planning. The question is a political one: how to transform the joyless present into a happy future. It is the great originality of *Jean Rivard* to have shown, stage by stage, through deliberate decisions and actions, throughout both parts of the work, how this particular republic was formed. It is an enterprise that has lasted approximately fifteen years, and though it has reached its prescribed limits, it is not yet completed. It is a profoundly historical utopia then, in two ways: its gestation has been minutely described and it is launched into a particular historical time-frame. Indeed, Rivardville can probably hope to become one day the improved equivalent of large American cities, which was what its founder had sought from the beginning (27).

Moreover, Gérin-Lajoie has the outstanding merit of having been sensitive to that other form of historicity that Ruyer called the 'incompressible duration' necessary for the formation of 'axiological capital.'[47] Contrary to utopian writers of his time and particularly European utopian socialists – who had hoped for a revolution as a catalyst of the new era, unless, like Marx, they postulated an inevitable, historical determinism – Gérin-Lajoie is fully aware that, if a utopia is to be formed and maintained, it needs to have capital slowly built up 'in all types of values: good social habits, good artistic traditions, a scientific and reasonable conception of the world, etc. This capital, like the other (economic capital), needs an incompressible duration if it is to be built up.'[48] To create his particular utopia, Gérin-Lajoie had recourse to a 'good habit' that is certainly the most widespread and fully developed: the pursuit of self-interest. Ruyer has clearly pointed out that utopian writers generally think they can make use of very low-powered aspirations (friendship, the search for the collective good) as forces of social cohesion; they fail to recognize that self-interest continues to exist in public figures; they neglect or ignore 'a fundamental social phenomenon that can be described as the "archway phenomenon." In an arch, each stone has a tendency to fall, but it is precisely for that reason that the arch does not fall ... The fundamental and truly durable institutions are in accordance with the archway system: massive, individual self-interest is made to work in favour of the general interest by the way the whole is organized.'[49]

There is none of this naïvety in Gérin-Lajoie's work. He does not rely on a motivation that is supposedly noble but purely idealistic. On the contrary, Jean Rivard is driven by the most widespread passion on the continent, the desire to be rich. This fundamental motivation ensures his personal success. The combination of this passion and analogous ones that surround and accompany it ensures the success of the republic of Rivardville by way of the archway phenomenon, which Tocqueville, without using the term, clearly described as at work in the American republic. This utopia is thus typically and profoundly American, relying on individualism as a force for collective progress and exalting greed as a means of enriching the community. It is poles apart from European socialistic utopias, which were collectivist and idealist and were stillborn, in any case, on the American continent. Gérin-Lajoie is fully aware that the axiological capital of individualism and personal gain is universal and already exists among his compatriots, but it is insufficiently used; they have to imitate the Americans. He is content, then, with provoking them to move in this direction: the axiological capital does not have to be created, it is enough to stimulate it. For that reason, he takes into account the reproaches that his father-in-law had directed ten years earlier at utopian writers, who, in their generous but specious projects, scorned natural laws and above all normal selfishness; in their reformist plans they were not faithful to the community's traditions.[50]

Thus, all the preachers and politicians of the nineteenth century who encouraged French Canadians to show their patriotism and not abandon the land, accusing emigrants of treachery or weakness, were in fact utopian in the most negative sense of the term: they were dreamers. Like utopian writers in general, they appealed to a 'noble' motive, patriotism, which is a very low-powered social motive under normal circumstances. On the contrary, Gérin-Lajoie, a utopia builder, presents us with a hero whose motivation is supposedly 'base,' but is undeniably highpowered: everybody has a most profound interest in succeeding personally, in becoming prosperous. This is sound realism, which does not presuppose an above-average virtue in a republic's inhabitants, but teaches the proper use of vigorous individualism. Enlightened self-interest makes for the happiness of all.

The author's heartening pragmatism is also evident in the precise configuration of his republic. Ruyer reproaches utopian writers for confusing family and state, community and society, for unhesitatingly merging values and dimensions, for applying to a large state what could be suitable for only a limited community, if not for a group of friends. 'Principled utopian writers, like Plato and Harrington, take care to point out the size of their model state.'[51] This is precisely the case with Rivardville, which is a parish or municipality approximately the size of a Greek city-state – that is, the town with its surrounding territory. Its small size enables citizens to become acquainted with one another, to get together, to feel they are directly involved in running public affairs, and to participate fully in them. It is therefore advisedly that Jean Rivard conceives his utopia as a republic: 'My whole ambition would be to make Rivardville a model parish. I would like to make it into a small republic, if possible, with all the institutions necessary for the good administration of its affairs, the development of its resources, the intellectual, social, and political progress of its people' (273). Tocqueville had already viewed in this way American municipalities that had enabled the English republican spirit to reach its full potential:

In the United States ... the communes become almost independent municipalities, a kind of democratic republic. The republican element, which forms the basis of the constitution and of English customs, appears without hindrance and is developed. In England, the administration as such does very little, while the people do a lot; in America, the administration no longer meddles in anything, so to speak, and the individuals, by uniting together, do everything.[52]

If Tocqueville could record this republican spirit at work at the time of his journey in 1835, it was probably because it corresponded to the intentions that inspired the founding of the American republic:

Brought up with great memories of Greco-Latin Antiquity, the republicans intended to make the United States into a republic, hence their name republican: their ideal was an American Arcadia, a democratic society of small landowners who were free and equal, living off their work without owing anything to anyone and enjoying an honestly earned prosperity.[53]

It is precisely this American spirit that motivates the citizens of Rivardville and ensures the success of their community.

While these precise, restricted dimensions of Rivardville guarantee the efficiency of the utopian plan and its plausibility, they perhaps also enable us to understand one aspect of the novel that, at the beginning of the century, constantly preoccupied Monsignor Camille Roy. In the second edition of his book, Gérin-Lajoie omitted the four chapters (fifty-three pages!) that narrated Jean Rivard's parliamentary life. Monsignor Roy was greatly interested in this omission, which apparently annoyed him. He proposed various hypotheses to explain it.[54] Perhaps it was the 'qualms of conscience of a civil servant who regretted all the nasty things he had said about the Members of Parliament whom he had rubbed shoulders with and assessed.' Perhaps it was 'remorse' at having painted too dark a portrait of the MPs. Or had Gérin-Lajoie realized that Jean Rivard was critical of parliamentary life, but proposed nothing: 'He had been a dauntless demolisher, but he did not appear to have been capable of constructing anything.' Or else the author perhaps felt that his hero came out of it with his stature diminished; in that case, he probably chose to omit what Jean Rivard 'had not done and what he ought to have done.' Or could it be that, by this omission, the author wanted to make it clear that however gifted a settler may be, he does not have the competence necessary to become an MP? In thus constructing various hypotheses, Monsignor Roy only takes over from the narrator himself, who seeks in vain to explain the withdrawal of his hero (*Le Foyer canadien*, 2 [1864], Chapter 20).

Whatever the reasons that persuaded Gérin-Lajoie to remove these numerous pages, Monsignor Roy severely reprimands him for it:

If we look at this excision in terms of the treatment of the work and the harmony of its plan and composition, we believe Gérin-Lajoie was wrong to cut out this picture of parliamentary life. It was no doubt pessimistic, but it included some very instructive and subtly ironic pages.[55]

According to him, if Gérin-Lajoie had wanted to cut out these pages describing Jean Rivard's short career as an MP, he should have taken everything out: not just the four years the hero lived in Quebec, but also the election and the candidacy itself. He ought not to have 'whetted the reader's curiosity for nothing.'

This question is interesting and quite legitimate. Why cut out these pages? They certainly have an anecdotal and historical interest. They ask serious questions about party spirit, an MP's responsibilities, and the way parliamentary life is conducted, and it is indisputable that they are deftly written. Monsignor Roy's disappointment is thus quite understandable. However, in the author's defence, it is possible to imagine another explanation that is connected to the novel's utopian dimension and the internal consistency it requires.

If *Jean Rivard* is only a success story based on the American model, it is perfectly normal for its hero to end up in Parliament. We have already seen the model for this career path in Chapter 2: he is successively a pioneer, a farmer, and industrialist, the founder of a town, a mayor, a magistrate, a notability, and an MP. As Tocqueville pointed out, this model has been realized everywhere on the continent. But *Jean Rivard* is also a utopia that follows the requirements of this kind of discourse, even in stylistic details. This particular ending, which would be the crowning achievement of an American pioneer's normal career, presents insoluble problems for the utopian writer. When Jean Rivard leaves Rivardville to become an MP in Quebec, two antinomic spaces are in confrontation. He leaves the world of nowhere to inhabit the here and now. If need be, the simultaneous existence of these two worlds can be supposed (Quebec, after all, is large enough to have a few hidden islands); it is, nevertheless, inconceivable that the principles that govern the first would be effective in the second. Indeed, the first has been imagined as a reaction against the second, which is the negation of all the principles exalted and practised in the ideal republic. Therefore, Jean Rivard is condemned to failure. He is literally incomprehensible to the other MP's, as much as if he had come from another planet. This is, in fact, the case: he does come from another space, from a planet based on different principles. For parliamentary life to be something other than a blind alley, the Parliament in Quebec must become in its turn a utopian parliament. But plausibility forbids this from happening.

In short, to stick to the logic of the utopian world, the novel evades an absolutely indispensable stage. Contrary to what Gérin-Lajoie believed, the extension of Rivardville is not the Parliament in Quebec, but other Rivardvilles, multiple small republics. Once these prosperous, happy, utopian spaces have been formed, they could then arrange to get together and delegate their representatives to a new parliament, which would, by the nature of things, be a utopian parliament. But here again, plausibility forbids it, unless the author reverts to science fiction, which is not at all what he intended. Rivardville, even a few Rivardvilles, could exist here and there. The reader is willing to admit that, by travelling laterally, it would be possible to be stranded there by chance on a stormy night. But readers are also in a position to note that in 1862, in Lower Canada, these Rivardvilles were not legion: they know of none.

In short, two diegeses are in confrontation: there is a novel about a personal success and there is a utopian novel. Both are worked out in the book and both can be integrated without any apparent contradiction, except in their respective conclusions. Thus, Jean Rivard must become an MP because it is the crowning achievement in his career and the culmination of his success story. Gérin-Lajoie is right to have him elected. But since the character is literally from nowhere, 'u-topian,' he cannot become an MP somewhere. This is why the author, upon reflection, has nothing to say about this parliamentary career. He must omit these four years, excise these pages and condemn them to the textual non-place, that is, the 'hors-texte.' 'We will not say anything about Jean Rivard's parliamentary career' (313), the narrator confides to us. In fact, it is literally impossible to say anything whatsoever about it without falsifying the whole purpose of the novel.

Immediately after he is elected, in the space of a sentence, Jean Rivard returns to Rivardville, the place where he is truly himself. It is his paradise, his ideal republic, but also his prison. A narrator may return from the 'u-topia' to tell his readers about it and to urge them to attempt the same adventure. He went, he saw, and he can attest to it. As for the hero, he is condemned to remain on his 'island of the Blessed.' It is up to readers who want to see this strange island in Quebec waters, this 'eu-topian' island, to reproduce it in their turn.

5

Republicanism or Feudalism in Laurentia?[1]

Gérin-Lajoie may well choose to relegate to the 'hors-texte' Jean Rivard's four years in Parliament. Nonetheless, this decision does not eliminate his novel's political dimension. His rejection of parliamentary politicking in the work's later versions in no way reduces the text's political discourse. On the contrary, a utopian novel raises the question of the novel's ideological dimension in its most radical form. How should social organization be achieved? How does the novelist perceive the structure of the *politikos*? How does the individual, the protagonist, fit into the community and how does the community respond to his aspirations?

The previous chapter outlined *Jean Rivard*'s political vision; by giving free rein to his dreams of transforming society, the novelist reinvents the *civitas*. Yet this republic, according to numerous commentators, is deeply reactionary: they claim that *Jean Rivard* conveys an essentially conservative ideology, upholding the established order, refusing progress and change. The novel has thus, over the years, contributed strongly to the stereotype of French Canadians as being backward. As Roger LeMoine affirms, for example, in an otherwise accurate presentation of the novel of that period, 'Gérin-Lajoie makes settlement and agriculture, which results from it, the quintessential occupations of French Canadians. Yet in putting forward this ideal, which means first and foremost accepting the established order, he widens the economic gap between francophones and anglophones, and he locks the former even more securely into their colonial, alienated situation.'[2] In short, the political colour of the novel is alleged to be a deep, conservative blue.

Of course, novels, to which we readily attribute a texture or a flavour, have no characteristic colour in critics' vocabulary; their hue is acquired from elsewhere. It may be derived from the series that flaunts its colour precisely because its purpose is to improve the marketability of individual titles, whether it be the *Bibliothèque bleue* novels peddled during the ancien régime or today's *Série noire* thrillers. Above all, however, novels acquire their colour from the ideology that they supposedly convey. That is why, although *Jean Rivard* has been called an agrarian novel, it has never been described as 'brown.' Agrarian novels are not brown – brown like the soil, which is supposed to form their substance but which, paradoxically, they almost never describe (this silence should give us pause). They are not grey either, despite the opinions of several critics who are only too hasty to associate soil with dullness and insipidity. They are more likely blue, the colour of their ideology. Loftily judging the whole of the last century's literary output from a staunchly progressive standpoint, the majority of today's critics and readers scarcely bother to make certain essential distinctions. For today's Québécois intellectuals, reformist by definition, quick to condemn and more often than not secretly ashamed of their people and of their past, the soil signifies reluctance to change and love of routine; settlement is but a backward-looking, delusive, Messianic dream, and all of nineteenth-century French Canada was mired in nostalgia and untouched by progress. All works are thus judged harshly, regardless of the particular time of a text's genesis and publication, regardless of the specific qualities of an outstanding work. And yet, if the trouble is taken to make certain distinctions, this perception is a far cry from reality.

The epilogue of *Charles Guérin*, P.-J.-O. Chauveau's novel, which was published in its entirety some ten years before *Jean Rivard*, is well known. It is extremely instructive to compare it with Gérin-Lajoie's novel. Entitled 'A New Parish,' this text, which is a few pages long, constitutes in a way a preliminary sketch of *Jean Rivard*, but with some very revealing differences.

Its protagonist, Charles Guérin, a vain, frivolous youth, has, against all likelihood, quickly settled down and become a propagandist for settlement. The author himself seems to have difficulty believing it, which explains no doubt the ironic, slightly casual tone of the ending. A few years after his marriage, Charles Guérin notes that several young people from his parish are about to emigrate to the United States. 'Charles assembled all the fugitives at the church door and gave them a magnificent three-point sermon.'[3] What might be expected happens. This three-point sermon has no more effect than the similar lecture given by Father Leblanc to Jean Rivard. Worse still, since Charles Guérin is neither a priest nor a 'venerable' citizen, the 'fugitives' make fun of this unlicensed preacher: 'Does this fine gentleman want us to starve to death just to please him?' (CG, 345). A makeshift preacher, yet astute all the same, 'Charles understood right away that the best sermon was not worth a good example. That same night, he proposed to Jacques Lebrun the formation of a small society for settling uncultivated land in the *seigneurie* and in the neighbouring township' (CG, 345). In this way, in barely six pages, with his father-in-law, his friend, his brother the priest (and his legacy, of course), Charles Guérin founds a flourishing parish. He becomes the adviser to all, and there is even talk of making him the MP for the area: a 'calamity' (CG, 352) says the narrator, ironically, as his last word.

In this sketch of the creation of a new settlement, numerous elements can be recognized that are taken up in *Jean Rivard*, but the differences are considerable. First, Charles Guérin encounters numerous obstacles all around him – incredulity, hesitations, and even defections. His father-in-law is reluctant to follow him; his wife, Marichette, and his sister, Louise, wife of his friend Jean Guilbeault, do not want to isolate themselves in the forest and demand some guarantees of comfort before going there. Those he wants to help lack enthusiasm. The *seigneur* and the government create 'delays and hindrances' (no Mister Lacasse or 'Honorable' Smith here). Moreover, the bishop and the neighbouring priest oppose the establishment of this new parish, and a lawsuit is narrowly avoided. The human adversaries of the plan are therefore numerous. Second, all the work of the settlement is done by the group. They are partners who venture into the forest; the first year, they survey the land and open up the roads, then, in the second year, they 'clear plots of equal size on each one's land' (CG, 347). In this new parish, moreover, it is Pierre Guérin, the priest, who exercises the most authority and has the most influence over decisions. Suitable sermons encourage the settlers and justify their striving for prosperity. Third, Charles Guérin, while readily giving advice, systematically refuses, despite numerous appeals, the slightest honour: 'He never wanted, either for himself, or his brother-in-law, or his father-in-law, any of the local offices and high positions' (CG, 351). The Guérin family has no power. Charles can advise, but he can neither impose his will nor give orders.

It can be seen that the differences between 'the new parish' and *Jean Rivard* all point in the same direction: *Jean Rivard* is a utopia, and a utopia that practises American values. First, there are scarcely any conflicts in *Jean Rivard*, beyond his own family's initial reservations. Human conflict is systematically downplayed, foregrounding the running battle with nature, which must be conquered. Second, Jean Rivard's venture becomes resolutely personal: his project is entirely the work of an individual. Pierre Gagnon is an employee, not an associate. Third, as we have already seen, the novel makes settlement a radically secular enterprise. Jean Rivard will preach his crusade of materialistic success by means that are exclusively human: church, priest, parishioners follow his lead; they are invited onto his land to settle where he chooses. The priest always remains in his shadow. Finally, Jean Rivard is the legislator and the organizer of a republic; in it he wields great power, sets its limits and its layout, and decides on its institutions. When we talk of nineteenth-century settlement, there are thus distinctions that need to be made. On the same canvas – the ecumen that is occupied and exploited – Gérin-Lajoie has painted a very different picture from that of Chauveau.

Do they, however, share the same ideology, one that numerous commentators have described as essentially retrograde – isolation, self-sufficiency, the establishment of parishes far from corrupting influences? Did these writers, spiritual heirs of the Patriotes, see themselves, like all members of the liberal professions of the time, as a new aristocracy, and thus create works expressing only their ambiguous dream? Fernand Ouellet has described this dream in particularly vigorous terms:

Despite rationalizations derived from liberal and democratic ideologies, their true intention is to rebuild an ancien régime society on the banks of the St Lawrence ... Under the cloak of democracy and liberal aspirations that have a certain authenticity, we thus see them searching for an impossible isolation that results in the creation of a feudal, theocratic society.[4]

Yet the novel as I read it is completely opposed to this perception. As an original attempt to transplant American values into Quebec and to graft onto an ancient stock an adventurous pioneering spirit associated with Anglo-Saxons, with triumphant nineteenth-century liberalism, and with the development of this new continent, *Jean Rivard* appears to me to have other meanings. No doubt the time has come to put an end to this negative estimate of the novel that makes it a deeply reactionary work, doubly so, since it allegedly cloaks itself in progressive liberalism in order to mislead readers about its true intentions.

This perception of the work has been confidently expressed, in particular by its English-speaking commentators like Mason Wade:

Republicanism or Feudalism in Laurentia? 185

Jean Rivard remains essential reading today for those who would understand the French-Canadian mind, with its distrust of the urban industrial civilization of the rest of the continent, which it cannot reconcile with its own patriarchal rural tradition.[5]

Or by Vida Bruce, who develops this judgment at much greater length:

The parish with its carefully controlled confines, both political and geographical, is seen as the only viable form of democracy. The image of the parish as a fortress against vague threats of aggression from without becomes the overpowering message of the novel ... The parish becomes a 'little republic,' a territorial entity to be protected and preserved. An essential part of that community, of Rivardville, is its isolation. The world that Jean Rivard constructs, on the model of the parish, is economically self-sufficient ... Economic, religious and political harmony within have been achieved, not by a process of democratization but by separation, and by the exercise of authoritarian political power thinly disguised as a democracy ... The attempt to make the most conservative aims wear the face of liberal and progressive idealism was an integral but inadmissible part of the French-Canadian national image in the difficult years that followed the Act of Union.[6]

In short, for Fernand Ouellet, Mason Wade, and Vida Bruce, who quotes Ouellet in support of her thesis, the ideology of a work like *Jean Rivard* is, under a progressive disguise, fundamentally conservative ('the most conservative aims'): it is a dream of a feudal, theocratic society, isolated from capitalist America. The accusation is serious, all the more since it undermines in advance and from within the whole argument of my study. Have I simply been deceived by appearances? What is the truth of the matter?

A Reactionary, Elitist Dream?

It must first be recognized that this perception of the work can be based on numerous pages of the novel. It is difficult, for example, not to have second thoughts after reading the following excerpt:

The enthusiasm, the warmth with which they (Jean Rivard and his friend, Father Octave Doucet) discussed all the questions that could exert some influence on the future of Rivardville were something to be seen. Never did king, emperor, president, dictator, or sovereign take as much interest in the happiness and prosperity of their subjects as did these two friends in the success of the people of their parish ...

The two friends could be seen sometimes alone in the middle of the night in Jean Rivard's bedroom, enthusiastically discussing certain measures for the enlargement of the parish, the development of the township's resources, happily conversing about the good they would do, the reforms they would bring about, the changes they would make for the welfare of their fellow men and for the greater glory of God.
   It was the spiritual and temporal powers supporting each other and working hand in hand. (204-5)

It is also difficult not to hesitate after reading several declarations in the sixth chapter of the 'Last Part': 'A Visit with the Priest – Economic Discussions.' It is the priest who launches into economic discourses for the benefit of the narrator, and, at times, his reflections appear to clash head-on with my perception of the novel, for example, this one, which Vida Bruce has already cited:

Each parish can form a small republic, where not only the natural, and material, but the moral resources of the nation can be utilized in the interests of our future existence as a people. The parish will be our fortress. Even if all other resources fail us, it seems to me that here we would find an impregnable rampart against aggression from without. (359)

To such apparently conservative passages must be added the massive presence of a feudal type of vocabulary that places heavy emphasis on Rivardville's social stratification and on the existence of very distinct classes. Jean-Charles Falardeau, in a very surprising judgment for a sociologist, said that society in Rivardville is 'absolutely homogeneous': 'The social universe that Jean Rivard reconstructs in his "republic" is absolutely homogeneous. Rural life has a fraternal character.'[7] This society is admittedly fraternal, but with all respects to the sociologist, in the strict sense of the word, it can hardly be said to be homogeneous. The republic as a whole is not made up of elements of the same kind: we find masters and servants, a landowner and employees, an emperor and his soldiers, a leader and supporters. The classes are in close fraternal contact, but they certainly do exist, as the novel explicitly recognizes:

Nowhere does the spirit of fraternity exist in such a touching manner as in the

Canadian countryside, remote from the cities. Here, *all classes* are in contact with one another. Diversity of professions or conditions is no divisive barrier as it is in the cities. The rich man greets the poor man he meets on his way. They eat at the same table and go to church in the same carriage. (56; my italics)

Throughout the novel, Jean Rivard is an emperor, a king, a bourgeois, a *seigneur* (passim), and his wife, a queen (180), a chatelaine (156). Before him stands 'good rustic Pierre Gagnon' (163), totally self-sacrificing, utterly happy to be of service, whom he enjoys calling his 'steward' (31). Jean Rivard consistently uses the informal 'tu' when speaking to him, while his servant systematically uses the formal 'vous' when speaking to his young master. Pierre is a 'good and faithful servant' (30) whose sensible, intelligent remarks are but 'chatter' (53) for his condescending master. He is a 'child of the people,' coarse, rustic, indefatigable, jolly, and smiling, a repository of folklore. He will receive as his lot Jean Rivard's servant ('I want to marry in my own class' [215], he declares), a 'neat and tidy' and 'suitable' (217) woman, but without romantic qualities, somewhat simple, naïve, and superstitious.[8] Jean Rivard has friends of his own class, Octave Doucet and Gustave Charmenil. Pierre Gagnon will never attain this rank. Moreover, he does not aspire to do so: 'You will always be my emperor as you were before' (213) he hastens to say, even when they are neighbours. In his mind, Jean Rivard, his illustrious emperor, will always belong to a higher social rank. On election day, Jean Rivard, after having thanked his 'friend Gustave Charmenil,' addresses his devoted servant: 'Gentlemen, there is another old comrade here as well, a working companion who demonstrated in this latest battle the same ardent devotion as always, the same readiness to support me at the cost of his life' (306). On one hand there is a friend, Gustave Charmenil; on the other there is a devoted workmate, Pierre Gagnon.

This representation of social interaction never ceases to astound. When the narrator assures us that 'this good servant's greatest happiness, his finest triumph was to succeed in bringing a smile to the lips of his young master' (46–7), these superlatives may seem suspect. When Jean Rivard condescendingly addresses the older man – 'That's very good, Pierre. Those sentiments do you honour. I am thoroughly convinced that with your energy and good sense, and especially your love of hard work, you will one day be prosperous, and your children, if you have any, will be able to enjoy the advantages of education and make fine citizens' (73) – these mawkish words go beyond the limits of probability. The self-sacrifice of the lower classes and the superior attitude of the masters are understandable in a novel like *Les anciens Canadiens*, the work of a *seigneur* that recounts the halcyon years of the seigneurial regime in New France. But *Jean Rivard* is the work of a farmer's son, who describes the relationship of his protagonist, himself a farmer's son, with a day labourer born in the same parish. By stressing the somewhat disconcerting social gulf between them, the narrator even comes close to implausibility. It is, for example, inconceivable that Jean Rivard, a farmer's son, the eldest of a large family, born in a traditional parish, should scarcely know any folksongs and should have to resort to the 'child of the people,' Pierre Gagnon, for this repertoire (31). How can it be that, though the eldest of a farming family, Jean Rivard is totally ignorant of the tapping of maple trees and has to be initiated by his hired help (48)? These liberties with plausibility can be explained only by the author's concern to establish a coherent class discourse, despite its historical improbabilities. In short, with Jean Rivard, readers appear to be offered a representative of this 'professional nobility, born of the people, which has taken over from the titled nobility,' as Chauveau had pointed out a couple of years before.[9] This new aristocracy cherishes the same nostalgic dreams as its predecessor, according to Fernand Ouellet.

Yet is this really the meaning of this social gulf? Is *Jean Rivard* a 'true blue' novel? A certain number of distinctions must be made in order to answer this question.

The Ramparts of the Parish

Let us begin with the passages in the novel that, according to Fernand Ouellet and Vida Bruce, appear to outline a society that seeks an 'impossible isolation' and a 'feudal and theocratic' identity. This isolation is real, all the more so since it corresponds to one of the requirements of the utopian genre. However, it is also very relative. It must not be forgotten that *Jean Rivard* is to some extent an epistolary novel, constructed around the continuous correspondence between two characters who occupy very different realms, but who are in frequent and constant contact with each other. By mail, Jean Rivard is in uninterrupted communication with the city; in return, Gustave Charmenil is amply informed of all the events, big and small, that occur in Bristol Township, then Rivardville. And the post, which is the favoured means of communications in *The Pioneer*, is but the first of many methods used to form closer links with the outside world. The construction of a 'public road through the township of Bristol' is the occasion for unlimited rejoicing: 'There were bonfires, demonstrations, public celebrations. New life seemed to surge through the entire community' (146). This road is soon followed by a railway. Every day, the community grows, immigrants arriving from everywhere, settling everywhere: 'Jean Rivard saw habitations spring up in the heart of the virgin forest, extend in every direction and form, little by little, this well-populated, flourishing parish' (187). Besides this immigrant population there is an intense exchange of ideas, since all the inhabitants of Rivardville are subscribers to a wide variety of newspapers, 'gazettes,' or periodicals (350–1).

So, if Rivardville is isolated, it must be recognized that this isolation is very relative; if the parish is a fortress, it must be noted that its contours are somewhat vague and its walls very porous. People come and go as they please; people, ideas, and goods cross it unimpeded, to the inhabitants' great pleasure. What are we to think, then, of this fortress, an ambiguous metaphor used by Father Doucet and taken up by Vida Bruce? Against what 'attacks from without' (359) does the parish have to protect its inhabitants?

The image must be put back in its context. In discoursing on the economy, Father Doucet eventually speaks of the importance of agriculture as a tool for economic prosperity. He then tackles education, the key to individual prosperity and collective wealth. A question from the narrator leads him to the subject of race relations and gives him the opportunity to stress the harmony between the Irish and the French Canadians in Rivardville: the parish receives these immigrants warmly and the priest fights with all his power against 'race hatred and national prejudices, these groundless animosities' (358). Finally, an examination of municipal government enables him to see an advantageous way to develop 'political common sense and an understanding of government' (359) in the community. It is at this point that he declares that this municipal government can 'safeguard all we hold dear' and that each parish can form a 'republic,' a 'fortress,' 'an impregnable rampart against attacks from without' (359). Do these attacks represent the materialistic spirit and the ravages of capitalism, as most commentators would have it? It is unlikely. Father Doucet has previously assured the narrator that 'those who believe that a priest is indifferent to material progress ... are sadly mistaken.' On the contrary, he wants 'material comfort to be as widespread as possible. What is more, wealth in his view constitutes a moral force: 'We realize all the moral force that wealth, well administered and applied, carries with it' (358). Does the aggression reside in the penetration of new ideas? That is impossible.

The priest stresses the supreme importance of education in increasing the *self-reliance* of his fellow citizens: 'How is it people do not understand that enlightened men in all walks of life – agriculture, business, industry, administration – constitute the strength, the wealth, and the glory of a country?' (358). Is it possible that foreigners are the threat? Not at all, because the priest encourages numerous contacts with foreigners. Their influence can only be beneficial, especially for national prosperity: 'There is something good to be drawn from the customs and habits of any people. Our contact with people of different origins and countries can introduce, without harming our national character, certain modifications in our habits that will affect our destiny and especially our material future' (359). We are reminded of Father Ferland's reflections on the advantages that the French Canadians could draw from their association with the Scots and the Anglo-Saxons.[10]

So, what is it exactly Father Doucet is afraid of? Just what is it that threatens, according to him, the 'future existence' (359) of French Canadians 'as a people'? This remains somewhat vague, but the scourges evoked at the century's end by ultramontane ideologues – materialism, industrialization, urbanization, Protestantism, in a word, Americanization – are not at issue. Is it simply a hyperbole provoked by the author's partiality for military metaphors? It is possible. Yet the answer is rather to be found in the words that follow immediately after the image of the fortress and are uttered in the most fervent invocatory tone: '"Let us pray God," he added earnestly, "that there is no gangrenous invasion of our body politic"' (359–60). The context is very precise. The attacks threaten the *body politic* first, and the nation only by extension. The threats are 'corruption, venality, demoralization ... party spirit' (360). It is by raising an 'impenetrable barrier' that the priest wishes to withstand 'the devastating torrent of immorality threatening to engulf our political liberties' (360). Thus the parish is a fortress, but not against the entire outside world. The context does not allow this meaning; moreover, it affirms exactly the opposite. Wealth is good and moral, education and new ideas are indispensable, foreigners are an element of progress and profitable emulation. The parish is a fortress, indeed, but against one danger: political immorality. It can thus protect its citizens since it trains them in the practice of politics and of government.

We are far from the interpretations of critics like Vida Bruce: the isolated parish, self-sufficient, agrarian, hostile toward foreigners. On the contrary, the parish is open to all influences and, with its institutions, becomes a privileged and primary place for a political apprenticeship: the school of democracy. It is the equivalent, in short, of the American communes that Tocqueville had described so well. The good Father Doucet's 'discourses,' therefore, have an entirely different significance from what has been too hastily attributed to them. They propose an original, entirely legitimate model of civic activity; the parish is seen as the first level of political life, and an extremely important one, since it is the breeding ground for higher-level service. Thus, after having completed his apprenticeship in the parish, Jean Rivard is judged worthy of representing his fellow citizens in Parliament: his high civic qualities have won him unanimous support.

In short, to better understand the novel's discourse with respect to the parish's importance, one should avoid reading it anachronistically in the light of ultramontane discourse at the end of the century. It should be read instead in terms of the analysis Tocqueville made of American institutions in the early chapters of *De la démocratie en Amérique*. Tocqueville insists on the importance of the township as established by the Puritans, the Pilgrims of New England: 'In the laws of Connecticut, as well as in all those of New England, we find the birth and development of that township independence that has been the life and mainspring of American liberty up to the present day.'[11] The parallel between township organization and education that Jean Rivard made in his long letter to Gustave Charmenil on education (Chapter 13 of the *Economist*) is spelled out in Tocqueville: 'Nevertheless townships constitute the strength of free nations. Township institutions are to liberty what primary schools are to knowledge; they bring it within the people's reach.'[12] We even find in Tocqueville the military imagery that may have been used to give a certain sharpness to the speeches of Father Doucet. The township is threatened, it must fight back, defend itself against invasions; it is a fortress against the corruption of its libertarian principle:

Again, no liberties are so *ill protected against the encroachments* of the supreme power as that liberty that has been so hard to establish in the townships. Township institutions are unable *to struggle* single-handedly against a strong, enterprising government, and they cannot *defend themselves successfully* unless they are fully developed and have become identified with the opinions and customs of the nation. Thus, until the liberty of townships has become part of the manners of a people, it is easily *destroyed*, and it is only after a long existence in the laws that it can become part of its manners.[13]

For Tocqueville, a European, the threat comes from the central government; for Father Doucet, a French Canadian, the danger comes from the fact that democratic institutions have not had a long enough apprenticeship among the people. Both use the same military imagery, share the same conviction that the township-commune is of vital importance, and are afraid that in the beginning this bastion of liberty may be fragile. In a word, instead of being a precursor of Bishop Laflèche[14] and a die-hard reactionary, this fictional character is a disciple of Tocqueville, a theorist of liberalism.

The Meaning of the Gulf between Classes

The parish does not appear to be the sanctuary of an inward-looking fiefdom, hostile toward the world around it, unhealthily building its derisory ramparts. Quite the contrary, in the image of the American township, it is the cradle and the stronghold of liberty, the sanctuary of democracy.

But of what democracy? Of a very non-egalitarian democracy apparently, to judge by the rank, prestige, and dominance of Jean Rivard. Here again, however, a distinction must be made. The protagonist's influence and power are real. The narrator and the characters readily use an aristocratic and feudal vocabulary, if not monarchic and imperial. Yet Rivardville remains a republic, and its society is democratic. As in the United States, the actual inequalities of this society in no way put into question the equality of all citizens before the law. Jean Rivard is powerful because he is worthy of this power, and it has been freely granted to him. It can just as easily be withdrawn, as happens once when he is beaten at the school-board elections. Moreover, his authority does not threaten the liberty of his fellow citizens, since he is their representative. The citizens of Rivardville, like those of the United States described by Tocqueville, 'obey the government, not because they are inferior to the people in charge of it, nor because they are less capable than their neighbours of governing themselves, but because they acknowledge the utility of an association with their fellow men, and because they know that no such association can exist without a regulating force'.[15] They obey all the more willingly when they know that this regulating force is worthy of their confidence.

On what does the social stratification in Rivardville depend? On what does the supremacy of Jean Rivard and the confidence he enjoys hinge? If Jean Rivard becomes 'bourgeois' and 'emperor' – in a word, head of the township – it is no doubt partly because of his education. But only partly. Gustave Charmenil, his counterpart, who is a failure, is more educated than he is, since he has finished his classical studies and even his articling; nevertheless, he is poor and miserable, unemployed, with no prospects and no social rank. Moreover, we know that the education Jean Rivard received left him ill-equipped and incapable of making a living. In order to qualify the endless remarks on the new Quebec aristocracy of the time it is thus important to stress that Jean Rivard *rejects the studies* that allegedly would have given him access to the 'professional nobility' represented by law, medicine, and the priesthood. *He rejects them and he becomes an emperor.*

On what does his climb up the social ladder depend? On his personal qualities and on his financial success. The protagonist comes from nowhere; he could have been less than nothing (falling to the level of a labourer in the parish where he was born). Thanks to his adventurous spirit and his leadership qualities, he reaches, in the community that he creates, the top of the social pyramid. His success gives him the highest rank. Yet despite the unofficial titles lavished on Jean Rivard, this society remains egalitarian. The novel's vision is futuristic, not a throwback to the ancien régime, since social rank is not determined by birth but by merit. The individual is judged to be deserving if he acquires exterior signs of success: property and wealth. Thus we come to the key phrase of the prefatory discourse: 'a young man ... who succeeded in making it to the top by his own merits, becoming financially independent, and receiving his country's highest honours' (1).

Receiving the highest honours does not mean creating a new aristocracy, however. The novel leads us to believe this is the case by its choice of feudal or imperial vocabulary, but this vocabulary is only metaphoric, and it would be a mistake to be taken in by these images. The novel's lesson lies elsewhere, and once again it is Tocqueville's observations that enable us to understand better what is at stake and the significance of the hierarchical social organization in America and in this fictional universe. Everything depends on the supremely differentiating power of money. 'When the prestige that belonged to what is old has vanished, birth, condition, and profession no longer distinguish men, or scarcely distinguish them at all: hardly anything but money remains to create strongly marked differences between them, and to raise some of them above the common level. The distinction originating in wealth is increased by the disappearance and diminution of all other distinctions.'[16] Moreover, since this distinction is neither permanent nor territorial, strictly speaking it does not constitute a basis for an aristocratic class: 'In a nation, immense fortunes may coexist with extreme wretchedness, but unless those fortunes are territorial, there is really no aristocracy, but simply the rich and the poor.'[17] On the contrary, since the power of money to make social distinctions is extremely fluid and since fortunes can rapidly change hands, the society that is created remains, in spirit at least, deeply egalitarian: 'Wealth circulates with incredible rapidity, and experience shows that it is rare to find two successive generations in full enjoyment of it.'[18] 'In the United States fortunes are easily won and lost; the country is boundless, and its resources are inexhaustible.'[19] 'Among democratic nations new families are constantly emerging out of nowhere, others are constantly falling away, and all those that remain change their condition; the fabric of the time is every instant broken, and the last traces of generations disappear.'[20]

In Tocqueville's reflections can be sensed the French aristocrat's fascination with an unprecedented social mobility and perhaps a trace of nostalgia for his own country's outdated social order. He occupied a privileged position as an observer, and we can benefit from his American findings, since they patently apply to the fictional universe of Gérin-Lajoie. Jean Rivard's meteoric success is a dazzling illustration of this. His father was a simple habitant; he is the founder of a town, head of the township, mayor and MP; what his son will become is unknown and depends only on him. Indeed, everything is possible for everyone, but nothing is given to anyone. Success is within everyone's reach, so long as you want it enough. All the paratextual apparatus (prefaces, notes, biographical sketches of pioneers) stress this fact, as does the novel itself. Parallel to the rise of Jean Rivard, hundreds of others, anonymous but nonetheless real, are evoked. Some even emerge from anonymity. Such is the case of Joseph Lachance, who is first a journeyman working for Jean Rivard, then, 'after settling in one of the neighbouring townships, becomes one of their prominent citizens and is appointed a member of the delegation' (298) that comes to ask Jean Rivard to stand for election. Having lost his father, having no education that is convertible into gainful employment, Jean Rivard becomes a pioneer and a founder of a town; the career of the day labourer and pioneer Joseph Lachance follows the same course. These 'outstanding men' have none of Chauveau's 'professional nobility': lawyers, notaries, doctors, priests. They are of a new breed, the breed that Gérin-Lajoie proposes: that of *self-made men*, American pioneers.

A Mauve Novel

Thus, if there is social stratification, it springs from a liberal order and from nascent capitalism. This order is deeply egalitarian in its principles: every competitor has a chance of winning. If a feudal vocabulary is proposed to describe this stratification, it is simply because mentalities and conceptual baggage move slowly: the novel's characters and the narrator have no other vocabulary at their disposal than that provided by their tradition (Jean Rivard, the *seigneur* of the area) or that of popular culture (Jean Rivard, a new Napoleon). This feudal or imperial vocabulary in a fundamentally liberal republic and in the avant-garde of democracy is yet another indication of the curious ideological mixture to be found in these fascinating years.

The first few chapters of Bernard Proulx' book on the 'territorial novel' need to be read if we are to fully understand what was at stake at the time and the deep meaning of the novels that deal with it.[21] These 'mauve texts' are quite wrongly called agrarian novels, since they are in fact novels of territorial expansion. They are 'mauve' since these novelists, unfortunate inheritors of the red radicalism of the Patriotes, had to compromise with the reality of their collectivity (poverty, peasantry, English power) and therefore moderate the radicalism of the previous generation. 'This nascent genre is a child of mauvism, that pragmatism that seeks to reconcile Quebec nationalism and the reality of political power; industrial expansion and the appeal to the peasant majority; and the secular and the clerical power.'[22] I could not possibly do better, in concluding this examination of the political significance of *Jean Rivard*, than to quote Bernard Proulx, whose perception of the first 'agrarian' novels is so similar to mine:

What underlies the settlement ventures, of which the agrarian novel sings the praises, is a socioeconomic project of wide scope, which is modern in terms of the youthful surge of capitalism. If today we generally see therein purely agricultural aims, it is because we are following an inattentive, unsubstantiated reading of this entire output of novels. The rural background that the first agrarian novelists chose, far from hinging on the faith that they allegedly had in virtues possessed only by agriculture, definitely corresponded to an entire range of imperatives: occupation of the territory, seizure of natural wealth, foundation of cities under francophone control, checking massive emigration, unemployment, and causes for revolt. All of this, including even the rhetoric favourable to the agricultural class, must be seen only in the more inclusive context of the foundation of a modern society, which was sought by moderates and radicals.[23]

The foundation of a modern society. In short, as Bernard Proulx has said elsewhere, in reaction against constantly anachronistic readings of these writers, 'the post-1837 liberal ideologues (and Gérin-Lajoie could be placed among the first ranks of these) marched toward us and not backwards into the past.'[24]

6
Conclusion

Jean Rivard is a work of severance. The protagonist leaves the land where he was raised and abandons his native village, despite his mother's tears and his family's derision. He breaks with the reigning prejudice against manual work. Had he remained faithful to the land his father had cleared, he would have been condemned to become a hired hand, as did so many of his contemporaries. Thus Jean Rivard breaks loose from his native parish and sets out to conquer an immense space.

Rather than let himself be moulded by the pressures of his environment, he shapes the space in his own image: he makes the parish and the church come to him. Stereotypical roles are reversed, and the church is built 'in the shadow' of his home, on his own land. In a sense, a space and a way of life are reproduced: in the middle of the wilderness, a village is built just like the one left behind. Yet that is precisely the point: it is built, it is made. It is still very different, though, since it is built better and elsewhere. Jean does not follow the beaten track, he blazes a new trail. To stay put, to fail to conquer hostile nature would mean accepting a life of confinement. So, far from getting into a rut, he is never seen with his 'feet in the furrow' like a traditional farmer. And devout though he may be, he is never seen either 'with his eyes lifted heavenward' like the stereotypical habitant with his unshakeable faith. On the contrary, Jean Rivard's eyes are constantly focused on his account book and his journal of 'operations' (338). He scrupulously 'examines his conscience' (339) – a highly revealing expression! – every night, not before the agriculturists' God but before that journal of transactions. The day-by-day ledger of his activities and operations is, in fact, *the* book, his bible.[1]

He is therefore sharply set apart from all of his acquaintances, his

Grandpré and college friends, Gustave Charmenil, and others of that ilk. He breaks with the French-Canadian isolationist, stand-pat, wait-and-see traditions. He breaks with the traditional culture of fixed routines, of life in the shadow of the village church, of farming a shrinking parcel of land. He breaks away by choosing not to be a lawyer waiting for clients who will never come. Through his life, he suggests other values. He is neither a 'settler,' a 'typical farmer,' nor a man of tradition. He is a man of change and conquest.

Jack Warwick clearly realized this when he recognized in Jean Rivard a hero who embodies the two fundamental tendencies of the French-Canadian temperament: he is courageous, independent, pragmatic, and flexible like the old voyageurs, yet anxious to put down roots and establish a secure base, like the sedentary peoples. Gérin-Lajoie's great originality lies in his application of the heroic qualities of the nomad to the life of the pioneer, and this no doubt explains this novel's lasting success.[2]

However, it must be stressed that the adventure lived out in this novel is neither exclusively nor even mostly spatial. Above all, it is economic. This novelistic hero wants to acquire space in order to become rich and live in comfort. Gérin-Lajoie therefore offers to his contemporaries the lesson that to him seems obvious: roll up your sleeves and make your own fortune. This is a method within everyone's reach, the method used by their neighbours south of the border, which has served them so well. And it must be admitted that on a largely uninhabited continent, for a population with no marketable education and lacking commercial traditions, wealth, contacts, and a state of its own, there could be no better advice than that of *Jean Rivard*: drive the frontier back and the future is yours.

The ideology expressed is profoundly American. Étienne Parent became an ardent propagandist of American virtues: careful and intelligent work, pragmatism, vigorous individualism, a thirst for success, and the exaltation of material gratification and money. It is to Gérin-Lajoie's credit that he was able to embody these values in a character and a story. Étienne Parent proposed a change of mentality, the adoption of Anglo-Saxon behaviour; his son-in-law showed, in everyday life and in concrete ways, how a young French Canadian could go about it. Through lectures and an educational novel, these two great minds of nineteenth-century Quebec both preached conversion to American values.

Critics could not, or would not, recognize this. 'I live in America, without being aware of it. And if I am unaware of it, it is because nobody ever told me about it.' 'French Canada never told itself about America,' claims influential critic Gilles Marcotte,[3] amazed that for him the word 'America' always brings to mind another world – the United States, South America – and that it is never spontaneously used in conjunction with the words that describe his part of North America. He is amazed, irritated, and disappointed that French Canada has not claimed this reality as its own. In short, in his experience of the spoken and the written word, he has come to the conclusion that the word 'America' does not belong to him: 'It immediately brings to mind a foreign reality – almost as much as old Europe does.'[4] He almost shares Jean Lemoyne's opinion that 'the invention and the shape of America are not French.'[5] Let us understand 'America' in this sentence as meaning an 'ideology of conquest, of unlimited development';[6] let us take 'French' to mean French Canadian. 'We need America and we have missed it.'[7] Jacques Brault had already expressed this in poetic terms: Quebec, 'a country longing for unlimited redskins.'[8]

The remark gives us pause. Quebec writers and story-tellers are perhaps not to blame. At least not all of them. Perhaps, on the contrary, some writers have told us the story of America. Perhaps they have helped us to discover it, its vastness, its challenge, and its opportunities. Have they perhaps not tried to make the word 'America' belong to Quebeckers? Contrary to Jean Lemoyne's opinion, perhaps Quebec writers, at least those of Gérin-Lajoie's generation, wanted 'the invention and the shape of America to be French,' that is, French Canadian, Québécois. Their works are works of conquest, of a vastness to be possessed and inhabited, of a new society to be invented. Does the responsibility not lie with critics who did not know how to read them because they themselves were insufficiently sensitive to this original form of Americanism that was being developed in the middle of the nineteenth century? Or perhaps the critics were only capable of reading them through the distorting lens of late-nineteenth- and early-twentieth-century readings, which had completely falsified the meaning of these works. How else can it be explained that a conqueror of the calibre of Jean Rivard, a pioneer of the breed of American heroes, an adventurer modelled after those of Fenimore Cooper, akin to the pragmatic founders described by Franklin and Emerson, could have become, in Quebec's literary history, a settler, a peasant, timidly traditionalist? How else can we explain that this relentless individualist described by Gérin-Lajoie, braving the huge forests of America on his own, determined to rival the continent's great

Anglo-Saxon cities, bearing with him his vision of a republic to be created, has become, for the literary establishment in both Quebec and English-speaking Canada, the brave habitant who timidly withdraws within the reassuring boundaries of his parish?

Jean Rivard has been misinterpreted and needs to be reread. If this study has helped ensure this essential rereading, if it has provided a glimpse of the rich ambiguity of this supposedly one-dimensional novel, if it stimulates a similar rereading of other works of the period, its goal will have been achieved.

Certainly, one could poke fun at the novelist's naïve optimism and take issue with the conquering spirit he brings into play. Today, we are much more tempted to put economic liberalism on trial and to believe that passionate adherence to it has helped make the world an intolerable place. A recent book by René Dumont[9] makes just such a scathing indictment of this world, painting a dark picture of unemployment, cyclical economic crises, scandalous military budgets, waste of resources, pollution, the despoilment of forests and oceans, destructive agriculture, technology devoid of conscience, chronic underdevelopment in the Third World, people made into robots. But Gérin-Lajoie and his contemporaries cannot possibly be held responsible for the subsequent exaggerations and excesses of their ideology, especially since their aim was precisely to give these economic ambitions a human face: a republic of small independent landowners, development that is concerned with nature, gradual and structured urbanization, industrialization that is harmonious and integrated with its environment, diversified and comprehensive economic activity, and an intense civic and political life that would accentuate the sense of public responsibility in all citizens.

Admittedly, this is all very naïve. But it is precisely an *ideal* that the novelist proposes, an ideal lived out by a few, but no doubt inaccessible to most. Is the American success story real? Most Americans of the time, as Thoreau expressed it so well, led 'lives of quiet desperation.'[10] However, their lives do not exclude dreams, but, rather, accentuate and exacerbate them. The life of a pioneer, a farmer, a producer, an industrialist, or the founder of a city is a dream that all can dream. In harsh reality, most are hard put to push their farm and their possessions along a bumpy road, slaves to their belongings. Once again it is the eccentric Thoreau who perhaps best perceives and describes the reality lived by men of his day:

I see young men, my townsmen, whose misfortune it is to have inherited farms, houses, barns, cattle, and farming tools; for these are more easily acquired than got rid of ... They have got to live a man's life, pushing all these things before them, and get on as well as they can. How many a poor immortal soul have I met well-nigh crushed and smothered under its load, creeping down the road of life, pushing before it a barn seventy-five feet by forty, its Augean stables never cleansed, and one hundred acres of land, tillage, mowing, pasture and wood-lot. The portionless, who struggle with no such inherited encumbrances, find it labor enough to subdue and cultivate a few cubic feet of flesh.[11]

On the whole, Thoreau is right. But his spiritual and transcendental point of view is surely not shared by the majority of his contemporaries, or even by his writer friends at Concord. 'It is of no use to argue the wants down,' Emerson, fourteen years his senior, seems to answer him with a previously cited comment, 'the philosophers have laid the greatness of man in making his wants few, but will a man content himself with a hut and a handful of dried pease?'[12] What is more, even Thoreau was not always content with his hut on the banks of Walden Pond – all the more reason for the 'portionless' to aspire to being, in turn, burdened with possessions. In this sense, nineteenth-century Americans, who are or seek to be heavily laden with possessions, are truly our contemporaries.

But Gérin-Lajoie's contemporaries, his fellow citizens, were for their part rather unencumbered: they had no prospects, with nothing to look forward to but proletarianization or unemployment in their own country, or expatriation and proletarianization in New England factories. The judicious advice that Horace Greely kept offering in the New York *Daily Tribune* during those years ('Go West, young man, go West') has found in this novel its French-Canadian counterpart, which is equally judicious in the circumstances and equally worthwhile and prophetic: 'Go to the forest, young man, and build a kingdom worthy of you.' And who knows – it is our turn to dream! – whether the face of Quebec would have been different if that advice had been better heeded, if the population had been in a better position to heed it, or if the American model had been more widely spread and put to better use? At least Quebec would thus have avoided a sorry depletion of its human resources through emigration.

This is all well and good, it will be said, but we have strayed far from literature. Not at all, in fact. *Jean Rivard* is certainly of its times: a serious, educational, reasoning work, driven by its moral aims. It is against this standard that it must be judged, and not according to present-day conventions. To reverse Gide's aphorism, bad morals do not necessarily make for good literature, and literary works – present fashion not withstanding – have not always been vehicles for unhappy consciences. We can agree that the conventions in *Jean Rivard* are somewhat removed from modern sensibility. But all writing tends toward mannerism and affectation, to standardization and to formulas; that is the price of literary recognition. And fashions change – admittedly, the 'poetic' periphrases and the stereotypical epithets used by Gérin-Lajoie may well irritate us. These days, one cannot (and would not *want* to) say 'our hero' or 'good mother' (passim) in a novel, or 'those interesting fowl' (83) when speaking of chickens, or 'that useful quadruped' (320) when referring to a cow. But how quickly have more recent mannerisms become outdated, how quickly did the conventions of the periodicals *Les Herbes rouges*[13] and *La Nouvelle Barre du jour*[14] or of any other literary movement start to age?

We should accept that gratuitousness, a fevered imagination, or even the playful suspension of reality have only recently become part of literature. Gérin-Lajoie was writing at a time when the many exclusions that, by way of purification or impoverishment, transformed belles-lettres into 'literature' had not yet been completed. A serious, didactic novel was at the time a worthwhile and acceptable project. Balzac is a good enough example of this. We should also note that a utopian like Gérin-Lajoie 'does not seek the same kind of momentary and aesthetic credibility as does the novelist.' The utopian 'is after more. He expects his reader to believe seriously and permanently in the "possible" that he describes.'[15] The result should not surprise us: seriousness, frankness, and moral conviction do not necessarily guarantee a literary masterpiece. The contrary is actually the norm. Raymond Trousson readily made this point in his assessment of the question:

> It has often been pointed out, and A. Cioranescu recently emphasized it, that no literary masterpieces have ever been produced in the utopian genre. All critics allude to the sermonizing tone, the monotony of the genre, the lack of novelistic innovation in traditional utopias ... The first modern utopia, that of More, does not go beyond this level. An omniscient narrator reports what he has seen in Utopia and his narrative is purely descriptive ... The technique is even more elementary in Campanella ... in Francis Bacon ... The reader is struck by the absence of the traditional novelistic elements in early utopian narratives: characters,

action, episodes, sudden developments, dénouement. The vision is flat, and this monotony will be repeated *ad nauseam* for two or three centuries ... From the seventeenth century on, in order to rejuvenate the genre, writers tended to combine utopia with the imaginary voyage; this time around, novelistic traits were abundant and even superabundant. Still, soon after we enter the Utopia itself, hero and story give way to dry description, and the traveller reappears only to ask for further information.[16]

Trousson asked: 'Must we admit that utopias are incompatible with the novelistic?' and answered in the affirmative. Ruyer had already identified the many difficulties faced by utopian writers when they took up their pens:

Utopia is several hobbies come together, and it is not surprising that, in this genre, alongside a few masterpieces so many mediocre and inferior works are to be found. Utopia often presupposes the combination in an author of an amateur writer and an amateur scientist or politician, of a casual novelist and a Sunday sociologist.[17]

Disparagers of utopias are therefore quick to point out that, judging from utopian narratives, the worst thing about the utopia of the future will probably be its literature!

In these conditions, we should marvel at Gérin-Lajoie's more-than-modest success. He was able to cross the personal success novel with the utopian novel, to exploit the romantic topoi of the poor student and the fatherless youth who must make his way in the world, and to integrate his contemporaries' preoccupations and the constraints of the community, while holding his sermonizing temperament in check (he is, after all, the author of a *Catechism*!) and controlling his taste for pouring out his emotions, all in order to offer us a finely developed work. It is well written and often colourful as well, if one is willing to approach it without prejudice and take the trouble to read it carefully. Gilles Marcotte claims that Gérin-Lajoie is 'the most scrupulous, the most honest, and also the most lifeless of nineteenth-century (Quebec) novelists.'[18] A harsh and unjust comment! Gérin-Lajoie knows the meaning and value of words, the weight words can wield among a repressed people, but this does not keep him from enjoying himself, from poking fun at his readers and at himself, and from often making fine use of irony. His subject is of the most serious kind; he is convinced that the destiny of his fellow citizens is at stake. However, as one gets to know his work better, the rather stern mask that tradition has imposed on him is seen to be lined with many wrinkles that reveal numerous conspiratorial winks to the reader: wrinkles of irony and of a discreet intelligence.

The most subtle irony of this work no doubt lies in its profoundly paradoxical discourse: in order to survive, to flower, to remain what they are, Quebeckers must take on another identity. Like his father-in-law, Étienne Parent, who considered nationality to be 'his life's motto,' a 'sacred trust,'[19] but nonetheless wanted his compatriots to learn from the Anglo-Saxons, Gérin-Lajoie invites Quebeckers to break with what they were in order to remain what they are! He invites his fellow citizens to break their collective suicidal habits in order to maintain their national identity. They must follow the example of the continent's conquerors – act like Jean Rivard, the American.

This is perhaps hard to take. Accepting such a reading of the novel may be too radical a challenge to common perceptions of the century. Is it possible that nineteenth-century Quebeckers were not as stupid as contemporary ideologues claim? Is it possible that they were capable of fervently dreaming and planning, preaching progress and new departures, yet doing so pragmatically and intelligently, concerned with proposing an ideal but one based on experience? Could their works have expressed a desperate thirst for conquest, possession, success, and power? But what of the leftist readings of Quebec literature and history, according to which the whole period from the defeat of the Patriotes in the 1830s to the first stirrings of the Quiet Revolution in the 1960s is nothing but clerical-bourgeois darkness, bleak agriculturalist mystification, idealization of the past, and condemnation of the present? All of these readings content themselves with paraphrasing Bishop Camille Roy: Jean Rivard as the worthy settler and farmer. They then simply see his interpretation in a negative light and go on, paradoxically, to accuse the author, Gérin-Lajoie, of contributing to Quebec's alienation and backwardness.

But, it must be repeated, reversing the moral lesson of a previous analysis without challenging that analysis does not constitute a new approach. It is a simplistic ideological reversal. Moreover, it is further evidence of a distressingly smug habit too common among the Quebec intelligentsia, who make it a practice of denigrating past generations, even when the latter have created remarkable works.

Perhaps a better solution would be to reread these works with an open mind. Indeed, the views of a foreigner who loves Quebec are no doubt appropriate here, to provide a clear look at *Jean Rivard* and its cultural significance. 'Many aspects of Quebec escape me,' exclaims Jean-Pierre Issenhuth:

> I have never quite understood why Quebeckers, for example, seem to be ashamed of their past ... I have never run into a shame of the collective past in the countries I have known, except here and in Germany. Is it shameful to have ancestors who were farmers, Catholic, poor, and uneducated? Many a German would love to have such a light burden to bear. Furthermore, the Quebec heritage is not devoid of virtues that evoke in me great admiration. In the area of books, the one to which I feel closest is an old work from Quebec. Antoine Gérin-Lajoie's *Jean Rivard* was one of the great books of my life. Gérin-Lajoie was naïve and thoroughly well-meaning? But Balzac too was naïve, as were Proust and even Stendhal, even though he was ashamed of it and tried to hide it. Michel Deguy reminds us that it is with bad morals that bus terminal-literature is written, and without some degree of naïvety, hidden or not, any creation is still-born. I therefore read *Jean Rivard*, and I realized that here an art of living to my liking had been dreamed up, a harmony among dreams, feelings, thoughts, decisions, projects, actions, the soil, the places, and the moments. Gérin-Lajoie was so right to point out that his protagonist was 'of an eminently poetic character!' A few years before *Jean Rivard* appeared in serial form in *Le Monde*, Isidore Ducasse had expressed some ideas in *Poésies* that Gérin-Lajoie would not have repudiated. He had prepared his arrival. Today, if Quebec has a future, it cannot be in amnesia: it has behind it, in its literature, the art of living that the planet lacks most.[20]

Is this appraisal excessive? Perhaps. But this excess serves only as a counterweight to all the negative judgments about a crucial novel in Quebec literature and about a literary generation that deserves far greater recognition.

Notes

Foreword

1 The name 'Patriotes' was given after 1826 to the Parti canadien and to the popular movement that led to the rebellions of 1837–8 in Lower Canada. The primarily francophone party, led mainly by members of the liberal professions and small-scale merchants, was widely supported by farmers, day labourers and craftsmen.

Introduction

1 Herman Melville, *Moby Dick, or the White Whale*, 55. Full descriptions of the works cited will be found in the Bibliography.
2 *Relations des jésuites*, I (1611–36), 15.
3 See Jack Warwick, *The Long Journey: Literary Themes of French Canada*.
4 See Marcel Rioux, *Une saison à la Renardière*.
5 Ernest Gagnon, *L'homme d'ici*, 157.
6 Jacques Godbout, 'Place Cliché,' *Liberté* 138: 23, 33.
7 Jean Larose, *La petite noirceur*, 104.
8 See Pierre Vadeboncoeur, *Trois essais sur l'insignifiance*.
9 Benoît Melançon, 'La littérature québécoise et l'Amérique. Prolégomènes et bibliographie,' *Études françaises* 26 (1990), 65–108.
10 See, for example, André Major's condemnation: 'The Decline of America' in Al Purdy, ed., *The New Romans: Candid Opinions of the U.S.*, 141–3.
11 Guildo Rousseau, *L'image des États-Unis dans la littérature québécoise (1775–1930)*, 11.
12 Paul-André Bourque, 'L'Américanité du roman québécois,' *Études littéraires* 8 (1975), 9–19.

13 Ronald Sutherland, 'Les États-Unis et la littérature québécoise,' in Claude Savary, ed., *Les rapports culturels entre le Québec et les États-Unis*, 202-9.
14 P.A. Bourque, ibid.
15 See Camille Roy, *Manuel d'histoire de la littérature canadienne de langue française*, 75, and Camille Roy, *Histoire de la littérature canadienne*, 106.
16 René Dionne, *Antoine Gérin-Lajoie, homme de lettres*, 316.
17 Mary Kandiuk, *French-Canadian Authors: A Bibliography of Their Works and of English-Language Criticism*, xii.
18 Henry J. Morgan, *Bibliotheca Canadensis or a Manual of Canadian Literature*, 137-8.
19 See articles on Henri Gérin-Lajoie and on Antoine Gérin-Lajoie's son Léon Gérin, in Henry David Morgan, *The Canadian Men and Women of the Time. A Hand-Book of Canadian Biography*.
20 See, for example, William A. Robb Kerr, *A Short Anthology of French-Canadian Prose Literature*; George Alfred Klinck, *Allons Gai* and *En Avant*; A.J.M. Smith, *The Oxford Book of Canadian Verse*.
21 Lorne Pierce, *An Outline of Canadian Literature (French and English)*, 20-1.
22 Ian Forbes Fraser, *The Spirit of French Canada: A Study of the Literature*, 163.
23 Norah Story, *The Oxford Companion to Canadian History and Literature*, 269.
24 Archibald MacMechan, *The Headwaters of Canadian Literature*, 82.
25 Ibid.
26 See Antoine Sirois, 'Deux littératures,' *Canadian Literature* 43 (1970), 36-41; René Dionne, 'Étude. *Jean Rivard* et son auteur,' postface to Antoine Gérin-Lajoie, *Jean Rivard, le défricheur, suivi de Jean Rivard, économiste*, 370-90; Martin Dubé, '*Jean Rivard, le défricheur*, récit de la vie réelle?' *Incidences* 4 (1980), 19-36; Rosanna Furgiuele, *Mythe et démythification. Une lecture idéologique de Jean Rivard et de Trente arpents*.
27 Claude Duchet, 'Réflexions sur les rapports du roman et de la société,' in *Roman et société*, 66.
28 Richard Hoggart, *The Literary Imagination and the Study of Society*.
29 Susan Rubin Suleiman, *Le roman à thèse*. The English version is called *Authoritarian Fictions. The Ideological Novel as a Literary Genre*.
30 Duchet, 'Réflexions ...,' 67.
31 Jacques Dubois, *L'assommoir de Zola: société, discours, idéologie*, especially chapter 4.
32 Ibid.
33 Karl Mannheim, *Idéologie et utopie*. Louis Wirth, the author of the preface of the 1936 English edition (which was subsequently used for the 1956 French translation), considers this the special contribution of Mannheim, who was

the true founder of the sociology of knowledge. The first edition appeared in German in 1929.
34 Duchet, 'Refléxions ...,' 66.
35 Jacques Dubois, *L'institution de la littérature*, 62.
36 Dubois, 'Code, texte, métatexte,' *Littérature* 12 (1973), 9.
37 Michel Foucault, *L'archéologie du savoir*, 34.
38 The expression is from Pierre Barberis, 'À propos de Lux: la vraie force des choses (sur l'idéologie des *Châtiments*),' *Littérature* 1 (1971), 105.
39 Jean-Paul Sartre, *Questions de méthode*, 161–2.
40 Dubois, *L'assommoir de Zola*, 12.
41 Pierre Machery, *Pour une théorie de la production littéraire*, 156.
42 Vida Bruce, 'Introduction,' in A. Gérin-Lajoie, *Jean Rivard*, 10.
43 Sir Philip Sidney, *An Apology for Poetry, or the Defense of Poesy*, 101, 108.
44 Georges Duveau, *Sociologie de l'utopie et autres essais*, 19–20.
45 *Lord Durham's Report*, 146.
46 See Yves Roby, 'Un Québec émigré aux États-Unis. Bilan historiographique,' in Claude Savary, ed., *Les rapports culturels entre le Québec et les États-Unis*, 106.
47 Pierre Barberis, *Balzac, une mythologie réaliste*, 174.
48 Marc Angenot and Darko Suvin, 'Thèses sur la "sociologie de la littérature,"' *Littérature* 44 (1981), 122.
49 Obviously, we all build on the foundations laid by others. My numerous debts will be recognized at appropriate points in this study.
50 Joseph-Gabriel Barthe, *Souvenirs d'un demi-siècle ou Mémoires pour servir à l'histoire contemporaine*, 206. Barthe was one of the first to draw attention to this family as an entity: '[Gérin-Lajoie] that untiring worker, who was carried off by an untimely death, had devoted his intelligence and his heart to his country, and, with his relatives, was part of an intellectual group that has not been surpassed by any other in this country. It must be remembered that its leader was somebody like Étienne Parent, with Gérin-Lajoie, Gélinas and Benjamin Sulte coming after him to keep up the traditions of one of the founders of our French-Canadian press, and to do it the greatest honour in the past half-century.' If we add the grandson Léon Gérin, the first French-Canadian sociologist, to the leader, Étienne Parent, and his relative Gérin-Lajoie, we have three intellectuals of unusual vigour who exerted a profound influence. The history of this family deserves to be written.
51 Gabriel Dussault, *Le curé Labelle. Messianisme, utopie et colonisation au Québec, 1850–1900*.
52 Norman Séguin, *Agriculture et colonisation au Québec, aspects historiques*.
53 On this question, Guildo Rousseau's book, *L'image des États-Unis dans la lit-*

térature québécoise (1775–1930), has cleared the ground and has opened up many new fields of research.
54 'Documents on propaganda for the United States are almost completely lacking. We can partially reconstruct it with the help of literature. In this sense, Lorenzo Surprenant's remarks in *Maria Chapdelaine* have a rare testimonial value in their realism' (Pierre Savard, *Jules-Paul Tardivel*, 205, note 2). But in the absence of documents, what is the basis for assuming that the remarks are realistic and have a testimonial value?

Chapter 1: The Genesis of a Discourse

1 Jacques Dubois, *L'assommoir de Zola*, 102.
2 René Dionne, *Antoine Gérin-Lajoie, homme de lettres*.
3 H.-R. Casgrain, *Antoine Gérin-Lajoie d'après ses Mémoires*, 32–56.
4 Casgrain, 103–4.
5 Léon Gérin, *Antoine Gérin-Lajoie. La résurrection d'un patriote canadien*, 92–3.
6 Casgrain, 103–4.
7 Casgrain, 32, 34. J.-G. Barthe believes that this desire for wealth was the main motivation behind this aborted trip, which was originally a two-year project. See J.-G. Barthe, *Souvenirs d'un demi-siècle*, 269–70.
8 Casgrain, 56.
9 Casgrain, 44.
10 'I had never before prayed with such unction and fervour' (Casgrain, 56).
11 Dionne, 65.
12 Claude Lessard, *Le séminaire de Nicolet, 1803–1969*, 235.
13 Lessard, 235.
14 Lessard, 146.
15 Lessard, 29.
16 Léon Gérin, 113.
17 Cyrille Étienne Légaré, 'J.-B.-A. Ferland,' reprinted with the title 'Notice sur l'auteur,' in J.-B.-A. Ferland, *La France dans l'Amérique du Nord* II, v. *La France dans l'Amérique du Nord* is the third edition (and the one cited) of Ferland's major work, first published under the title *Cours d'histoire du Canada*. The new title, as we will see, in reality better suits the author's North American viewpoint.
18 Letter to Monsignor Signay, Bishop of Quebec, 20 June 1840, in J.-A.-I. Douville, *Histoire du collège-séminaire de Nicolet, 1803–1903*, I, 278.
19 Father Harper's reply to Monsignor Signay's letter of 19 August 1841, in Douville, 285–6. The bursar's concern was primarily economic; his bishop's concern was no doubt the same but pastoral as well. The college historian,

Monsignor Douville, states that Monsignor Signay wanted to introduce 'the English language among teachers and students in a more practical way,' since he 'felt the need to spread English among the priests of his diocese, in order to respond to the ministry's needs among the mixed populations of the Eastern Townships and of some other areas' (Douville, 278).

20 Douville, 292.
21 A. Gérin-Lajoie, 'L'abbé J.-B.-A. Ferland,' *Le Foyer canadien* 3 (1865), xxx–xxxi.
22 The few pages that Ferland devotes to these events are linked to his narrative by the fact that Phipps, who attacked Quebec in 1690, was a friend of the Mathers and that the embarrassment caused by this business of witchcraft in all likelihood stopped him from attacking Quebec again in 1692.
23 Ferland, *La France ...*, I, 208, note 2.
24 'The natives, finding the word *English* too difficult to pronounce, instead said *yingees*; hence came the word Yankees, given to the English in the northern United States' (Ferland, *La France ...*, 153).
25 Ferland, *Observations sur un ouvrage intitulé 'Histoire du Canada, etc,' par M. l'abbé Brasseur de Bourbourg*, 4.
26 Ferland, *Notes sur les registres de Notre-Dame de Québec*, 34.
27 Ferland, *La France ...*, I, 186–7.
28 Léon Gérin, 19.
29 Douville, 299–300.
30 Dionne, 98.
31 Dionne, 133 ff.
32 Jean-Charles Falardeau, *Étienne Parent, 1802–1874*, 26, 11. The following Étienne Parent quotations are taken from Falardeau's collection; the numbers in parentheses refer to pages.
33 The fourth lecture, 'Reflections on Our Popular Education System, on Education in General and on the Legislative Means to Provide It,' is far more selective, being dedicated to criticism of one law and to the short-term reforms that the legislator could make to further the education of the people. As for the fifth lecture, 'About the Priest and Spiritualism in Their Connection with Society,' it is addressed particularly to the clergy, inviting it, by all kinds of historical and moral considerations, to reform itself and to support the general movement toward freedom and social progress.
34 Étienne Parent, *Discours prononcés par M. É. Parent devant l'Institut canadien de Montréal*.
35 Falardeau, 26. Étienne Parent has been readily seen as 'a sort of spiritual father for the nation' (Marcel Cadieux and Paul Tremblay, 'Étienne Parent, un théoricien de notre nationalisme,' *L'Action nationale* 13 [1939], 204–5).
36 F. Cooper, *The Chainbearer, or the Littlepage Manuscripts*, 85. As for Gérin-

Lajoie, he textually took up, in his novel, the terms used by Parent and Cooper in their eulogy: 'From dawn until dusk, our two pioneers made the forest resound with the sound of that useful instrument that might with good reason be considered the emblem and tool of civilization' (*Jean Rivard*, 33).

37 See Robert Major, 'Étienne Parent, utopiste,' *Mélanges de littérature canadienne-française et québécoise offerts à Réjean Robidoux*, 188–203.
38 A study of Parent's numerous borrowings from Tocqueville's work is needed. His lectures seem deeply marked by his reading of *De la démocratie en Amérique*, right down to the details of the phraseology.
39 C.-F. de Volney, *Tableau du climat et du sol des États-Unis d'Amérique, suivi d'Éclaircissements sur la Floride, sur la colonie française à Scioto, sur quelques colonies canadiennes et sur les sauvages*, ii. The first edition appeared in 1803.
40 So as not to overload the text, the quotations taken from *Jean Rivard* will be followed by a number in parentheses referring to the page in the one-volume 1977 edition that I have used throughout this work: A. Gérin-Lajoie, *Jean Rivard le défricheur (récit de la vie réelle)*, followed by *Jean Rivard, économiste*, postface by René Dionne. It reproduces the original two-volume edition (1874 and 1876) by J.B. Rolland. On occasion, I will cite the first edition in serial form of each of the titles: *Jean Rivard, le défricheur canadien*, in *Les Soirées canadiennes* 2 (1862), 65–319, and *Jean Rivard, économiste*, in *Le Foyer canadien* 2 (1864), 15–371.
41 The passage that Gérin-Lajoie cites here is taken from C.-F. de Volney, *Tableau*, 373–7.
42 H.R. Casgrain, 'Biographie de Gérin-Lajoie. Fragment,' *Mémoires de la Société royale du Canada*, 3 (1885), 57.
43 Volney, *Tableau*, 356. Elsewhere Volney adds: 'According to the accounts of the Americans and the *Canadians* [italics in the text], the Illinois and Upper Louisiana settlements were in a similar state; discouragement, apathy, poverty were equally prevalent among the French settlers of Kaskaskias, Cahokias, La Prairie du Rocher, St Louis, etc.' (Volney, *Tableau*, 366).
44 I am not claiming that Volney is the first to establish this parallel. Volney himself cites the travellers who preceded him – Alexander Mackenzie among others – whose accounts contain certain elements of this portrait (in particular when Mackenzie talks about his half-Native Canadian rowers). Moreover, the first French administrators and the missionaries deplored the nomadism of the French in Canada and their debauchery (see Jack Warwick's *The Long Journey*). Volney initiates the topos for the purposes of this study.
45 A. de Tocqueville, *Oeuvres complètes*, I, 1, *De la démocratie en Amérique*. See the

long notes in Chapter X, second part, and in particular pages 348–50. After summarizing Volney's thought, Tocqueville adds: 'In Canada where the intellectual difference between the two races is far less pronounced, I saw for myself the Englishman, master of business and industry in Canada, expand on all sides, and confine the Frenchman within too narrow limits. Likewise, in Louisiana, almost all commercial and industrial activity is concentrated in the hands of the Anglo-Americans' (349, note 19).

46 *De la démocratie en Amérique* had been published in 1835 and 1840; 'Quinze jours dans le désert' had been published by Beaumont in the *Revue des Deux Mondes*, 1 December 1860; Beaumont had finally published, in 1861, *Oeuvres et correspondance inédites d'Alexis de Tocqueville* in two volumes. Thus, Gérin-Lajoie could have read the Tocqueville texts I am citing before the publication of *Jean Rivard*.
47 Tocqueville, *Démocratie*, 320.
48 Tocqueville, *Démocratie*, 426.
49 Tocqueville, *Oeuvres complètes*, V, 1, *Voyages en Sicile et aux États-Unis*, 352–3.
50 Tocqueville, *Voyages*, 358.
51 Tocqueville, *Voyages*, 378–9.
52 Maurice Sand, the son of George Sand, made the same remarks thirty years later when he visited Canada with Prince Napoleon (see Maurice Sand, *Six mille lieues à toute vapeur*).
53 Tocqueville, *Voyages*, 78.
54 Tocqueville, *Voyages*, 82.
55 Tocqueville, *Voyages*, 214.
56 Tocqueville, *Voyages*, 216.
57 Cited by Jacques Vallée, *Tocqueville au Bas-Canada*, 108.
58 Tocqueville, *Voyages*, 257. Making a global comparison of Canadians and Americans, Tocqueville writes: 'In short, this race of men seemed to us inferior to the Americans in know-how, but superior when it came to noble feelings. One does not, in any respect, sense here that *mercantile* spirit that appears in every action and every speech of the Americans' (*Voyages*, 214; 'mercantile' is italicized in the text).
59 One of hundreds of examples: Fenimore Cooper, in the last volume of the 'Leather-Stocking Tales' (*The Prairie*, 438), settles in a few words, in his final chapter, the fate of his various characters: '[Paul] soon became a land-holder, then a prosperous cultivator of the soil, and shortly after a town officer ... he went on, from step to step, until his wife enjoyed the maternal delight of seeing her children placed far beyond the danger of returning to that state from which both their parents had issued. Paul is actually at this moment a member of the lower branch of the legislature of the State where he has long

resided.' There you have, in a few words, the life of Jean Rivard: *land-holder, prosperous cultivator, town-officer, member of the legislature.*
60 Tocqueville, *Démocratie*, 295.
61 *Le Journal de Québec*, 12 July 1855, cited by Fernand Ouellet, *Histoire économique et sociale du Québec, 1760–1850*, II, 481.
62 Ouellet, II, 481.
63 Ferland, in the abbé Racine, *Le Canadien émigrant*, 1851, cited by Ouellet, 481.
64 The first part of Guildo Rousseau's book, *L'image des États-Unis dans la littérature québécoise 1775–1930*, is teeming with varied information on the different aspects of this fascination. However, Rousseau is concerned with *explicit* references to the United States in Quebec literature, so that Gérin-Lajoie's work hardly merits his attention. The presence of the United States in this novel is, in effect, of another order.
65 See Yolande Lavoie, *L'émigration des Québécois aux États-Unis de 1840 à 1930*.
66 Benoît Brouillette, *La pénétration du continent américain par les Canadiens français 1763–1846. Traitants, explorateurs, missionnaires*.
67 Gustave Lanctôt, 'Introduction,' in Gustave Lanctôt et al., *Les Canadiens français et leurs voisins du Sud*, viii.
68 Jean Bruchési, 'Influences américaines sur la politique du Bas-Canada, 1820–1867,' in Lanctôt, *Les Canadiens français*, 187–235.
69 Fernand Dumont, 'Quelques réflexions d'ensemble,' in Fernand Dumont et al., eds, *Idéologies au Canada français, 1850–1900*, 3.
70 See, for example, his articles of 20 July 1835, 11 July 1836, and 16 January 1837 in *Le Canadien*, and his debate with *La Minerve* (late 1836) and the *Vindicator* (March–April 1837) in *Le Canadien*.
71 See Casgrain, *Antoine Gérin-Lajoie*, 97, and Dionne, 190–1.

Chapter 2: Paratext and Plot: What Happens in *Jean Rivard*?

1 See Chapter 3 of my study *'Jean Rivard' ou l'art de réussir* for a critical examination of the novel's traditional reception.
2 See the studies of Claude Duchet, '*La fille abandonnée* et *La bête humaine*, éléments de titrologie romanesque,' *Littérature* 12 (1973), 49–73; Charles Grivel, 'Puissance du titre,' in Charles Grivel, *Production de l'intérêt romanesque, 1870–1880*, 166–81; and Gérard Genette, *Seuils*, 54–97. For a good illustration of what may be gleaned from a title, see François Gallays' '*Les îles de la nuit*: prestige d'un titre,' *Incidences* 2–3 (1979), 23–5.
3 Duchet, 49.
4 Ibid.
5 Yves Dostaler, *Les infortunes du roman dans le Québec du XIXe siècle*.

6 Pierre Fontanier, *Les figures du discours*, 296.
7 This distinction between an identifying apposition and a descriptive apposition is taken from R.L. Wagner and J. Pinchon, *Grammaire du français classique et moderne*, 81.
8 Ibid.
9 'Canadian,' in the context, means in fact 'French Canadian.' Up until a few generations ago, French Canadians called themselves 'Canadiens.' English speakers were 'les Anglais.' Indeed, different historical circumstances have, over the years, brought about a distinctive process of ambiguous identification. The early settlers called themselves 'les habitants,' to distinguish themselves from the French administrators, whose stay was temporary; then, 'Canadiens,' to distinguish themselves from the British conquerors, whose stay was also hopefully to be short-lived; then 'Canadiens français,' when the English also started calling themselves 'Canadians' and not only British subjects; and finally, 'Québécois,' after having painfully realized that the French presence in Canada was to all practical purposes reduced to one stronghold, the territory of the province of Quebec (see Robert Major, 'Notes sur l'identité nationale et la fortune d'un vocable,' *Contemporary French Civilization*).
10 A. Buies, *L'Outaouais supérieur*, 121.
11 A letter dated 8 January 1882, to Rameau de Saint-Père, quoted by Gabriel Dussault, *Le curé Labelle*, 119.
12 Dussault, 163.
13 Samuel Eliot Morison and Henry Steele Commager, *The Growth of the American Republic*, II, 152 ff.
14 Tocqueville, *Démocratie*, 295.
15 Maurice Grévisse, *Le bon usage*, 274.
16 Tocqueville, *Voyages*, 353.
17 Dussault, 7, 184.
18 Tocqueville, *Voyages*, 353.
19 C.-M. Ducharme, *Ris et croquis*, 118.
20 Duchet, 56.
21 This aspect of the novel clearly has other functions. Gustave Charmenil is in effect Gérin-Lajoie unburdening himself, as in his *Mémoires*. In a way, an autobiographical function has been added to this 'commercial' aspect. However, Gustave's letters serve a primarily structural purpose. Obviously, the author is seeking a contrast between frivolity and waste (Gustave and urban society) as opposed to seriousness and productivity (Jean in the forest). This structure, more clever than it first seems, will be examined in the analysis of the novel's utopian dimension.

22 The title that gives rise to this indignation is 'Potash and pearlash'' (Chapter XIV, first edition, 1862). The reader might recognize as a recollection of the author's school-days his pompous and ironic borrowing from a speech of Cicero (the first oration against Cataline): 'Quo usque tandem abutere, Catalina, patientia nostra.'
23 These claims can even be used in a playful way – 'The truth obliges us also to tell the reader in the strictest confidence, that there was in the house next door a beautiful young woman' (25) – or to obtain a comic effect – 'But since I promised to tell the truth, the whole truth, I should not omit mentioning here an evil that lurks in the woods ... I mean mosquitos' (84).
24 The reader is aware of Roman Jakobson's observation: 'The classicists, the sentimentalists, in part the romantics, even the 'realists' of the nineteenth century, to a large extent the decadents, and finally the futurists, the expressionists, etc., have often emphatically asserted that faithfulness to reality, maximum probability, in a word realism, is the basic principle of their aesthetic program' (Roman Jakobson, 'Du réalisme artistique,' in Tzevetan Todorov, *Théorie de la littérature. Textes des formalistes russes*, 99).
25 Stanislas Drapeau, *Études sur les développements de la colonisation du Bas-Canada depuis dix ans (1851–1861)*, 124–5. Drapeau's studies are chock-full of statistics: on population, cultivated and uncultivated land, different types of production, the value of goods and land, the exploitation of mines, etc. One must not, 'in a presentation of this type, dread details,' he says to the reader (14). But, oddly enough, he refers to *Jean Rivard* for 'reflexions or data of a striking accuracy'!
26 Arthur Saint-Pierre, 'La Littérature sociale canadienne-française avant la Confédération,' *Mémoires et comptes rendus de la Société royale du Canada*, third series, vol. 44, section 1 (1950), 67–94. To his regret, Saint-Pierre states that, according to his research, Le Play had expounded his method in *Les ouvriers européens*, which was published in 1855 and was included in the *Catalogue de la Bibliothèque du Parlement* of 1857, and that Gérin-Lajoie thus consulted or could have consulted it. If Gérin-Lajoie cannot be credited with the invention of this method, it must at least be recognized, according to Saint-Pierre, that he was one of the first to make good use of it. The reader can find in his novel the same attributes as in Le Play's monographs: serious research, findings based on field work, good faith, a concern for precision and accuracy, accumulation of revealing facts, presentation of the development budget. 'If *Jean Rivard* is not a manual, if it is hardly a novel, it is undeniably a monograph, a novel-like monograph, even before such a term was invented' (Saint-Pierre, 82).
27 See Chapter 1, note 50.

28 'There are certain tendencies that are condemned by the reason and by the universal conscience of mankind, but answer to the particular needs of the time in American society. It only half-heartedly disapproves of these tendencies and sometimes it praises them. I will make special mention of the love of wealth and secondary tendencies that are associated with it. In order to clear, make fertile, and transform this vast uninhabited continent that is his domain, the American needs the daily pressure of an invigorating passion; thus this passion for riches is never censured in America, and, as long as it does not go beyond the limits prescribed by public order, it is honoured. Americans call noble and praiseworthy what our forefathers in the Middle Ages called abject greed' (Tocqueville, *Démocratie*, 243–4).
29 Geneviève Idt, 'Fonction rituelle du métalangage dans les préfaces hétérographes,' in *Littérature* 27 (1977), 67.
30 Henri Mitterand, 'La préface et ses lois: avant-propos,' *Le discours du roman*, 32.
31 Jacques Derrida, 'Hors-livre,' in *La dissémination*, passim.
32 Susan Suleiman, *Authoritarian Fictions*, 188.
33 Tocqueville, *Démocratie*, 245.
34 The value of the louis is that established by Dussault (*Le Curé Labelle*, 55).
35 *Mélanges religieux*, 11 May 1847; my italics.
36 Simon Lesage, 'Historique de la colonisation dans la Province de Québec,' in *Rapport du Congrès de colonisation 1898*, 101.
37 Henri Lessard, 'Le recrutement des colons,' in *Le problème de la colonisation au Canada français*, 131.
38 Drapeau, *Études sur les développements de la colonisation* , 199–201.
39 Tocqueville, *Démocratie*, 95.
40 My italics. I must stress again that this novel, like the lectures given by Étienne Parent, is about changing national habits: becoming the other, adopting the mentality of another people.
41 The distribution of all the other epigraphs, the three found in *The Pioneer* and the eight (out of twenty-three chapters) in the *Economist*, is consistent: under the roman numeral for the chapter comes its title, then the epigraph.
42 Maurice Lemire, *Jean Rivard d'Antoine Gérin-Lajoie, un plan de conquête économique*, 66.
43 Étienne Parent, 'Du travail chez l'homme,' in Falardeau, *Étienne Parent*, 149.
44 See Bernard Dupriez, *Gradus. Les procédés littéraires*, 105–6.
45 L.-M. Darveau, *Nos hommes de lettres*, 221.
46 This fact was quite evident for contemporaries who knew the American situation, but Tocqueville, writing for a French public, felt the need to emphasize it: 'An erroneous notion is generally entertained that the wilds of America

are peopled by European emigrants who annually disembark upon the coasts of the New World, while the American population increases and multiplies upon the soil their forefathers tilled. On the contrary, the European settler arrives in the United States without friends and often without resources; in order to subsist, he is obliged to work for hire, and he rarely proceeds beyond that large industrial belt that adjoins the ocean. The bush cannot possibly be cleared without capital or credit; and the body must be accustomed to the rigours of a new climate before it can be exposed in the midst of the forest. It is thus the Americans themselves who daily quit their birthplace to acquire extensive domains in a remote region' (Tocqueville, *Démocratie*, 293).

47 This recalls Emerson's description of wealth as opportunism: 'Wealth is in applications of mind to nature; and the art of getting rich consists not in industry, much less in saving, but in a better order, in timeliness, in being at the right spot. One man has stronger arms or longer legs; another sees by the course of streams and growth of markets where land will be wanted, makes a clearing to the river, goes to sleep and wakes up rich' (R.W. Emerson, 'Wealth,' *The Complete Works of R.W. Emerson*, VI, *Conduct of Life*, 86). In this sense Jean Rivard fully deserves his wealth, since he was intelligent enough to select the right place at the right time. And he did not fall asleep on the job.

48 Tocqueville, *Démocratie*, 194.

49 'It would seem as if every imagination in the United States were bent upon inventing means of increasing the wealth and satisfying the wants of the public. The most enlightened inhabitants of each township constantly use their knowledge to discover new truths that may increase general prosperity; and if they have made any such discoveries, they eagerly surrender them to the mass of the people ... The free institutions that the inhabitants of the United States possess, and the political rights of which they make so much use, remind every citizen, constantly and in a thousand ways, that he lives in society. Every instant they impress upon his mind the notion that it is the duty as well as the interest of men to make themselves useful to their fellow creatures; and as he sees no particular grounds for animosity to them, since he is never either their master or their slave, his heart readily leans to the side of kindness. Men attend to the interests of the public, first by necessity, afterwards by choice; what was intentional becomes instinctive, and by dint of working for the good of one's fellow citizens, the habit and the taste for serving them are at length acquired' (Tocqueville, *Démocratie*, 112).

50 Casgrain, *Antoine Gérin-Lajoie d'après ses Mémoires*, 103-4.

51 Ibid.

52 Léon Gérin, 96-7.

Notes to pages 88–94   219

53 Casgrain, 114.
54 Léon Gérin, 96–7.
55 Dionne, *Antoine Gérin-Lajoie, homme de lettres*, 213–20.
56 *Catalogue de la Bibliothèque du Parlement. Ouvrages relatifs à l'Amérique. Brochures et manuscrits. Index des auteurs et des matières*, VIII, 1075–1896.
57 Perry Miller et al., *Major Writers of America*, I, 119. In the Parliamentary Library Catalogue, besides the ten-volume edition of Franklin's works, a separate edition of *Poor Richard* is listed (I, 250).
58 Benjamin Franklin, *The Works of Benjamin Franklin*, II, 92–103. In my text, the numbers in parentheses following the letters *BF* refer to the pages of this volume.
59 Jean Rivard's first two secrets – the choice of a good piece of land and good health – are outside factors, and are dealt with in two short, five-line paragraphs. What matters is his way of life, on which he lays great emphasis.
60 William Charvat, *Emerson's American Lecture Engagements*.
61 R.W. Emerson, letter dated 7 January 1852 to the chief editor of *The Commonwealth* (Boston), in Ralph L. Rusk, *The Letters of Ralph Waldo Emerson*, IV (1848–1855), 270.
62 See Bessie D. Howard, 'The First French Estimate of Emerson,' *New England Quarterly* 10 (1937), 447–63.
63 Rusk, VI, 311.
64 Léon Gérin, 91–2.
65 Charvat, 25–7.
66 I have been unable to discover whether he also tried to meet Emerson. Gérin-Lajoie's United States journal has been lost, and a thorough search of Emerson's works and of his manuscripts in the Houghton Library (Harvard) and the Free Public Library in Concord turned up no evidence. But Emerson did not usually note his meetings: 'It is remarkable how little is recorded of his company in his journals,' remark the editors of his work (Emerson, *Complete Works*, VI, *Conduct of Life*, 26, note 2).
67 *La Minerve*, 24 (23 April 1852), 2.
68 *Montreal Gazette*, 67 (21 April 1852), 2.
69 *Daily News/Montreal Transcript*, 16 (20 April 1852), 2.
70 *Daily News*, 16 (22 April 1852), 2.
71 *Daily News*, 16 (24 April 1852), 2.
72 *The Pilot*, 8 (24 April 1852), 2.
73 Moreover, later on in 1858, when Gérin-Lajoie was a librarian in Toronto, Emerson was to give a lecture (22 December 1858) with a title very reminiscent of *Jean Rivard*: 'Laws of Success' (Charvat, 27).
74 Emerson, *Works*, VI.

75 Emerson, *Works*, 47.
76 Brooks Atkinson, 'Introduction,' *Selected Writings of Ralph Waldo Emerson*, xi.

Chapter 3: Intertextuality I: Jean Rivard's Library

1 Laurent Mailhot, 'Bibliothèques imaginaires: le livre dans quelques romans québécois,' *Études françaises* XVIII (1983), 82–3.
2 See *La Minerve*, 14 May 1847.
3 P.-J.-O. Chauveau, *Charles Guérin*, 54.
4 Maurice Blanchot, *L'entretien infini*, 45. The term 'désoeuvrement' is a play on 'lack of work' (idleness) and 'lack of [literary] works.'
5 Washington Irving, 'The Mutability of Literature. A Colloquy in Westminster Abbey,' in *Representative Essays, Selected from the Series of Prose Masterpieces from Modern Essayists*, 3.
6 F. Scott Fitzgerald, *The Great Gatsby*, 45–6.
7 Gustave Flaubert, *Emma Bovary*, I, 6.
8 Umberto Eco, *The Name of the Rose*. In this fascinating novel, the library is the domain of a blind man, the supreme reader; not only is the library a coded labyrinth and the murder scene, but a book is the murder weapon.
9 Montaigne, *Essais*, III, 50.
10 Philippe Hamon, 'La bibliothèque dans le livre,' *Interférences* 11 (January–June, 1980), 9.
11 It is worth noting that Jean Rivard's choice has a lot of merit, quite apart from the meanings I will examine here. According to Marthe Robert, who is cited approvingly by Laurent Mailhot, *Robinson Crusoe* and *Don Quixote* originated the Western novelistic tradition. André Malraux thought that only three books remained true for those who had been in prison and concentration camps: *Robinson Crusoe*, *Don Quixote*, and *The Idiot* (of Dostoyevski) . *The Idiot*, of course, had not yet been written when Jean Rivard made his choice. Much could be made of Gérin-Lajoie's critical acumen as his character heads off to the equivalent of a labour camp.
12 I am referring here to the other travel narratives mentioned in *Jean Rivard*. Obviously, *Robinson Crusoe* is a novel. But it has the peculiarity of being the most prosaic, down-to-earth, and intentionally banal work that one could imagine, especially in its evocation of the most perilous adventures. Therein lies its originality at the time, and its subsequent renown as a founding work of the realist novelistic tradition. What is more, Defoe's contemporaries were convinced that they were reading an authentic narrative. In a curious reversal of the problem later faced by Gérin-Lajoie, Defoe had a hard time convincing others that his book was not a 'true-life narrative,' but a novel.

13 Chauveau, 59.
14 J.-J. Rousseau, *Émile, ou de l'éducation*, 238. *Robinson Crusoe*, published in 1719, was translated into French the following year.
15 This will be shown in another way and in more detail in the next chapter on utopia.
16 No one has done a better job of it than Ian Watt, to whose book *The Rise of the Novel* I am greatly indebted.
17 The edition cited is Daniel Defoe, *The Best Known Works of Daniel Defoe* (New York, 1942), which includes *Life and Adventures of Robinson Crusoe*, *The Further Adventures of Robinson Crusoe*, as well as *A Journal of the Plague Year*. Quotations will be indicated in this way.
18 Watt, 91.
19 Falardeau, *Étienne Parent*, 122.
20 For the benefit of students of history, the novel's chronology situates this event around 20 February 1695.
21 It would seem this refers to the *Histoire populaire de Napoléon 1er, suivie des anecdotes impériales, par un ancien officier de la garde*. Two-thirds of this book is dedicated to Napoleon's public life, and the last third to anecdotes about the emperor's private life ('besides the hero, we also show the private man, the husband, the father, the friend ... the protector' [234]). It ends with a summary of what Napoleon left to France and Europe, his only treasures 'brought into the light of day' (319).
22 Léon Gérin (20–1) cites his father's journal: 'During the winter of that same year [1842], the students organized themselves and formed a small regiment of about sixty soldiers and ten officers. They all had painted wooden guns that were perfect imitations, and sabres, swords, helmets, etc. I was named general. I made them march on parade from time to time. I had drawn up very strict rules. Those who broke them were brought before a court-martial, at which I presided. They chose a lawyer; the court also had a lawyer. We sat under the trees in the countryside, as Saint Louis once had. Almost the whole community attended our sessions. We often marched under arms out into the countryside with a very well organized band alongside the regiment.'

Claude Lessard, the historian of the Nicolet seminary, recalling that Gérin-Lajoie started the first militia corps at Nicolet (1842–4), noted that there was little military activity as such at the seminary: 'It was only twenty years later, at a time of agitation and fear of an American invasion, that a second battalion was formed: the Sons of Chateauguay' (Lessard, 367). It thus seems that it was the presence of Gérin-Lajoie, the general, president of the court-martial and an excellent organizer, that was the determining factor.
23 Jean Tulard, *Le mythe de Napoléon*, 68.

24 Victor Hugo, 'Lui,' in *Les orientales*, *Oeuvres complètes*, III, 602. The first edition of *Les orientales* appeared in 1829. 'Napoleon, dark and dazzling, still stands at the threshold of the century.'
25 Tulard, 44.
26 See Maurice Descotes, *La légende de Napoléon et les écrivains français du XIXe siècle*.
27 Hugo, in a letter to Charles de Lacretelle, 3 January 1848, *Oeuvres complètes*, VII, 745.
28 Tulard, 77.
29 Descotes, 266.
30 Chateaubriand, *De Buonaparte et des Bourbons*, quoted by Tulard, 48.
31 Hugo, 'Napoleon II,' in *Les chants du crépuscule*, *Oeuvres complètes*, V, 410:

> When this great labourer, who knew how to create,
> Had, with great blows of an axe, just about created the world
> As he had seen it in his dreams.

32 Hugo, 'L'expiation,' in *Les châtiments*, *Oeuvres complètes*, VIII, 698:

> The Emperor was there, standing, watching.
> He was like a tree that had fallen victim to an axe.
> Upon this giant, whose greatness had hitherto been spared,
> Misfortune, a sinister woodsman, had fallen;
> And he, a living oak who had been insulted by the axe,
> Quivered beneath the sceptre of lugubrious revenge,
> He watched his branches fall around him.

33 Marcel Trudel, *L'influence de Voltaire au Canada*.
34 Ringuet, *Confidences*, 108.
35 Philippe Aubert de Gaspé, *Mémoires*, 384–6.
36 Gaspé, 165.
37 Gaspé, 165–8. In English in the original.
38 Thomas Chapais, *Cours d'histoire du Canada*, II (1791–1814), 213.
39 J.-P. Eckerman, *Conversations avec Goethe dans les dernières années de sa vie*, II, 303–4. This conversation took place on 4 May 1827.
40 Chauveau, 317.
41 Ibid.
42 The Annexation Association was founded in 1849 to promote a Canada–U.S. political union. Most of those who signed the 'Annexation Manifesto' were those from the powerful English-speaking business community in Montreal and Quebec who were disappointed at Britain's abolition of preferential duties on Canadian lumber, wheat, and flour products. They were supported

by the radical French-Canadian nationalists, led by Louis-Joseph Papineau, who preferred American republican institutions.
43 Gabriel Dussault, *Le curé Labelle*, 33.
44 François-Edme Rameau de Saint-Père, *La France aux colonies. Études sur le développement de la race française hors de l'Europe. Les Français en Amérique. Acadiens et Canadiens.*
45 Jean Bruchési, 'Rameau de Saint-Père et les Français d'Amérique,' *Les Cahiers des Dix* 13 (1948), 228.
46 This is particularly true of Michel Brunet's widely acclaimed essay 'Trois dominantes de la pensée canadienne-française: l'agriculturisme, l'anti-étatisme et le messianisme,' in *La présence anglaise et les Canadiens*, 113–66.
47 Dussault, 84, 86, 97, note 40.
48 Rameau de Saint-Père, 'Voyages au Canada' (presented by his daughter L. Decencière-Rameau de Saint-Père), *La Revue de l'Université Laval* III (February 1949), IV (March 1950).
49 *La Revue de l'Université Laval* III (1949), 530.
50 See for example *Le Canadien*, 23 January 1860.
51 *La Revue de l'Université Laval* III (February 1949), 539, and IV (1949), 175, 177, 182.
52 *La Revue de l'Université Laval* IV (1950), 552.
53 Rameau often uses this expression. It should be noted that, despite the little regard that he has for Americans in general, he nevertheless recognizes their good influence on French Canadians. One observation that he makes in Sherbrooke, in Jean Rivard country, recalls what for me is the essential aspect of the novel, that is, the advantage for French Canadians of modelling themselves on Americans: 'The following day [13 July 1860], I realized that the Canadian population is growing in the Sherbrooke area and that close contact with Americans makes them even more industrious and hard-working without changing them as a nation. They are beginning to learn about mechanical things and are improving their knowledge in many areas' (*La Revue de l'Université Laval* III [1949], 541).
54 Tulard, 63.
55 Descotes, 249.
56 Descotes, 174.
57 Tulard, 6.
58 Tulard, 83. *Les déracinés* (1897) is a novel by Maurice Barrès. Seven young Lorrainers come to Paris and find themselves adrift, lacking the cultural or spiritual roots to aid their development. Disillusionment follows, to which they react in diverse ways.
59 Hugo, 'Avant l'exil,' quoted by Descotes, 207.

60 Balzac, *Le médecin de campagne*, 171–2.
61 Emerson, 'Napoleon, Man of the World,' Emerson, *Works*, IV, 224. My italics.
62 Emerson, 246–7.
63 *Mandements, lettres pastorales, circulaires et autres documents publiés dans le diocèse de Montréal depuis son érection jusqu'à l'année 1869*, IV, 42–95.
64 *Mandements*, 111.
65 On this tour see Robert Sylvain, 'La visite du prince Napoléon au Canada,' *Mémoires de la Société royale du Canada*, 4th series, II, section 1, June 1964, 105–26. Prince Napoleon has left his own impressions of the trip: Napoleon Joseph Charles Paul Bonaparte, 'Voyage du prince Napoléon aux États-Unis et au Canada, 1861,' *Revue de Paris*, 15 September 1935 and 1 October 1935 (see the 1 October issue, 576–84, for the Canadian portion of the voyage). One of the members of his retinue, Maurice Sand, has likewise left an amusing and colourful narrative of this journey, in the form of a letter to his famous mother (Maurice Sand, *Six mille lieues à toute vapeur*).
66 *Le Pays*, 19 December 1861; italics in original.
67 Bonaparte, 580–1.
68 Bonaparte, 582.
69 Bonaparte, 578.
70 *Quebec Mercury*, 14 September 1861.
71 Jean Bruchési, 'Les correspondants canadiens de Rameau de Saint-Père,' *Les Cahiers des Dix* 14 (1949), 106 (Étienne Parent's letter of 25 October 1861).
72 *The Morning Chronicle*, 14 September 1860.
73 Louis-Antoine Dessaulles (1819–95) was the nephew of Louis-Joseph Papineau, one of the leaders of the Parti rouge and editor of *L'Avenir*, then *Le Pays*, the party's organ, which opposed Confederation and the influence of the clergy in temporal affairs.

   Louis-Joseph Papineau (1786–1871) was the leader of the French-Canadian reformers or Patriotes. His anti-British policy resulted in the Rebellion of 1837 in Lower Canada, though he himself took no active part in it and fled to the United States. After a five-year stay in France, he returned to Montreal in 1844, when the Canadian government granted an amnesty to the rebels of 1837, and he resumed his political career in 1848.

   Antoine-Aimé Dorion (1818–91) was a Parti rouge leader in the 1850s who praised American political institutions, supported liberal ideas, promoted the colonization of virgin lands, and attacked financial and business interests as well as certain aspects of the Roman Catholic Church's presence in society. He led Lower Canadian opposition to Confederation, which he saw as a legislative union that would accord virtually no autonomy to the provinces even in matters of local concern.
74 Father Octave Doucet's scruples about politics, as expressed in the novel

(354), would no doubt have pleased Prince Napoleon, a believer but an anticlerical: 'I attended mass in a wooden Catholic church [in Prairie-du-Chien, on the Mississippi, in Wisconsin]. The priest is a Frenchman from Toulouse, who settled in these parts thirteen years ago ... How favourable to true religion are true liberty and the absence of all government influence or direction! This mass in this remote place profoundly impressed me; as soon as religion is separated from politics and from this dominating spirit that causes people to detest priests, I am drawn to it' (Bonaparte, 565).
75 The Rouges were members of the radical Parti rouge formed in Lower Canada in 1848 under the influence of Louis-Joseph Papineau and led by Antoine-Aimé Dorion. It was the counterpart of the moderate reformers called Bleus, supporters of Louis-Hippolyte Lafontaine.
76 André Belleau, 'Code social et code littéraire dans le roman québécois,' L'Esprit créateur 23 (1983), 28.
77 Belleau, 27.
78 Belleau, 27.
79 Quoted by Michel Simonin, 'Les bibliothèques dans le livre (XVIe-XVIIe siècles). Notes,' Interférences (1980), 51-2. It is from Michel Simonin that I have also borrowed the idea of the library as an ethopoeia, that is, a rhetorical figure that seeks to portray the nature of a character.

Chapter 4: Intertextuality II: *Jean Rivard* as a Utopia

1 Philippe Sollers, 'Écriture et révolution,' Tel quel: théorie d'ensemble, 75.
2 Sollers, 75.
3 Raymond Trousson, Voyages aux pays de nulle part. Histoire littéraire de la pensée utopique, 185.
4 Frank E. Manuel and Fritzie P. Manuel, Utopian Thought in the Western World, 6.
5 Lewis Mumford, The Story of Utopias, 115.
6 A letter from Emerson to Thomas Carlyle, quoted by Ivan Doig, Utopian America. Dreams and Realities, 11.
7 Doig, 8.
8 Roger LeMoine ('Le roman au XIXe siècle,' in René Dionne, ed., Le Québécois et sa littérature, 80) emphasizes Jean Rivard's 'controls, typical of creators of utopias.' Above all, Gabriel Dussault (Le curé Labelle, 153 ff.) writes, after careful consideration of the nature of utopia: 'Gérin-Lajoie's entire utopian novel, a social day-dream, which includes Jean Rivard's first dream at the very beginning of the novel, indicates settlement as a way of resolving multiple, interlocking social contradictions, which he detects around him.' Already in 1924 Édouard Montpetit had used the expression 'utopian novel,'

but without dwelling on it: 'To interest the general public he resorted to the utopian novel where literature endeavours to embellish a thesis, a kind of treatise-novel' (Édouard Montpetit, 'Discours,' in Léon Gérin, *Antoine Gérin-Lajoie. La résurrection ...*, 198).

9 Casgrain, *Antoine Gérin-Lajoie*, 52.
10 A. Gérin-Lajoie, *Jean Rivard, économiste*, in *Le Foyer canadien* 2 (1864), 353 (Appendix).
11 Melville, *Moby Dick*, 70.
12 Montpetit, 211.
13 Maurice Lemire, *Jean Rivard d'Antoine Gérin-Lajoie, un plan de conquête économique*, 88.
14 As for readers, they are more critical than the narrator and better mathematicians than Father Doucet. They know that despite the marvellous salubrity of the air in the Eastern Townships, these people, who are one hundred years old, must certainly have drawn their strength from elsewhere, since Rivardville has existed for only fifteen years at the time of the narrator's visit!
15 Quoted by Joseph Gabel, 'Conscience utopique et fausse conscience,' in Maurice de Gandillac, Catherine Piron et al., *Le discours utopique*, 43. Berdiaeff's reflection obviously has its source in the tribulations of the Bolshevik utopia.
16 Susan Rubin Suleiman, *Authoritarian Fictions*, 54; Suleiman's italics.
17 Raymond Ruyer, *Utopie et les utopies*, 37-8.
18 André Canivez, 'Introduction,' in Georges Duveau, *Sociologie de l'utopie et autres essais*, xi-xii.
19 Duveau, 105.
20 Duveau, 82.
21 Ian Tod and Michael Wheeler, *Utopia*, 7.
22 Ruyer, 3.
23 Ruyer, 9; Ruyer's italics.
24 Ernest Bloch, *L'esprit de l'utopie*, 11.
25 J.C. Davis, *Utopia and the Ideal Society. A Study of English Utopian Writing, 1516-1700*, in particular the introduction and the first chapter.
26 Ruyer, 55.
27 Ruyer, 24.
28 Robert Lefevre Shurter, *The Utopian Novel in America, 1865-1900*, 1.
29 Antoine Lion, 'Extraits de la discussion,' in Maurice de Gandillac, Catherine Piron et al., *Le discours utopique*, 19.
30 Ruyer, 39.
31 Ruyer, 41.
32 Ruyer, 236-7. The reader may also remember that Voltaire's Candide leaves El Dorado.

33 Duveau, 39.
34 Ruyer, 41 ff.
35 René Scherer, 'L'utopie pédagogique,' in Gandillac, Piron et al., 375; Scherer's italics.
36 Gilles Marcotte, *Une littérature qui se fait*, 13–14.
37 'But what is the significance of this opposition to your education laws among your people, which is so vigorous and apparently so general in many places in this country? Here you see these people so full of reverence for their spiritual pastors remaining deaf to their exhortations in favour of education. There, the minister of the gospel, in order not to compromise his holy ministry, decides it is wise to stay out of the discussion. Further away, the most influential and rightly respected men become the object of public distrust. Elsewhere, our good habitants, who are always so calm, so submissive to the laws, resort openly to force against the officers of the law. In other places there are deplorable night attacks on property and even on schoolhouses. One day, upon meeting one of our most noteworthy citizens from one of our important parishes, I congratulated him on the fact that there had not been any trouble in his parish regarding the education act and that all was going well there: "Yes" he replied. "All is going well for us, because, seeing the pointlessness of speaking in favour of the education law, we kept quiet"' (Étienne Parent, 'Considérations sur notre système d'éducation populaire, sur l'éducation en général et sur les moyens législatifs d'y pourvoir,' lecture delivered on 19 February 1848, in Jean-Charles Falardeau, *Étienne Parent, 1802–1874*, 172).
38 Gilbert Leclerc, 'L'Éducation permanente comme modèle utopique,' in Guy Bouchard, Laurent Giroux, and Gilbert Leclerc, *L'Utopie aujourd'hui*, 85 ff. Leclerc traces the origin of the continuing-education concept back to the early 1950s.
39 Chauveau, *Charles Guérin*, 53.
40 In particular, by A.N. Kaul, *The American Vision: Actual and Ideal Society in Nineteenth-Century Fiction*, and Lionel Trilling, *The Liberal Imagination. Essays on Literature and Society*.
41 Kaul, 310.
42 Balzac, *La comédie humaine*, I, 52 (Foreword).
43 These characters are the protagonists in the works of James Fenimore Cooper, Mark Twain, Herman Melville, and Nathaniel Hawthorne, respectively.
44 Kaul, 4.
45 Frank E. Manuel and Fritzie P. Manuel, 28.
46 Jean Servier, *Histoire de l'utopie*, 315.
47 Ruyer, 100.

48 Ruyer, 100.
49 Ruyer, 87.
50 Étienne Parent, 'De l'intelligence dans ses rapports avec la société,' in Falardeau, 264–6.
51 Ruyer, 107.
52 Tocqueville, *L'ancien régime et la révolution*, quoted by Jacques Vallée, *Tocqueville au Bas-Canada*, 174–5.
53 René Rémond, *Histoire des États-Unis*, 36.
54 Camille Roy, *Nouveaux essais*, 97–9.
55 Roy, 98.

Chapter 5: Republicanism or Feudalism in Laurentia?

1 The term 'Laurentie' was used in the nineteenth century by French-Canadian writers and patriots for the St Lawrence River valley in Lower Canada. It is a poetic term for the homeland.
2 Roger LeMoine, 'Le roman au XIXe siècle,' in René Dionne, ed., *Le Québécois et sa littérature*, 80.
3 P.-J.-O. Chauveau, *Charles Guérin*, 344. In this chapter, the numbers in parentheses, preceded by CG, refer to the pages of this novel.
4 Fernand Ouellet, *Histoire économique et sociale du Québec 1760–1850*, II, 434.
5 Mason Wade, *Les Canadiens français de 1760 à nos jours*, 296.
6 Vida Bruce, 'Introduction,' in A. Gérin-Lajoie, *Jean Rivard*, 13.
7 Jean-Charles Falardeau, *Notre société et son roman*, 23.
8 I have shown elsewhere how the erotic content of this novel – unavailingly obscured – is conveyed through a secondary character, Pierre Gagnon, who is a good companion but a burlesque figure. See Robert Major, 'D'un ours bien léché. Bestiaire et idéologie dans *Jean Rivard*,' *Voix et images* 11 (1985), 76–95.
9 Chauveau, 55–6.
10 See above, chapter I.
11 Tocqueville, *Démocratie*, 39.
12 Tocqueville, *Démocratie*, 59.
13 Tocqueville, *Démocratie*, 58–9; my italics.
14 Bishop Laflèche (1818–98) was educated at the Nicolet College, where he later taught, becoming superior in 1859. He was appointed coadjutor bishop of Trois-Rivières in 1866, and was bishop from 1870 until his death. He was the acknowledged leader of ultramontanism in Canada and was involved in bitter controversies with civil and ecclesiastical authorities.
15 Tocqueville, *Démocratie*, 63.
16 Tocqueville, *Démocratie*, 236–7.

17 Tocqueville, *Démocratie*, 29.
18 Tocqueville, *Démocratie*, 50.
19 Tocqueville, *Démocratie*, 244.
20 Tocqueville, *Démocratie*, 106.
21 Bernard Proulx, *Le roman du territoire*.
22 Proulx, 41.
23 Proulx, 61.
24 Ibid., 61.

Chapter 6: Conclusion

1 This is reminiscent of the American pioneers who recorded important events in the family Bible; the Bible thus became a symbiosis of the sacred word and family history. To gather in its presence was an act of worship of the Creator and a confirmation of one's own existence as His creation. Jean Rivard writes out his own existence, but in a book of his own making.
2 See Warwick, 53.
3 Gilles Marcotte, *Littérature et circonstances*, 91.
4 Ibid.
5 Marcotte, 92.
6 Ibid.
7 Ibid.
8 Jacques Brault, *Mémoire*, 50.
9 René Dumont, *Un monde intolérable. Le libéralisme en question*.
10 Thoreau, *Walden, or Life in the Woods*, 10.
11 Thoreau, 8.
12 Emerson, *Works*, VI, 88.
13 *Les Herbes rouges* is an avant-garde Quebec literary magazine founded in 1968 and edited by François and Marcel Hébert.
14 *La Barre du jour* is a literary magazine founded in 1965 by Nicole Brossard, Marcel Saint-Pierre, Roger Soublière, and Jan Stafford. In 1977 it was reorganized with the new title *La Nouvelle Barre du jour* by Brossard, Michel Gay, and Jean Yves Colette.
15 Ruyer, 3.
16 Raymond Trousson, 'Utopie et esthétique romanesque,' in Gandillac, Piron et al., *Le discours utopique*, 392–3.
17 Ruyer, 58.
18 Marcotte, 207.
19 Falardeau, *Étienne Parent*, 306.
20 Jean-Pierre Issenhuth, 'En quête d'un art de vivre,' *Liberté* 175 (30), (1988), 6–7.

Bibliography

This bibliography lists only the works consulted. A more complete bibliography of Antoine Gérin-Lajoie can be found in René Dionne, *Antoine Gérin-Lajoie, homme de lettres*, pp. 379–421.

Works of Antoine Gérin-Lajoie

Catéchisme politique ou élémens du droit public et constitutionnel du Canada, mis à la portée du peuple. Montréal: Imprimerie de Louis Perrault, 1851.
Catalogue de la Bibliothèque du Parlement. Vol. I, *Bibliothèque générale*. Toronto: John Lovell 1857.
Catalogue de la Bibliothèque du Parlement. Vol. 2, *Ouvrages relatifs à l'Amérique*. Toronto: John Lovell, 1858.

Jean Rivard

First publication in periodicals:
'Jean Rivard, le défricheur canadien.' *Les soirées canadiennes*. Vol. 2, 65–319. Québec: Brousseau Frères, 1862.
'Jean Rivard, économiste.' *Le Foyer canadien*. Vol. 2, 15–371. Québec: Bureaux du Foyer canadien, 1864.

Early Editions:

Jean Rivard, le défricheur (récit de la vie réelle). Second revised edition. Montréal: J.B. Rolland & Fils, 1874.
Jean Rivard, économiste (pour faire suite à Jean Rivard, le défricheur). Second revised edition. Montréal: J.B. Rolland & Fils, 1876.

Jean Rivard (scènes de la vie réelle). Montréal: J.B. Rolland & Fils, 1877.

Working Edition:

Jean Rivard, le défricheur (récit de la vie réelle), suivi de Jean Rivard, économiste. Postface by René Dionne. Montréal: Hurtubise HMH (Cahiers du Québec, Coll. Textes et documents litteraires), 1977.

Translation:

Jean Rivard. Translation and introduction by Vida Bruce. Toronto: McClelland and Stewart (New Canadian Library), 1977.

Dix ans au Canada, de 1840 à 1850 (histoire de l'établissement du gouvernement responsable). Québec: L.J. Demers et Frères, 1888.
'Discours sur l'histoire du Canada.' *L'Aurore des Canadas* (22 August 1843), pp. 2–3.
'Le bon départ.' *Le Charivari canadien* (11 June 1844), p. 1.
'Discours (prononcé devant l'Institut canadien, le 16 de janvier courant).' *La Revue canadienne* 1 (4) (25 January 1845), pp. 29–30; (5), (1 February 1845), pp. 37–8.
'Premier rapport annuel de l'Institut canadien.' *La Minerve* (24 December 1845), p. 2; *La Revue canadienne* 2 (17) (27 December 1845), pp. 199–200.
'Bibliothèques publiques – leur importance (article lu à l'Institut canadien).' *La Minerve* (14 May 1847), pp. 1–2.
'Le Foyer canadien, recueil littéraire et historique (prospectus).' *Le Journal de Québec* (30 October 1862), pp. 2–3.
'Prospectus.' *Le Foyer canadien* 1 (1863), pp. 5–9.
'L'abbé J.-B.-A. Ferland.' *Le Foyer canadien* 3 (1865), pp. i–lxxii.

Works Consulted

Anonymous works and periodicals are listed in alphabetical order by title. The newspapers consulted are all listed under the entry 'Newspapers.'

Allaire, Jean-Baptiste-Arthur. *Dictionnaire biographique du clergé canadien-français*. 6 volumes. Montréal et Saint-Hyacinthe: La Tribune, 1910-34.
Andrès, Bernard. 'Jean Rivard, le défricheur suivi de Jean Rivard, économiste/ Arsène Bessette, Le débutant.' *Livres et auteurs québécois 1977*, 64–5. Québec: Les Presses de l'Université Laval, 1978.

Angenot, Marc, and Darko Suvin. 'Thèses sur la sociologie de la littérature'. *Littérature* 44 (December 1981), pp. 117-27.
Aubert de Gaspé, Philippe. *Mémoires*. Montréal: Fides, 1971.
Auclair, E.J. 'Le rôle de l'Église dans les cantons de l'Est.' Société canadienne d'histoire de l'Église catholique, *Rapport 1939-1940*, 89–97. Ottawa: 1940.
Baczko, Bronislav. *Lumières de l'utopie*. Paris: Payot, 1979.
Baillargeon, Samuel. *Littérature canadienne-française*. Montréal: Fides, 1957.
Balzac, Honoré de. *La comédie humaine*. Paris: Seuil (Coll. L'Intégrale, vol. I), 1965.
Balzac, Honoré de. *Le médecin de campagne*. Paris: Garnier-Flammarion, 1965.
Barberis, Pierre. *Balzac, une mythologie réaliste*. Paris: Larousse, 1971.
Barberis, Pierre. 'À propos de Lux: la vraie force des choses (sur l'idéologie des *Châtiments*).' *Littérature* 1 (February 1971), pp. 92–105.
Barthe, Joseph-Guillaume. *Souvenirs d'un demi-siècle ou mémoires pour servir l'histoire contemporaine*. Montréal: J. Chapleau et Fils, 1885.
Beaulieu, André, and Jean Hamelin. *La presse québécoise des origines à nos jours*. Québec: Les Presses de l'Université Laval, Vol. I (1764–1859), 1973; vol. II (1860–79), 1975.
Belleau, André. 'Code social et code littéraire dans le roman québécois.' *L'Esprit créateur* 23 (3) (Autumn 1983), pp. 19–31.
Bellemin-Noël, Jean. 'Réplique à des "socio-thèses."' *Littérature* 46 (May 1982) pp. 124–5.
Bernier, Benoît. 'À propos d'Étienne Parent.' *Revue d'histoire de l'Amérique française*. 27 (1) (June 1973) pp. 86–90.
Berthiaume, Pierre. 'La ville et la campagne au XIXe siècle, lieux d'une rhétorique.' *Critère* 17 (Spring 1977), pp. 203–17.
Bessette, Gérard, Lucien Geslin, and Charles Parent. *Histoire de la littérature canadienne-française par les textes*. Montréal: Centre éducatif et culturel, 1968.
Blanchet, frère Urbain. 'Étienne Parent, ses opinions pédagogiques et religieuses.' D.E.S. thesis. Université Laval, 1965.
Blanchot, Maurice. *L'entretien infini*. Paris: Gallimard, 1969.
Bloch, Ernst. *L'esprit de l'utopie*. Paris: Gallimard, 1977.
Bonaparte, Napoléon Joseph Charles Paul. 'Voyage du prince Napoléon aux États-Unis et au Canada, 1861.' *Revue de Paris* (1 October 1935), pp. 549–87.
Bouchard, Guy, Laurent Giroux, and Gilbert Leclerc. *L'utopie aujourd'hui*. Montréal: Les Presses de l'Université de Montréal, 1985.
Bouffard, Jean. *Traité du domaine*. Québec: Le Soleil, 1921.
Boulanger, Jean-Baptiste. *Napoléon vu par un Canadien*. Bordeaux: Delmas, 1937.
Bourque, Paul-André. 'L'Américanité du roman québécois.' *Études littéraires* 8 (1) (April 1975), pp. 9–19.

Brault, Jacques. *Mémoire*. Montréal: Déom, 1965.
Breton, Raymond, and Pierre Savard. *The Quebec and Acadian Diaspora in North America*. Toronto: The Multicultural History Society of Canada, 1982.
Brouillette, Benoît. *La pénétration du continent américain par les Canadiens français (1763–1846). Traitants, explorateurs, missionnaires*. Montréal: Granger Frères, 1939.
Bruce, Vida. 'Introduction' to *Jean Rivard*. Toronto: McClelland and Stewart, 1977.
Bruchési, Jean. 'Rameau de Saint-Père et les Français d'Amérique.' *Les Cahiers des dix* 13 (1948), pp. 225-48.
Bruchési, Jean. 'Les correspondants canadiens de Rameau de Saint-Père.' *Les Cahiers des dix* 14 (1949), pp. 87-114.
Brunet, Gustave. *Essai sur les bibliothèques imaginaires*. Paris: J. Techner, 1862.
Brunet, Michel. *La présence anglaise et les Canadiens. Études sur l'histoire et la pensée des deux Canadas*. Montréal: Beauchemin, 1964.
Buies, Arthur. *Chroniques, humeurs et caprices*. Québec: C. Darveau, 1873.
Buies, Arthur. *L'Outaouais supérieur*. Québec: C. Darveau, 1889.
Cabau, Jacques. *La prairie perdue. Histoire du roman américain*. Paris: Seuil, 1966.
Cadieux, Marcel, and Paul Tremblay. 'Étienne Parent, un théoricien de notre nationalisme.' *L'Action nationale* 13 (3) (March 1939), pp. 203–19; (4) (April 1939), pp. 307–18.
Campanella, Tommaso. *La cité du soleil*. Edited with an introduction and notes by Luigi Firpo. Genève: Droz, 1972.
Carpenter, Frederic Ives. *Emerson Handbook*. New York: Hendricks House, 1953.
Casgrain, H.-R. 'Biographie de Gérin-Lajoie. Fragment.' *Mémoires de la Société royale du Canada*. First series, vol. 3, section 1, 1885, pp. 55–60.
Casgrain, H.-R. *Antoine Gérin-Lajoie d'après ses Mémoires*. 3rd ed. Montréal: Beauchemin, 1912.
Chamberland, Paul. *Terre Québec*. Montréal: Déom, 1964.
Chapais, Thomas. *Cours d'histoire du Canada*. Vol. II, 1791–1814. Québec: Garneau, 1921.
Charles, Michel. 'Bibliothèques.' *Poétique* 33 (February 1978), pp. 1–27.
Chartier, J.B. *La colonisation dans les cantons de l'Est*. Saint-Hyacinthe: Courrier de Saint-Hyacinthe, 1871.
Charvat, William. *Emerson's American Lecture Engagements: A Chronological List*. New York: New York Public Library, 1961.
Chauveau, Pierre-Joseph-Olivier. *Charles Guérin, roman de moeurs canadiennes*. Montréal: Fides (Coll. du Nénuphar), 1978.
Cioranescu, Alexandre. *L'avenir du passé. Utopie et littérature*. Paris: Gallimard, 1972.

Bibliography 235

Compagnon, Antoine. *La seconde main, ou le travail de la citation*. Paris: Seuil, 1979.
Cooper, James Fenimore. *The Chainbearer, or the Littlepage Manuscripts*. Reproduction of the original edition of 1845. New York: AMS Press, 1973.
Cooper, James Fenimore. *The Prairie*. New York: A.L. Burt, n.d.
Coup d'oeil sur la colonisation. Terres à coloniser. Moyens de hâter la colonisation. Montréal: Imprimerie de La Minerve, 1864.
Dagenais, Pierre. 'Le mythe de la vocation agricole du Québec.' *Mélanges géographiques canadiens offerts à Raoul Blanchard*, 193–202. Québec: Les Presses de l'Université Laval, 1959.
Darveau, L.-M. *Nos hommes de lettres*. Vol. 1. Montréal: A.A. Stevenson, 1873.
Davis, J.C. *Utopia and the Ideal Society. A Study of English Utopian Writing 1516–1700*. Cambridge: Cambridge University Press, 1981.
Decencière-Rameau de Saint-Père, L. 'Voyages au Canada.' *La Revue de l'Université Laval* 3 (6) (February 1949)–4 (7) (March 1950).
Defoe, Daniel. *The Best Known Works of Daniel Defoe*. New York: The Book League of America, 1942.
Derrida, Jacques. *La dissémination*. Paris: Seuil, 1972.
Descotes, Maurice. *La légende de Napoléon et les écrivains français du XIXe siècle*. Paris: Minard, 1967.
Desroches, Henri. *Dieux d'hommes. Dictionnaire des messianismes et millénarismes de l'ère chrétienne*. La Haye and Paris: Mouton, 1969.
Dionne, René. *Antoine Gérin-Lajoie, homme de lettres*. Sherbrooke: Naaman, 1978.
Dionne, René. 'Une nécessaire et fructueuse décolonisation.' *Vie française* 36 (1–3) (January–March 1982), pp. 11–15.
Dionne, René. 'Étude. *Jean Rivard* et son auteur.' Postface to working edition, above, pp. 379–90.
Doig, Ivan. *Utopian America. Dreams and Realities*. Rochelle Park: Hayden Books, 1976.
Dorion, Gilles. 'Nationalité et nationalisme en littérature québécoise.' *L'Esprit créateur* 23 (3) (Autumn 1983), pp. 9–18.
Dostaler, Yves. *Les infortunes du roman dans le Québec du XIXe siècle*. Montréal: Hurtubise HMH, 1977.
Doubrovski, Serge. *Pourquoi la nouvelle critique? Critique et objectivité*. Paris: Mercure de France, 1966.
Douville, Joseph-Antoine-Irénée. *Histoire du collège-séminaire de Nicolet, 1803–1903. Avec les listes complètes des directeurs, professeurs et élèves de l'institution*. 2 volumes. Montréal: Beauchemin, 1903.
Drapeau, Stanislas. *Études sur les développements de la colonisation du Bas-Canada depuis dix ans (1851 à 1861)*. Québec: Léger Brousseau, 1863.
Drapeau, Stanislas. *Le guide du colon français, belge, suisse, etc*. Ottawa: 1887.

Drolet, Antonio. *Les bibliothèques canadiennes, 1604–1960*. Ottawa: Le Cercle du livre de France, 1965.
Dubé, Martin. '*Jean Rivard, le défricheur*: récit de la vie réelle?' *Incidences*. Nouvelle série, 4 (1) (January–April 1980), pp. 19–36.
Dubois, C.G. *Problèmes de l'utopie*. Paris: Archives des lettres modernes, 1968.
Dubois, Jacques. *L'assommoir de Zola: société, discours, idéologie*. Paris: Larousse, 1973.
Dubois, Jacques. 'Code, texte et métatexte.' *Littérature* 12 (December 1973), pp. 3–11.
Dubois, Jacques. *L'institution de la littérature*. Paris: Nathan/Bruxelles: Éditions Labor, 1978.
Ducharme, Charles-M. 'Antoine Gérin-Lajoie et *Jean Rivard*.' *Ris et croquis*, 98–137. Montréal: Beauchemin et Fils, 1889.
Duchet, Claude. 'Romans et objets: l'exemple de *Madame Bovary*.' *Europe* 485–7 (September–November 1969), pp. 172–202.
Duchet, Claude. 'Pour une sociocritique ou variations sur un incipit.' *Littérature* 1 (February 1971), pp. 5–14.
Duchet, Claude. 'Une écriture de la socialité.' *Poétique* 16 (1973), pp. 446–54.
Duchet, Claude. '*La fille abandonnée* et *La bête humaine*. Éléments de titrologie romanesque.' *Littérature* 12 (1973), pp. 49–73.
Duchet, Claude. 'Réflexions sur les rapports du roman et de la société.' *Roman et société*, 63–73. Paris: A. Colin, 1973.
Duchet, Claude. 'La mise en texte du social.' In Claude Duchet and Ruth Amossy, *Balzac et la peau de chagrin*, 79–92. Paris: Société d'édition d'enseignement supérieur, 1979.
Duchet, Claude, ed. *Sociocritique*. Paris: Nathan, 1979.
Duchet, Claude. 'The Object-Event of the Ram's Charge: An Ideological Reading of an Image.' *Yale French Studies* 59 (1980), pp. 155–74.
Duchet, Claude, and Jacques Neefs, eds. *Balzac, l'invention du roman*. Paris: Belfond, 1982.
Ducrocq-Poirier, Madeleine. *Le roman canadien de langue française de 1860 à 1958*. Paris: Nizet, 1978.
Dumont, Fernand, and Jean-Charles Falardeau, eds. *Littérature et société canadiennes-françaises*. Québec: Les Presses de l'Université Laval, 1964.
Dumont, Fernand, et al., eds. *Idéologies au Canada français, 1850–1900*. Québec: Les Presses de l'Université Laval (Coll. Histoire et sociologie de la culture, 1), 1971.
Dumont, René. *Un monde intolérable. Le libéralisme en question*. Paris: Seuil, 1988.
Duneton, Claude. *Parler croquant*. Paris: Stock, 1978.

Bibliography   237

Dupriez, Bernard. *Gradus. Les procédés littéraires*. Paris: Union générale d'éditions (Coll. 10/18), 1980.
Durham, John George Lambton, Earl of. *Lord Durham's Report*. Edited and with an introduction by G.H. Craig. Toronto: McClelland and Stewart, 1963.
Dussault, Gabriel. *Le curé Labelle. Messianisme, utopie et colonisation au Québec, 1850–1900*. Montréal: Hurtubise HMH, 1983.
Duveau, Georges. *Sociologie de l'utopie et autres essais*. Paris: Les Presses universitaires de France, 1961.
Eckermann, J.-P. *Conversations avec Goethe dans les dernières années de sa vie*. Translated by Jean Chuzeville. 2 volumes. Paris: Henri Jonquières, 1930.
Eco, Umberto. *Le nom de la rose*. Paris: Bernard Grasset, 1982.
Emerson, Ralph Waldo. *The Selected Writings of R.W. Emerson*. New York: The Modern Library, 1950.
Emerson, Ralph Waldo. *The Journals and Miscellaneous Notebooks of Ralph Waldo Emerson*. Vol. VI, 1824–1838. Edited by Ralph H. Orth. Cambridge: Harvard University Press, 1966.
Emerson, Ralph Waldo. *The Complete Works of R.W. Emerson*. Reproduction of the original edition of 1904. 12 volumes. New York: AMS, Press, 1968.
Europe 480–1 (April–May 1969).
Falardeau, Jean-Charles. *Notre société et son roman*. Montréal: HMH, 1967.
Falardeau, Jean-Charles. *Étienne Parent, 1802–1874*. Biography, texts, and bibliography presented by Jean-Charles Falardeau. Montréal: Éditions La Presse, 1975.
Faucher, Albert. 'L'émigration des Canadiens français au XIXe siècle: position du problème et perspectives.' *Recherches sociographiques* 5 (3) (September–December 1964), pp. 277–317.
Fénelon. *Les aventures de Télémaque*. Paris: R. Simon, n.d.
Ferland, Jean-Baptiste-Antoine. *Observations sur un ouvrage intitulé 'Histoire du Canada, etc.' par M. l'abbé Brasseur de Bourbourg*. Québec: Augustin Côté et Cie, 1853.
Ferland, Jean-Baptiste-Antoine. *Notes sur les registres de Notre-Dame de Québec*. Québec: G. et G.-E. Desbarats, 1863 [1854].
Ferland, Jean-Baptiste-Antoine. *La France dans l'Amérique du Nord*. 3rd ed. 2 volumes. Tours/Montréal: Mame/Granger, 1929–1930.
'La fin des utopies.' *Magazine littéraire* 139 (July–August 1978), pp. 14–45.
Fitzgerald, F. Scott. *The Great Gatsby*. New York: Charles Scribner's Sons, 1925.
Flaubert, Gustave. *Emma Bovary*. 2 volumes. Paris: Garnier Frères, 1957.
Fontanier, Pierre. *Les figures du discours*. Paris: Flammarion, 1977.
Foucault, Michel. *L'archéologie du savoir*. Paris: Gallimard, 1969.

Le Foyer canadien, recueil littéraire et historique. Vol. 1 (1863) to vol. 4 (1966). Québec: Bureaux du Foyer canadien.
Franklin, Benjamin. *The Works of Benjamin Franklin.* 10 volumes. Boston: Hilliard, Gray and Co., 1840.
Franklin, Benjamin. *Memoirs of the Life and Writings of Benjamin Franklin.* London: J.M. Dent, 1913.
Franklin, Benjamin. *The Life and Letters of Benjamin Franklin.* Eau Claire, WI: E.M. Hale, n.d.
Fraser, Ian Forbes. *The Spirit of French Canada: A Study of the Literature.* New York: Columbia University Press, 1939.
Frégault, Guy, and Marcel Trudel. *Histoire du Canada par les textes.* Vol. I. Montréal: Fides, 1963.
Furgiuele, Rosanna. 'Mythe et démystification. Une lecture idéologique de *Jean Rivard* et de *Trente arpents*.' Ph.D. thesis. University of Toronto, 1983.
Gagnon, Ernest. *L'homme d'ici.* Montréal: HMH, 1963.
Galarneau, Claude. *La France devant l'opinion canadienne (1760–1815).* Québec: Les Presses de l'Université Laval, (Coll. Les Cahiers de l'Institut d'histoire, 16), 1970.
Gallays, François. '*Les îles de la nuit*: prestiges d'un titre.' *Incidences* 2–3 (1) (January–April 1979), pp. 23–35.
Gandillac, Maurice de, Catherine Piron, et al. *Le discours utopique.* Colloque de Cérisy-la-Salle. Paris: Union générale d'éditions (Coll. 10/18), 1978.
Garon, J. *Historique de la colonisation dans la province de Québec de 1825 à 1940.* Québec: Province de Québec, 1940.
Genette, Gérard. *Seuils.* Paris: Seuil, 1987.
Gérin, Léon. *Antoine Gérin-Lajoie. La résurrection d'un patriote canadien.* Montréal: Éditions du Devoir, 1925.
Gérin, Léon. *Le type économique et social des Canadiens. Milieux agricoles de tradition française.* Montréal: Éditions de l'A.C.F., n.d.
Godbout, Jacques. 'Place Cliché.' *Liberté* 138 (November–December 1981).
Goldmann, Lucien. *Le Dieu caché. Étude sur la vision tragique dans les Pensées de Pascal et dans le théatre de Racine.* Paris: Gallimard, 1959.
Grandpré, Pierre de. *Histoire de la littérature française du Québec.* Vol. I, 1534–1900. Montréal: Beauchemin, 1967.
Grevisse, Maurice. *Le bon usage.* 8th ed. Gembloux: Duculot/ Paris: Hatier, 1964.
Grivel, Charles. *Production de l'intérêt romanesque, 1870–1880.* La Haye: Mouton, 1973.
Guide du colon. Province de Québec. Québec: Département des Terres de la couronne 1877, 1880, 1885, 1892.

Halden, Charles ab der. *Études de littérature canadienne-française*. Paris: F.R. de Rudeval, 1903.
Hamelin, Jean, and Yves Roby. *Histoire économique du Québec, 1851–1896*. Montréal: Fides, 1971.
Hamon, Philippe. 'La bibliothèque dans le livre.' *Interférences* 11 (January–June 1980), pp. 9–13.
Hamon, Philippe. 'Texte et idéologie. Pour une poétique de la norme.' *Poétique* 13 (49) (February 1982), pp. 105–25.
Harding, Walter. *Emerson's Library*. Charlottesville: University Press of Virginia, 1967.
Heffner, Richard D. *A Documentary History of the United States*. New York: Mentor Books, 1956.
Hertzler, Joyce Oramel. *The History of Utopian Thought*. New York: Cooper Square Publishers, 1965 [1923].
Histoire populaire de Napoléon 1er, suivie des Anecdotes impériales, par un ancien officier de la garde. Paris: Bernardin-Bechet, n.d.
Hoek, Léo H. *La marque du titre. Dispositifs sémiotiques d'une pratique textuelle*. Paris and La Haye: Mouton, 1981.
Hoek, Léo H. 'Le discours social dans le texte.' *Rapports* 52 (1982), pp. 164–7.
Hoggart, Richard. *The Literary Imagination and the Study of Society*. Birmingham: Centre for Contemporary Cultural Studies, 1968.
Howard, Bessie D. 'The First French Estimate of Emerson.' *New England Quarterly* 10 (September 1937), pp. 447–63.
Hugo, Victor. *Oeuvres complètes*. 18 volumes. Paris: Le Club français du livre, 1967–70.
Idt, Geneviève. 'Fonction rituelle du métalangage dans les préfaces hétérographes.' *Littérature* 27 (October 1977), pp. 65–74.
Interférences 11 (January–June 1980); 12 (July–December 1980).
Irving, Washington. 'The Mutability of Literature. A Colloquy in Westminster Abbey.' In *Representative Essays Selected from the Series of Prose Masterpieces from Modern Essayists*, 1–14. New York: G.P. Putnam's Sons, 1885.
Issenhuth, Jean-Pierre. 'En quête d'un art de vivre.' *Liberté* 175 (February 1988), pp. 4–7.
Jakobson, Roman. 'Du réalisme artistique.' In Tzvetan Todorov, *Théorie de la littérature. Textes des formalistes russes*, 98–108. Paris: Seuil, 1964.
Kahn, Paul. 'Idéologie et sociologie de la connaissance dans l'oeuvre de Karl Mannheim.' *Cahiers internationaux de sociologie* 8 (1950), pp. 147–68.
Kandiuk, Mary. *French-Canadian Authors: A Bibliography of Their Works and of English Language Criticism*. Metuchen, NJ: Scarecrow Press, 1990.

Kaul, A.N. *The American Vision. Actual and Ideal Society in Nineteenth-Century Fiction.* New Haven and London: Yale University Press, 1963.

Kerr, William A. Robb. *A Short Anthology of French-Canadian Prose Literature.* Toronto: Longman Green and Co., 1927.

Klinck, George Alfred. *Allons Gai. A Topical Anthology of French-Canadian Prose and Verse.* Toronto: The Ryerson Press, 1945.

Kraushaar, Otto F., and Gairdner B. Moment. *Utopias, the American Experience.* Metuchen, NJ: Scarecrow Press, 1980.

Lafortune, Monique. *Le roman québécois, reflet d'une société.* Montréal: Mondia, 1985.

Lanctôt, Gustave, et al. *Les Canadiens français et leurs voisins du Sud.* Montréal: Bernard Valiquette, 1941.

Lapouge, Gilles. *Utopie et civilisation.* Paris: Weber, 1973.

Lareau, Edmond. *Histoire de la littérature canadienne.* Montréal: John Lovell, 1874.

Larocque, Hubert. *Index et concordance de Jean Rivard.* Ottawa: University of Ottawa (Département des lettres françaises), n.d., n.p.

Larose, Jean. *La petite noirceur.* Montréal: Boréal, 1987.

LaRue, Hubert. *Mélanges historiques, littéraires et d'économie politique.* Vol. 2. Québec: P.G. Delisle, 1881.

Lavoie, Yolande. *L'émigration des Québécois aux États-Unis de 1840 à 1930.* Québec: Éditeur officiel, 1979.

Légaré, Cyrille Étienne. 'J.-B.-A. Ferland.' *La France dans l'Amérique du Nord.* Vol. II, p. v. Tours/Montréal: A. Mame/Granger, 1929–30.

Lemieux, Germain. *La vie paysanne, 1860–1900.* Sudbury: Prise de parole/Laval: Éditions FM, 1982.

Lemire, Maurice. 'Jean Rivard d'Antoine Gérin-Lajoie, un plan de conquête économique.' D.E.S. thesis. Université Laval, 1962.

Lemire, Maurice. 'Jean Rivard, le défricheur et Jean Rivard, économiste, romans d'Antoine Gérin-Lajoie.' *Dictionnaire des oeuvres littéraires du Québec.* Vol. I, 410–15. Montréal: Fides, 1978.

LeMoine, Roger. 'Le roman au XIXe siècle.' In René Dionne ed., *Le Québécois et sa littérature*, 76–86. Sherbrooke: Naaman, 1984.

Lessard, Claude. *Le séminaire de Nicolet, 1803–1969.* Trois-Rivières: Éditions du Bien public, 1980.

Letarte, Jacques. *Atlas d'histoire économique et sociale du Québec 1851–1901.* Montréal: Fides, 1971.

La littérature canadienne de 1850 à 1860. Publié par la direction du Foyer canadien. 2nd ed. 2 volumes. Québec: Desbarats et Derbishire, 1863–4.

Little, J.I. 'The Parish and French Canadian Migrants to Compton County, Quebec 1851–1891.' *Histoire sociale/Social History* 11 (21) (1978), pp. 134–43.

Little, J.I. 'The Social and Economic Development of Letters in Two Quebec Townships, 1851–1870.' In D.H. Akenson, ed., *Canadian Papers in Rural History*, 90–113. Gananoque: Langdale Press, 1978.

Lower, Arthur, and Reginald Marsden. *Settlement and the Forest Frontier in Eastern Canada*. Toronto: Macmillan, 1936.

Macherey, Pierre. *Pour une théorie de la production littéraire*. Paris: Maspero, 1966.

MacMechan, Archibald. *The Head waters of Canadian Literature*. 3rd ed. Toronto: McClelland and Stewart, 1974 [1924].

Magnan, Hormisdas. *Le guide du colon de la province de Québec*. Québec: Ministère de la Colonisation, des Mines et des Pêcheries, 1927.

Mailhot, Laurent. 'Bibliothèques imaginaires: le livre dans quelques romans québécois.' *Études françaises* 18 (3) (Winter 1983), pp. 80–92.

Major, André. 'The Decline of America.' In Al Purdy, ed., *The New Romans: Candid Opinions of the U.S.*, 141–3. Edmonton: M.G. Hurtig, 1968.

Major, Robert. 'Québec ou Canada français: note sur l'identité québécoise et la fortune d'un vocable.' *Contemporary French Civilization* 2 (1) (1977), pp. 59–62.

Major, Robert. 'D'un ours bien léché ... Bestiaire et idéologie dans *Jean Rivard*.' *Voix et images* 11 (1) (Autumn 1985), pp. 76–95.

Major, Robert. 'Étienne Parent, utopiste.' In Yolande Crisé and Robert Major, eds, *Mélanges de littérature canadienne-française et québécoise offerts à Réjean Robidoux*. Ottawa: University of Ottawa Press, 1992.

Malraux, André. *Les noyers de l'Altenburg*. Paris: Gallimard, 1948.

Mandements, lettres pastorales, circulaires et autres documents publiés dans le diocèse de Montréal depuis son érection jusqu'à l'année 1869. 9 volumes. Montréal: J.A. Plinquet, 1887.

Mann, William Edward. *Robinson Crusoé en France. Étude sur l'influence de cette oeuvre dans la littérature française*. Paris: A. Davy, 1916.

Mannheim, Karl. *Idéologie et utopie*. Preface by Louis Wirth. Paris: Marcel Rivière, 1956.

Manuel, Frank E., ed. *Utopias and Utopian Thought*. Boston: Houghton Mifflin, 1966.

Manuel, Frank E., and Fritzie P. Manuel. *French Utopias. An Anthology of Ideal Societies*. New York: Schocken Books, 1971.

Manuel, Frank E., and Fritzie P. Manuel. *Utopian Thought in the Western World*. Cambridge: Harvard University Press, 1979.

Marcotte, Gilles. *Une littérature qui se fait*. Montréal: HMH, 1962.

Marcotte, Gilles. *Littérature et circonstances*. Montréal: L'Hexagone, 1989.

Marquis, M.C. *Mémoire sur la colonisation des terres incultes du Bas-Canada. Pour être présenté à Nosseigneurs les évêques de la province ecclésiastique ...* . Québec: A. Côté et Cie, 1867.

Marx, Karl, and Friedrich Engels. *Sur la littérature et l'art.* Textes choisis, traduits et présentés par Jean Fréville. Paris: Éditions sociales, 1954.
Mayer, J.-P. *Alexis de Tocqueville.* Paris: Gallimard, 1948.
Melançon, Benoît. 'La littérature québécoise et l'Amérique. Prolégomènes et bibliographie.' *Études françaises* 26 (2) (1990), pp. 65–108.
Melville, Herrman. *Moby Dick, or the White Whale.* New York: Signet Classics, 1964.
Miller, Perry, et al. *Major Writers of America.* 2 volumes. New York: Harcourt, Brace & World, 1962.
Mitterand, Henri. *Le discours du roman.* Paris: Les Presses universitaires de France, 1980.
Moncelet, Christian. *Essai sur le titre en littérature et dans les arts.* Le Cendre: Éditions BOF, 1972.
Montaigne, Michel de. *Essais.* 3 volumes. Paris: Livre de poche, 1965.
Montigny, Gaston de. *Le livre du colon. Recueil de renseignements utiles.* Montréal: Imprimerie de La Patrie, 1902.
Montigny, Gaston de. 'Le régime paroissial et la colonisation dans la province de Québec.' *La Revue canadienne* 1 (1907), pp. 628–651; 2 (1907), pp. 32–46.
Montigny, Louvigny Testard de. *Antoine Gérin-Lajoie.* Toronto: The Ryerson Press, 1925.
Montreuil, Gaetane de. *Fleur des ondes. Roman historique canadien.* Québec: L'Action sociale, 1924.
More, Thomas. *The Complete Works of St. Thomas More.* Vol. IV, *Utopia.* E. Surtz et J.H. Hexter, eds. New Haven and London: Yale University Press, 1965.
More, Thomas. *Utopia, with the Dialogue of Comfort.* London: J.M. Dent, n.d.
Morgan, Henry David. *Bibliotheca Canadensis or A Manual of Canadian Literature.* Ottawa: G.E. Desbarats, 1867.
Morgan, Henry David. *The Canadian Men and Women of the Time. A Hand-book of Canadian Biography.* Toronto: William Briggs, 1912.
Morgan, Henry J. *Sketches of Celebrated Canadians.* Quebec: Hunter, Rose & Co., 1862.
Morison, Samuel Eliot, and Henry Steele Commager. *The Growth of the American Republic.* 5th ed. 2 volumes. New York: Oxford University Press, 1962
Morissonneau, Christian. *La terre promise: le mythe du Nord québécois.* Montréal: Hurtubise HMH, 1978.
Mumford, Lewis. *The Story of Utopias.* New York: Boni and Liveright, 1922.
Nantet, Jacques. *Tocqueville.* Paris: Seghers, 1971.
Negley, Glenn. *Utopian Literature. A Bibliography with a Supplementary Listing of Works Influential in Utopian Thought.* Lawrence: Regents Press of Kansas, 1977.

Negley, Glenn, and J. Max Patrick. *The Quest for Utopia*. New York: H. Schuman, 1952.
Nelson, W. *Twentieth Century Interpretations of Utopia*. Englewood Cliffs, NJ: Prentice-Hall, 1968.
Newspapers consulted: *L'Aurore des Canadas, Le Canadien, Le Courrier du Canada, Daily News/Montreal Transcript, L'Écho du cabinet de lecture paroissial de Montréal, Le Journal de Québec, Mélanges religieux, La Minerve, Montreal Gazette, Morning Chronicle, Le Pays, The Pilot, Quebec Mercury*.
Nourry, Louis. 'La pensée économique d'Étienne Parent, 1822–1852.' M.A. thesis. Université de Montréal, 1969.
Nourry, Louis. 'La pensée politique d'Étienne Parent, 1831–1852.' Ph.D. thesis. Université de Montréal, 1971.
Ouellet, Fernand. *Histoire économique et sociale du Québec, 1760–1850*. 2 volumes. Montréal: Fides, 1971.
Parent, Étienne. *Discours prononcés par M. É. Parent devant l'Institut canadien de Montréal*. Montréal: Imprimerie de Lovell et Gibson, 1850.
Parizeau, Gérard. 'Étienne Parent ou le sens des réalités, 1802–1874.' *Assurances* 39 (3) (October 1971), pp. 45–100.
Pierce, Lorne. *An Outline of Canadian Literature (French and English)*. Toronto: The Ryerson Press, 1927.
Le problème de la colonisation au Canada français, Rapport officiel du Congrès de colonisation, tenu par l'A.C.J.C. à Chicoutimi du 29 juin au 2 juillet 1919. Montréal: A.C.J.C., 1920.
Proulx, Bernard. *Le roman du territoire*. Les Cahiers d'études littéraires, 8. Montréal: Université du Québec à Montréal, 1987.
Proulx, Jean-Baptiste. *Le guide du colon français au Canada*. Paris: Imprimerie de l'Oeuvre de Saint-Paul, 1885/Ottawa: Département d'Agriculture du gouvernement du Canada, 1886.
Quintal, Claire, ed. *L'émigrant québécois vers les États-Unis, 1850–1920*. Special issue of *Vie Française*. Québec: Ferland, 1982.
Rameau de Saint-Père, François-Edme. *La France aux colonies. Études sur le développement de la race française hors de l'Europe. Les Français en Amérique. Acadiens et Canadiens*. 2 volumes. Paris: A. Jouby, 1859.
Rapport du Congrès de colonisation, tenu à Montréal les 22, 23 et 24 novembre 1898. Montréal: La Patrie, 1900.
Relations des jésuites, 1611–1672. 6 volumes. Montréal: Éditions du Jour, 1972.
Rémond, René. *Histoire des États-Unis*. 7th ed. Paris: Les Presses universitaires de France, (Coll. Que sais-je?, 38), 1972.
Revue des sciences humaines. L'utopie. Special issue, no. 155 (1974).

Rigolot, François. 'Rhétorique du nom propre.' *Poétique* 28 (1976), pp. 466–83.
Ringuet. *Confidences*. Montréal: Fides, 1965.
Ringuet. *Trente arpents*. Montréal: Fides (Coll. du Nénuphar), 1966.
Rioux, Jean-Roch. 'L'Institut canadien (les débuts de l'Institut canadien et du journal *L'Avenir*, 1844–1849).' D.E.S. thesis. Université Laval, 1967.
Rioux, Marcel. *Une saison à la Renardière*. Montréal: L'Hexagone, 1988.
Robert, Véronique. 'Le virage technologique, c'est le retour à la terre.' *L'Actualité* 9 (5) (May 1984), pp. 35–6.
Robidoux, Réjean. '*Les Soirées canadiennes* et *Le Foyer canadien* dans le mouvement littéraire québécois de 1860.' D.E.S. thesis. Université Laval, 1957.
Roby, Yves. 'Un Québec émigré aux États-Unis. Bilan historiographique.' In Claude Savary, ed., *Les Rapports culturels entre le Québec et les États-Unis*. Québec: Institut québécois de recherche sur la culture, 1984.
Romantisme 44 (1984).
Rousseau, Guildo. *L'image des États-Unis dans la littérature québécoise (1775–1930)*. Sherbrooke: Naaman, 1981.
Rousseau, Jean-Jacques. *Émile, ou de l'éducation*. Paris: Garnier-Flammarion, 1966.
Roy, Camille. *Nouveaux essais sur la littérature canadienne*. Québec: L'Action sociale, 1914.
Roy, Camille. *Histoire de la littérature canadienne*. Nouvelle édition revue et mise à jour. Québec: L'Action sociale, 1930.
Roy, Camille. *Manuel d'histoire de la littérature canadienne de langue française*. Nouvelle édition. Montréal: Beauchemin, 1939.
Roy, Pierre-Georges. *Le Centenaire de Gérin-Lajoie*. Special issue of the *Bulletin des recherches historiques* 30 (10) (October 1924), pp. 289–352. Québec: Commission des monuments historiques.
Rusk, Ralph L. *The Letters of Ralph Waldo Emerson*. 6 volumes. New York: Columbia University Press, 1966.
Ruyer, Raymond. *L'utopie et les utopies*. Paris: Les Presses universitaires de France, 1950.
Ryan, William F. *The Clergy and Economic Growth in Quebec (1896–1914)*. Québec: Les Presses de l'Université Laval, 1966.
Saint-Pierre, Arthur. 'La littérature sociale canadienne-française avant la Confédération.' *Mémoires et comptes rendus de la Société royale du Canada*. 3rd series, vol. 44, section 1, 1950, pp. 67-94.
Sand, Maurice. *Six mille lieues à toute vapeur*. Paris: Michel Lévy Frères, 1862.
Sanford, Charles L. *The Quest for Paradise: Europe and the American Moral Imagination*. Urbana: University of Illinois Press, 1961.
Sartre, Jean-Paul. *Questions de méthode*. Paris: Gallimard (Coll. Idées), 1960.

Savard, Pierre. *Jules-Paul Tardivel, la France et les États-Unis, 1851–1905*. Québec: Les Presses de l'Université Laval, (Coll. Les Cahiers de l'Institut d'histoire, 8), 1967.
Séguin, Maurice. *'La nation canadienne' et l'agriculture (1760–1850)*. Trois-Rivières: Boréal Express, 1970.
Séguin, Normand. *La conquête du sol au XIXe siècle*. Québec: Boréal Express, 1977.
Séguin, Normand. *Agriculture et colonisation au Québec, aspects historiques*. Montréal: Boréal Express, 1980.
Séguy, Jean. 'Une sociologie des sociétés imaginées: monarchisme et utopie.' *Annales* (March–April 1971), pp. 328-54.
Servais-Maquoi, Mireille. *Le roman de la terre au Québec*. Québec: Les Presses de l'Université Laval, (Coll. Vie des lettres québécoises, 12), 1974.
Servier, Jean. *Histoire de l'utopie*. Paris: Gallimard, 1967.
Servier, Jean. *L'utopie*. Paris: Les Presses universitaires de France (Coll. Que sais-je?, 1757), 1979.
Shurter, Robert Lefevre. *The Utopian Novel in America, 1865–1900*. New York: AMS Press, 1973.
Sicard, Maurice Ivan. *Napoléon, Balzac et l'empire de la Comédie humaine*. Paris: A. Michel, 1979.
Sidney, Sir Philip. *An Apology for Poetry, or the Defense of Poesy*. Edited by Geoffrey Shephard. Manchester: Manchester University Press, 1973.
Simard, Sylvain. *Mythe et reflet de la France: l'image du Canada en France, 1850–1914*. Ottawa: University of Ottawa Press, 1987.
Simonin, Michel. 'Les bibliothèque dans le livre (XVIe et XVIIe siècles).' *Interférences* 11 (January–June 1980), pp. 47-55.
Sirois, Antoine. 'Deux littératures.' *Canadian Literature* 43 (Winter 1970), pp. 36–41.
Smith, A.J.M. *The Oxford Book of Canadian Verse*. Toronto: Oxford University Press, 1960.
Les Soirées canadiennes, recueil de littérature nationale 1 (1) (January 1861) to 5 (1865). Québec: Brousseau et Frères.
Sollers, Philippe. 'Écriture et révolution.' In *Tel quel. Théorie d'ensemble*. Paris: Seuil, 1968.
Sowder, William J. *Emerson's Impact on the British Isles and Canada*. Charlottesville: University Press of Virginia, 1966.
Story, Norah. *The Oxford Companion to Canadian History and Literature*. Toronto: Oxford University Press, 1967.
Suleiman, Susan Rubin. *Authoritorian Fictions: The Ideological Novel as a Literary Genre*. New York: Columbia University Press, 1983.

Suleiman, Susan Rubin. *Le roman à thèse ou l'autorité fictive*. Paris: Les Presses universitaires de France, 1983.
Sutherland, Ronald. 'Les États-Unis et la littérature québécoise.' In Claude Savary, ed., *Les rapports culturels entre le Québec et les États-Unis*, 202–9. Institut québécois de recherches sur la culture, 1984.
Sylvain, Philippe. 'Un frère méconnu d'Antoine Gérin-Lajoie: Elzéar Gérin.' *Mélanges d'histoire du Canada français offerts au professeur Marcel Trudel*, 214–25. Ottawa: Éditions de l'Université d'Ottawa, 1978.
Sylvain, Robert. 'La visite du prince Napoléon au Canada.' *Mémoires de la Société royale du Canada*. 4th series, vol. 2, section 1, June 1964, pp. 105–26.
Thibault, Charles. *Biographie de Stanislas Drapeau*. Ottawa: A. Bureau et Frères, 1891.
Thoreau, Henry David. *Walden, or Life in the Woods*. Followed by *On the Duty of Civil Disobedience*. New York: Signet Classics, 1964.
Tocqueville, Alexis de. *Oeuvres complètes*. Definitive edition published under the direction of J.-P. Mayer. Vol. I, 1: *De la démocratie en Amérique* (1951); I, 2: *De la démocratie en Amérique* (1951); V, 1: *Voyages en Sicile et aux États-Unis* (1957). Paris: Gallimard.
Tocqueville, Alexis de. *Democracy in America*. New York: Vintage Books, 1954.
Tod, Ian, and Michael Wheeler. *Utopia*. New York: Harmony Books, 1978.
Tougas, Gérard. *Histoire de la littérature canadienne-française*. Paris: Les Presses universitaires de France, 1960.
Toye, William, gen. ed. *The Oxford Companion to Canadian Literature*. Toronto: Oxford University Press, 1983.
Tremblay, Marc-Adelard. 'L'idéologie du Québec rural.' *Académie des sciences morales et politiques. Travaux et communications*, 212–65. Sherbrooke: Éditions Paulines, 1973.
Tremblay, Victor-Laurent. *Au commencement était le mythe*. Ottawa: University of Ottawa Press, 1991.
Trilling, Lionel. *The Liberal Imagination. Essays on Literature and Society*. New York: Viking Press, 1950.
Trousson, Raymond. *Voyages aux pays de nulle part. Histoire littéraire de la pensée utopique*. Bruxelles: Éditions de l'Université de Bruxelles, 1975.
Trudel, Marcel. *L'influence de Voltaire au Canada*. 2 volumes. Montréal: Fides, 1945.
Trudelle, abbé Charles. 'Les Bois-Francs.' *Le Foyer canadien* 1 (January–February 1863), pp. 15–57.
Tulard, Jean. *Le mythe de Napoléon*. Paris: A. Colin, 1971.
Tulard, Jean. *Dictionnaire Napoléon*. Paris: Fayard, 1987.
Vadeboncoeur, Pierre. *Trois essais sur l'insignifiance*. Montréal: L'Hexagone, 1989.

Vallée, Jacques. *Tocqueville au Bas-Canada*. Montréal: Éditions du Jour, 1973.

Vattier, Georges. *Esquisse historique de la colonisation de la province de Québec (1608-1925)*. Paris: Champion, 1928.

Volney, Constantin-François Chasseboeuf, comte de. *Tableau du climat et du sol des États-Unis d'Amérique, suivi d'Éclaircissements sur la Floride, sur la colonie française à Scioto, sur quelques colonies canadiennes et sur les sauvages*. Paris: Bossange Frères, 1822. 1st ed. Paris: Courcier, 1803, 2 volumes.

Wade, Mason. *Les Canadiens français de 1760 à nos jours*. 2nd ed. 2 volumes. Ottawa: Le Cercle du livre de France, 1963.

Wagner, R.L., and J. Pinchon. *Grammaire du français classique et moderne*. Paris: Hachette, 1962.

Warwick, Jack. *The Long Journey: Literary Themes of French Canada*. Toronto: University of Toronto Press, 1968.

Watt, Ian. *The Rise of the Novel. Studies in Defoe, Richardson and Fielding*. Harmondsworth: Penguin Books, 1966.

Weber, Max. *L'éthique protestante et l'esprit du capitalisme*. Paris: Plon, 1964.

Weinmann, Heinz. *Du Canada au Québec. Généalogie d'une histoire*. Montréal: L'Hexagone, 1987.

Wilson, John Dover. *What Happens in Hamlet?* Cambridge: Cambridge University Press, 1964.

Wyczynski, Paul. 'Panorama du roman canadien-français.' *Le roman canadien-français. Évolution. Témoignages. Bibliographie*, 11-35. Montréal: Fides (Coll. Archives des lettres canadiennes, 3), 1964.

Zaslow, Morris. *The Opening of the Canadian North, 1870-1914*. Toronto and Montreal: McClelland and Stewart, 1971.

Index

Adams, John, 42
Agoult, Countess of. *See* Stern, Daniel
Alexander the Great, 129
Alger, Horatio, 17, 88
Andreae, Johann Valentin, 148, 158
Angenot, Marc, 21
Aquin, Hubert, 97
Archambault, Gilles, 6
Aristotle, 89
Attila, 127
Aubert de Gaspé, Philippe, 9, 10, 129, 188

Bacon, Francis, 145, 148, 158, 202
Balzac, Honoré de, 14, 71, 127, 133–4, 172, 173, 202, 205
Barberis, Pierre, 209nn38, 47
Barrès, Maurice, 134
Barthe, Joseph-Gabriel, 209n50, 210n7
Baudrillard, Jean, 143
Beaudry, Jean-Jérôme, x
Beaulieu, Victor-Lévy, 6, 7
Beaumont, Gustave de, 47, 213n46
Béland, J.-O., 28
Bellamy, Edward, 145, 156
Belleau, André, 142
Bellemare, Raphael, 93

Béranger, Pierre-Jean de, 129
Berdiaeff, Nicholas, 149
Bernardin de Saint-Pierre, Jacques-Henri, 89
Blais, Marie-Claire, 6, 10
Blanchot, Maurice, 99
Bloch, Ernst, 153
Boileau, Nicolas, 89
Bonaparte, Jérôme, 137
Bonaparte, Napoléon. *See* Napoléon I
Bonaparte, Napoléon Joseph Charles Paul, 98, 136–40, 213n52
Bornier, Henri de, 89
Bourdieu, Pierre, x
Bourget, Ignace, 137, 138
Bourque, Paul-André, 6, 7
Brasseur de Bourbourg, Charles-Étienne, 30
Brault, Jacques, 199
Brouillette, Benoît, 53
Bruce, Vida, xi, 9, 185–6, 188, 189, 190
Bruchési, Jean, 53
Brunet, Michel, 223n46
Burroughs, William, 7
Buies, Arthur, 61

Cabet, Étienne, 145–6, 158
Caesar, Julius, 129

Campanella, Tommaso, 148, 164, 202
Canivez, André, 151
Carlyle, Thomas, 147
Carnegie, Dale, 18
Carrier, Roch, 10
Cartier, Jacques, 4
Casgrain, Henri-Raymond, 7, 23–6, 44, 58, 132, 214n71
Cervantes, Miguel de, 105
Charlemagne, 133
Chateaubriand, François René de, 14, 89, 127, 173
Châtelet, Mme du, 106
Chauveau, Pierre-Joseph-Olivier, 10, 98, 130, 171, 182–4, 194
Chesterton, Gilbert Keith, 150
Cicero, Marcus Tullius, 67, 89
Cioranescu, Alexandre, 202
Colette, Jean Yves, 229n14
Comte, Auguste, 152
Conan, Laure, 9
Considérant, Victor, 146
Cooper, James Fenimore, 34, 173, 199, 213n59
Craig, James Henry, 129
Crémazie, Octave, 10
Cyrano de Bergerac, Savinien de, 145, 153

Darveau, Louis-Michel, 83
Davis, J.C., 153
Defoe, Daniel, 38, 106–20, 142–3, 148
Deguy, Michel, 205
Derrida, Jacques, 71
Dessaulles, Louis-Antoine, 141
Dickens, Charles, 172, 173
Diderot, Denis, 152
Dionne, René, 9, 12, 26, 214n71
Dorion, Antoine-Aimé, 141
Dostaler, Yves, 58

Dostoyevski, Feodor Mikhailovich, 220n11
Douville, Joseph-Antoine-Irénée, 210n18
Drapeau, Stanislas, 216n25
Drummond, William Henry, x
Dubé, Marcel, 7
Dubé, Martin, 12
Dubois, Jacques, x, 14, 23
Ducasse, Isidore, 205
Ducharme, Réjean, 7, 97, 142
Duchet, Claude, 13, 58, 214n2
Dumont, Fernand, 54
Dumont, René, 200
Dupanloup, Félix-Antoine-Philibert, 169
Durham, John George Lambton, 19
Dussault, Gabriel, 22, 62, 131, 225n8
Duveau, Georges, 19, 151

Eaton, Nathaniel, 30
Eco, Umberto, 100
Elder, Rev. P., 10
Emerson, Ralph Waldo, 40, 69, 89, 91–6, 134–6, 147, 199, 201

Falardeau, Jean-Charles, 32, 186
Faulkner, William, 6, 7
Fénelon, François de Salignac de la Mothe, 80, 89, 107, 147, 152
Ferland, Jean-Baptiste-Antoine, 26–32, 51, 53, 132, 190
Fitzgerald, Francis Scott, 100
Flaubert, Gustave, 100
Foigny, Gabriel de, 145
Fontanier, Pierre, 60
Fontenelle, Bernard Le Bovier de, 148
Ford, Henry, 18
Foucault, Michel, 16
Fourier, Charles, 145–7, 152

France, Anatole, 152
Franklin, Benjamin, 38, 89–91, 96, 199
Fraser, Ian Forbes, 11
Fréchette, Louis, 10
Fuller, Margaret, 146

Gagnon, Ernest, 5
Gallays, François, 214n2
Garneau, François-Xavier, 10
Gélinas, Évariste, 209n50
Genette, Gérard, 214n2
Genghis Khan, 127
Gérin, Léon, 23–4, 27, 208n19, 209n50
Gill, Léandre, 28
Godbout, Jacques, 5–7
Goethe, Johann Wolfgang von, 129
Goldmann, Lucien, 13
Greely, Horace, 201
Grivel, Charles, 214n2

Haldane, Richard, 153
Hamon, Philippe, 102
Harper, Charles, 27–8
Harrington, James, 176
Harvard, John, 30
Hawthorne, Nathaniel, 30, 146, 173
Hébert, Anne, 10
Hébert, Nicolas-Tolentin, 77–8
Hemingway, Ernest, 6
Hitler, Adolf, 151
Hogan, John Sheridan, 51
Hoggart, Richard, 13
Homer, 89
Horace, Quintus Horatius Flaccus, 89
Hosmer, J.K., 30
Hugo, Victor, 89, 126–8, 134
Huston, James, 33
Huxley, Aldous, 149, 152

Huyghe, René, 133

Iacocca, Lee, 18
Idt, Geneviève, 71
Irving, Washington, 100
Issenhuth, Jean-Pierre, 205

Jakobson, Roman, 216n24
Jasmin, Claude, 6

Kandiuk, Mary, 10
Kennedy, Joseph Patrick, 18
Kerouac, Jack, 6
Kerr, William A. Robb, 208n20
Klinck, George Alfred, 208n20

Labelle, François-Xavier-Antoine, 61–2, 77
Laflèche, Louis-François, 192
La Fontaine, Jean de, 89
Lamartine, Alphonse de, 89, 127
Lanctôt, Gustave, 53
Larose, Jean, 5
Lee, Ann, 146
Leibniz, Gottfried Wilhem, Baron von, 89, 167
Le Jeune, Paul, 4
Lemire, Maurice, 82
LeMoine, Roger, 181, 225n8
LeMoyne, Jean, 199
Le Play, Frédéric, 21, 68
Lessard, Claude, 221n22
Loranger, Thomas-Jean-Jacques, 132

Macherey, Pierre, 17
Mackenzie, Alexander, 212n44
MacLennan, Hugh, x
MacMechan, Archibald, 11
Mailer, Norman, 72

Mailhot, Laurent, 97, 220n1
Maine de Biran, 134
Major, André, 6, 7, 207n10
Malraux, André, 220n11
Mannheim, Karl, 15, 18
Marcotte, Gilles, 166, 168, 199, 203
Martineau, Édouard, 28
Martineau, Harriet, 88
Marx, Karl, 145, 175
Mather, Cotton, 30
Melançon, Benoît, 6
Melville, Herman, 3, 6, 148, 173
Mercier, Louis-Sébastien, 145, 163
Michelet, Jules, 92
Miller, Henry, 6
Mitterand, Henri, 71
Molière (Jean Baptiste Poquelin), 89
Montaigne, Michel de, 154
Montcalm, Louis Joseph, 19
Montesquieu, Charles Louis de Secondat, Baron de, 89
Montpetit, Édouard, 56, 149, 225n8
More, Thomas, 18, 145, 164, 174, 202
Morelly, 145
Morgan, Henry David, 18
Morgan, Henry J., 10
Morgan, John Pierpont, 18
Morris, William, 153, 163

Napoleon I, 102, 105, 120–43
Napoléon III, 137
Napoléon, Prince. *See* Bonaparte, Napoléon Joseph Charles Paul
Neilson, John, 49
Nelson, Worfred, 19
Nero, Claudius Caesar, 127

O'Reilly, Bernard, 28
Ouellet, Fernand, 51, 184–5, 188
Owen, Robert, 145–6, 152

Papineau, Louis-Joseph, 19, 141, 223n42
Parent, Étienne, 20, 22, 25, 32–41, 45, 50, 51, 54, 58, 60, 61, 69, 80, 82, 83, 95, 112, 116, 131–2, 139, 166, 176, 198, 204
Parent, Henri, 132
Pellico, Silvio, 89
Phipps, William, 211n22
Pius VII, 136
Pius IX, 137–8
Pierce, Lorne, 11
Plato, 89, 145, 152, 153, 164, 165, 167, 176
Poulin, Jacques, 6
Proudhon, Pierre-Joseph, 152
Proulx, Bernard, 195
Proust, Marcel, 205

Quiblier, Joseph-Vincent, 49
Quinet, Edgar, 92

Rabelais, François, 145, 152, 154
Racine, Antoine, 77
Racine, Jean, 89
Rameau de Saint-Père, François-Edme, 33, 131–3, 139, 215n11
Rapp, George, 146
Renan, Ernest, 152
Restif de La Bretonne, Nicolas, 145
Reybaud, Louis, 89
Ringuet (Philippe Panneton), 7, 128
Rioux, Marcel, 207n4
Robert, Marthe, 220n11
Robespierre, Maximilien de, 152
Rochambeau, Jean Baptiste Donatien de Vimeur, Count of, 43
Rockefeller, John Davison, 18
Rousseau, Guildo, 6, 214n64
Rousseau, Jean-Jacques, 108, 152

Roy, Camille, 9, 16, 57, 71, 141, 177, 178, 204
Roy, Gabrielle, 10
Ruyer, Raymond, 150, 153, 163, 165, 175, 176, 203

Saint-Just, Louis de, 164
Saint-Pierre, Arthur, 68
Saint-Simon, Claude Henri, Count of, 145, 152
Salinger, J.D., 6, 7
Sand, George, 61, 152, 213n52, 224n65
Sand, Maurice, 138, 213n52, 224n65
Sartre, Jean-Paul, 17, 100
Savard, Pierre, 22
Scherer, René, 167
Séguin, Normand, 22
Servier, Jean, 173
Shurter, Robert Lefevre, 155
Sidney, Sir Philip, 18
Signay, Joseph, 27-8
Simonin, Michel, 225n79
Sirois, Antoine, 12
Sollers, Philippe, 144
Solomon, 80, 113
Soublière, Roger, 229n14
Staël, Mme de, 89, 127
Stafford, Jan, 229n14
Stendhal (Henri Bayle), 100, 127, 133-4, 205
Stern, Daniel, 92
Story, Norah, 11
Suleiman, Susan Rubin, 14, 71, 150
Sulte, Benjamin, 209n50
Sutherland, Ronald, 6
Suvin, Darko, 21
Swift, Jonathan, 152

Tamerlane, 127

Tardivel, Jules, 22
Thériault, Yves, 6, 10
Thoreau, Henry David, 200, 201
Tocqueville, Alexis de, 41, 46-52, 61, 62, 63, 69, 70, 73, 77, 79, 83, 87, 88, 95, 116, 176, 177, 191, 192, 193, 194
Tougas, Gérard, 9
Toye, William, 11
Tremblay, Michel, 7, 10
Trevor, Thomas, 28
Trousson, Raymond, 144, 202, 203
Trudel, Marcel, 128
Tulard, Jean, 126, 133
Twain, Mark, 173

Vadeboncoeur, Pierre, 5
Vairasse, Denis, 145
Vanderbilt, Cornelius, 18
Victor-Emmanuel, 138, 140
Vigneault, Gilles, 4
Virgil, Publius Vergilius Maro, 89
Volney, Constantin-François Chasseboeuf, Count of, 41-6, 48, 50, 61, 63, 77, 88, 95, 113, 115, 116
Voltaire (François Marie Arouet), 89

Wade, Mason, 184-5
Warren, Joseph, 146
Warwick, Jack, 11, 198, 207n3, 212n44
Washington, George, 42, 88
Watt, Ian, 221n16
Weber, Max, 18
Wells, Herbert George, 163, 164
Williams, Tennessee, 7
Wilson, John Dover, 56
Winthrop, John, 30
Wirth, Louis, 208n33
Wolfe, James, 19

Zola, Émile, 14, 71

www.ingramcontent.com/pod-product-compliance
Lightning Source LLC
Chambersburg PA
CBHW071154070526
44584CB00019B/2782